Women's Bodies, Women's Worries

NORDIC INSTITUTE OF ASIAN STUDIES

Recent studies of Vietnamese history and society

Authority Relations and Economic Decision-Making in Vietnam:
An Historical Perspective
Dang Phong and Melanie Beresford

Women's Bodies, Women's Worries:
Health and Family Planning in a Vietnamese Rural Community
Tine Gammeltoft

Thailand and the Southeast Asian Networks
of the Vietnamese Revolution, 1885–1954
Christopher E. Goscha

Vietnam or Indochina? Contesting Concepts of Space
in Vietnamese Nationalism, 1887–1954
Christopher E. Goscha

Vietnam in a Changing World
Irene Nørlund, Carolyn Gates and Vu Cao Dam (eds)

Profit and Poverty in Rural Vietnam:
Winners and Losers of a Dismantled Revolution
Rita Liljeström, Eva Lindskog,
Nguyen Van Ang and Vuong Xuan Tinh

The Vietnamese Family in Change:
The Case of the Red River Delta
Pham Van Bich

Women's Bodies, Women's Worries

Health and Family Planning in a Vietnamese Rural Community

Tine Gammeltoft

CURZON

Nordic Institute of Asian Studies
Vietnam in Transition series

First published in 1999
by Curzon Press
15 The Quadrant, Richmond
Surrey TW9 1BP

Typesetting by
the Nordic Institute of Asian Studies

Printed and bound in Great Britain by
Biddles Ltd, Guildford and King's Lynn

Publication of this volume was assisted by a grant from the Danish
Council for Development Research (Danida)

British Library Cataloguing in Publication Data

Tine Gammeltoft
    Women's Bodies, Women's Worries : Health and Family Planning in a
    Vietnamese Rural Community
    1.Birth control - Vietnam 2.Women - Health and hygiene - Vietnam
    3.Women - Vietnam - Social conditions
    I.Title
    363.9'6'09597

ISBN 0-7007-1111-2

Contents

Acknowledgements

This study owes its existence to the contributions of numerous people and institutions.

A travel grant from the Nordic Institute of Asian Studies made possible an initial trip to Vietnam to carry out preliminary studies and establish the institutional affiliations necessary for the conduct of the present study. The study as such was made possible by a grant from the Research Council of the Danish International Development Agency (Danida), which I gratefully acknowledge. The Institute of Anthropology at University of Copenhagen funded a return visit to Vietnam in 1996 which enabled me to follow up on main research findings. On several occasions, Paule Mikkelsens Mindelegat generously offered residential facilities which made the writing up of fieldwork results a rare pleasure.

I am very grateful to the Institute of Sociology in Hanoi for sponsoring my research and for kindly arranging for my research permissions. Particular thanks to Phạm Bích San and Vũ Phạm Nguyên Thanh for many stimulating discussions over the years. For the practical guidance and emotional support without which research in Vietnam is virtually impossible, I am most deeply indebted to Professor Lê Thị Nhâm Tuyết. Without her unfailing assistance and that of the dedicated staff of the Center for Gender, Family and Environment in Development, this research would not have taken place. In Hà Tây province, the support of the Women's Union and the provincial Population and Family Planning Committee (PFPC) were invaluable. The kindness and cheerfulness of the PFPC staff was encouraging, as were the warmth and commitment I found in the Women's Union.

Also friends and research colleagues in Hanoi made important contributions to this study. The shared feelings of being privileged to be in Vietnam at this moment in time, the amazement at things going on around us, the questions pondered, the laughter, frustrations, and puzzles shared over good meals or late-afternoon *bia hơi*'s, formed a vital basis for the study. Of the many who deserve a mention, I would particularly like to thank Regina M. Abrami, Bùi Thị Hảo, Jonathan Caseley, David Craig, Debra Efroymson, Daniel Goodkind, Pamina Gorbach, Hoàng Tư Anh, Lê Minh Giảng, John and Debbie Humphries, Nguyễn Ngọc Hương, Nguyễn Phương Khanh, Melissa J. Pashigian, Harriet Phinney, Gill Tipping, Vũ Song Hà and Vũ Quý Nhân.

During the process of analysis and writing up these findings, the stimulating ideas, questions, and criticisms I received from students and colleagues at the Institute of Anthropology in Copenhagen proved invaluable. I have particularly benefited from the suggestions and support provided by Kirsten Hastrup and Ida Nicolaisen, who both followed the project from the beginning. For their careful readings of draft chapters I am grateful to David Craig, Anne Line Dalsgaard, Rolf Hernø, Annika Johansson, David Marr, Helle Rydström, Tine Tjørnhøj-Thomsen and Jayne Werner. I am indebted to Anton Baaré for assistance with the processing of survey data and to Ngô Thị Hoà for help with Vietnamese characters and language. Both academically and personally, I am most deeply indebted to my thesis adviser Susan Reynolds Whyte for her unflagging generosity, support, and encouragement over the years and for the way she has taught me – by her own example – what anthropology is all about.

A very profound debt of gratitude is owed to the people in Vải Sơn, who welcomed me among them, helped me overcome my mistakes and clumsiness, and discussed at length the joys, hopes and difficulties of their lives with me. I can never fully express my gratitude for the care, concern, and trust I have been shown and for all that I have been taught. However, it is my hope that the account I shall present here is capable of conveying the agency and resilience of the people I met in Vải Sơn. Particular thanks are due to 'Bà Chính' and her family for sharing their home and meals with me for more than a year and for still regarding me as a daughter of the house. Out of respect for the privacy of the people involved, I have changed most place and personal names in this study. But I do want to acknowledge the friendships of Nguyễn Thị Lê and Vũ Thị Dung, who have greatly enriched both my life and my work.

Last but not least, I would like to thank Rolf Hernø for being such an astute critic and supportive friend throughout. I am grateful to be able to share with him the love of Vietnam and all the gifts it continues to bring.

Prologue

As she sees us entering her yard, Thanh jumps up from her work by the kitchen fire, invites us into the house, and seats us on the bed. Apologizing for the poverty of her home and with a glance at her sleeping husband lying wrapped in blankets on the other bed, she pours water from the thermos into the teapot and offers us each a cup of bitter green tea while she herself takes nothing.

It is a grey and misty morning in January, one of those mornings where the cold seems to creep in through all crevices. I have joined Nhưng, one of the commune's family planning workers, on her house-to-house visits to hamlet women who 'have not yet understood' the benefits of family planning. Thanh is one of these women. She is a timid and fragile-looking little woman with huge eyes and a worn-out expression on her face. Her five children, who are all too small for their age, her unreliable husband who drinks too much, and her large debts and unsuccessful farming make her an obvious target for Nhưng's work.

Thanh's family lives in one large room with a dirt floor and hardly any furniture. Besides the two wooden beds there is only a small altar for the ancestors with some faded orange plastic flowers on it. Nhưng goes straight to the matter, telling Thanh that she has come to inform her that today there is a family planning campaign going on, and this afternoon district health staff will be at the commune health centre to insert IUDs. Thanh really should go there and have an IUD inserted, Nhưng says.

'Think of your family, you have to think of the happiness of your family,' she continues in an insistent voice, taking Thanh's hand. 'You should be able to take proper care of your children – how will you do that if you have more?'

'Of course I don't want to have more children,' Thanh replies, 'but I have already had an IUD twice, and I cannot bear it, I am too weak to have it.'

I ask what she means that she cannot bear the IUD, and Thanh says that each time she had an IUD she had very strong and prolonged menstrual bleedings, so she lost a lot of blood. This made her weak, she could not work as she used to, and she often got dizzy, and sometimes even lost her balance and fell over. Being so weak, how could she take care of her children? So each time she had an IUD inserted it wasn't long bfore she had it removed again, and then got pregnant again.

'I never wanted to have five children,' Thanh says. 'When I had the first two boys and my daughter, I wanted to stop, and so did my husband. Our finances cannot support having many children.'

Nhưng interrupts her, saying that she should try again with the IUD. 'Don't worry, it really is a very safe method. Very safe. It is used all over the world. I will take the responsibility, why don't you just go to the health station this afternoon?' she says.

'I am afraid,' Thanh insists. 'What if I can't work and take care of the children, who will take care of them?'

■ CHAPTER 1

Introduction

When I asked Chuyến, the commune Party Secretary, why so many women seemed to have problems with their IUDs (intra-uterine devices),[1] he answered, 'Do you know the saying "The last drop of water breaks the camel's back" (*Giọt nước để lên lưng con lạc đà*)? You should put that on the front page of your book.'

Background

The IUD is central to the Vietnamese family planning programme; three out of four users of modern methods of contraception rely upon it (GSO 1995). However, as both lay people, health workers and researchers in Vietnam have noted, an alarming number of Vietnamese women have serious problems using the IUD (e.g., Phạm Bích San 1993; Sundström 1994; Knodel *et al.* 1995; Johansson *et al.* 1996a, 1996b). When I was first in Vietnam in 1992, women's problems with the IUD were less known among foreign observers. The country had only just begun its policy of opening up to the West and very few foreign-language studies of health or family planning existed. Embarking on fieldwork in a Red River delta rural commune, I was therefore surprised to note the widespread dissatisfaction with the IUD among women.

One of the first women I talked to during my fieldwork told me about the serious health problems she had encountered with the IUD:

'After I had the IUD inserted I felt weak and tired and my periods became much stronger. Once I felt so exhausted that I had to rest for a whole month and could not work. I had pains in my back and stomach and a lot of discharge, and after a year I had the IUD removed.'

Another woman, complaining of the frequent pregnancies among IUD users, said:

'You know, in the old days, heaven decided how many children one would have. Today we have the IUD, so heaven still decides.'

Many other women told stories of heavy bleedings and heavy bodies, aching backs and stomachs, and feelings of weakness and exhaustion, which they all ascribed to their use of the IUD. After a few weeks of work in the commune, I summed up in my diary:

'This week I heard even more examples of heavy bleedings and unwanted pregnancies with IUDs. It is disastrous. Women sometimes have their IUDs inserted in secret because their husbands do not allow them to have an IUD, fearing that it may impair their working ability.'

ॐ

The massive problems Vietnamese women experience with their IUDs – including health problems, expulsions, and accidental pregnancies – are quite disturbing, particularly in a situation where the IUD is the most common form of contraception in a fairly ambitious national family planning programme. Explanations of women's IUD problems abound in Vietnam. Women's Union[2] cadres often say that 'it is a disease of the mind', that women simply blame all their troubles in life on the IUD. Others relate IUD problems to the poor quality of care in reproductive health services, including a lack of technical skills among providers (Đỗ Trọng Hiếu *et al.* 1995a). Some see in IUD problems a form of quiet 're-sistance' to a heavy-handed family planning programme (Johansson *et al.* 1996a). Some providers suggest that the IUD – which is today imported from the US – is too large for the uterus of Viet namese women (Jain *et al.* 1993). Commune women themselves often say that their bodies are 'weak already' and thus cannot bear the additional disturbance which an IUD causes. This was also what Chuyến referred to when he compared the IUD to the 'last drop of water' breaking the camel's back.

But the problems which Vietnamese women experience with their IUDs reach far beyond the particular context of family planning in Vietnam, signalling a range of much more general issues. Today, efforts to control human fertility are immense throughout the world, and technologies for fertility control – whether for limiting or enhancing fertility – are under constant development and change. Reproductive technologies provide wide-ranging potential for control of human bodies and their reproductive capacities. As noted by Fathalla (1994), these technologies are double-edged weapons: while they may considerably enhance the ability of women and men to control their own lives and fertility, they may also be violently used by governments and other agencies to control the bodies and fertility of citizens.

Both in terms of health costs and social costs, women tend to bear the major burden of efforts to control fertility. Most fertility control technologies are developed for use by women and in most societies women are held responsible for matters related to re-production and childcare. Given the global use of modern fertility control technologies and their vital importance to the lives of women all over the world, our knowledge of women's own ex-periences with these technologies is strikingly limited. Since the mid-1970s, large 'acceptability studies' have been carried out, investi-gating the acceptability of different contraceptive methods to their potential users. This approach to contraceptive research has been questioned by feminist researchers and women's health advocates, who maintain that assessments of contraceptive acceptability need to take into account contextual factors such as the social conditions of women's lives and attributes of the service delivery system, rather than seeing acceptability as something inherent in the technology as such (cf. Spicehandler and Simmons 1994; Heise 1997). Also the 'user perspective' studies which have been conducted in recent years tend to remain relatively narrow in scope, often neither context-ualizing women's perspectives on fertility regulating technologies within their wider life situations nor providing qualitative insights into the experiences and perceptions of contraceptive users. Anita Har-don has noted:

> Though they present us with a spate of descriptive statistics we learn relatively little from this existing body of knowledge about women's experiences and views. More in-depth studies that contextualize fertility-regulation practices in people's day to day lives are essential for understanding of user-views of fertility regulation methods (Hardon 1996, p. 7).

In order to improve women's health and quality of life, it seems important to enhance our insights into the ways in which women themselves perceive and use fertility control technologies and to better understand how the uses of technology are mediated by both social relations and cultural meanings.

This book presents a social science perspective on a field and a set of issues which have until now been dominated by biomedicine and demography. While demographic and biomedical studies may provide valuable insights into the medical safety and effectiveness or the demographic impact of contraceptive methods, there are important issues which these studies do not illuminate. Despite a recent interest in 'micro' analyses, demographic studies often tend to focus on population dynamics at aggregate and general levels, ignoring more specific social interactions and relations. Biomedical studies tend to see the body as an object and bodily experiences as phenomena to be objectively measured and treated, ignoring the subjective experiences which are always also involved in efforts to manage bodies and control fertility.

In contrast, my aim with the present study has been to understand Vietnamese women's own experiences with the IUD as a method of fertility control and to ground such understandings in the wider contexts of their lives. My analysis starts from an enquiry into women's physical experiences of having an IUD inside their bodies and extends into the everyday worlds of family and community life, examining the social, moral, and political issues with which women's experiences with the IUD are intertwined. Whereas most contraceptive research to date has focused rather narrowly on the technology as such, the focus of the present study will be on the lives in which technology is used. When an IUD is inserted into the body of a Vietnamese woman, it is also inserted into a life full of physical burdens and social stresses. A central argument of the study is therefore that neither physiological nor attitudinal reactions to a contraceptive device can be meaningfully distinguished from the social and cultural context in which contraceptive use takes place.

Theoretical and analytical premises

Technology plays a central role in the profound social changes the world is undergoing today. New technologies are transforming not only our everyday worlds, but also our bodies and sense of self. Importantly, however, as Donna Haraway points out, technology should not be seen as opposed to humans but as an integrated aspect of our selves:'The machine is not an *it* to be animated, worshipped, and dominated. The machine is us, our processes, an aspect of our embodiment' (Haraway 1991: 180).

One important effect of the technologization of human life is a blurring of boundaries between human and non-human, a collapsing of conventional distinctions between nature and culture, body and technology, self and other, local and global (Haraway 1991, 1997; Strathern 1992; Featherstone and Burrows 1995). In recent social science writings on body–technology interfaces there has been a proliferation of the 'cyborg' image, not least inspired by Donna Haraway's seminal 'Manifesto for Cyborgs' (Haraway 1985). Haraway writes: 'By the late twentieth century, our time, a mythic time, we are all chimeras, theorized and fabricated hybrids of machine and organism; in short, we are cyborgs' (1991: 150). The term cyborg refers to 'cybernetic organism', a self-regulating human-machine system. The transformation of humans into cyborgs has led Downey *et al.* (1995) to propose a 'cyborg anthropology', an anthropology which focuses on the ways in which technology mediates and transforms social relationships, bodies, and subjectivities. Cyborg anthropology explores 'the production of humanness through machines', arguing that 'technologies participate actively in every existing realm of anthropological interest' (Downey *et al.* 1995: 342–44). In today's technologically mediated social worlds, the questions we confront concern the implications for human life and social relations of the uses of various kinds of technology. In which ways do specific technologies contribute to the shaping of new modes of agency and new forms of social relations? Which issues of power and control are involved? How are cultural meanings produced and changed through the social uses of technological artifacts?

The role of technology in biomedicine is one of the most obvious topics of interest for a cyborg anthropology. Biomedical technologies interfere directly with our bodily processes and functions, affecting not only human bodies but also the communities they constitute. The elderly man with the pacemaker, the woman undergoing infertility treatment, the young travellers carrying several different vaccines in their bodies – these are all examples of the blurrings of conventional boundaries between humans and machines which biomedical technologies involve (cf. Casper and Koenig 1996). Also in the realm of human reproduction, technologies and organic bodies are becoming closely interwoven. The technology at the centre of attention in this study, the intrauterine device, is but one example of the reproductive technologies which are currently changing not only our lives, but the concept of life itself (Franklin 1993 in Haraway 1997). Reproductive technologies are defined here to include technologies to create, prevent, monitor, and terminate pregnancies, as well as birthing technologies. As noted by Traweek (1993), most research and feminist theory on women, sciences, and technologies concerns reproductive technologies. Existing studies and feminist theories present widely differing perspectives on reproductive technologies: some view technologies as devices that increase women's autonomy and choice (e.g., Haraway 1997); others see reproductive technologies as extensions of patriarchal control over female bodies (e.g., Arditti *et al.* 1985; Corea *et al.* 1985) or as first-world domination of third-world women (e.g., Morsy 1997).

Rather than starting from a preset and universal attitude towards reproductive technologies, the present study explores the specific uses and meanings of a particular kind of contraceptive technology in a particular social setting, investigating women's own experiences of the technology within the context of their daily social lives. As with other kinds of technologies, reproductive technologies are not neutral or 'innocent' devices with similar uses and effects irrespective of cultural context. Rather, technology takes on differing meanings and has differing social implications depending on the context of its use (cf. Pfaffenberger 1992). In the present study the recognition of the varying and unstable effects of technologies on women's lives opens up several areas of enquiry. As I shall outline below, in order to analyse reproductive technologies from an anthropological perspective, issues of human agency, human physiology and epistemology need consideration.

Human agency

The first premise of this study concerns human agency. The study starts from the premise that even in situations of high structural constraint, women do make active choices concerning the tools that may enhance or limit their fertility. Such choices, however, are always contextual, and the analytical challenge therefore lies in tracing out the social conditions that produce and enable specific modes of acting. In this context it is particularly important to illuminate the local and global distributions of knowledge and power which shape and condition the choices women make. As Ginsburg and Rapp (1995: 5) note, 'choices in reproductive technologies cannot be considered apart from international political and economic forces; ... in any given situation, the market and politics structure what knowledge is relevant, ruling out many potential choices.'

In the context of this study, the focus on socially situated human agency involves a double consideration of (a) the social, economic, and political conditions under which women come to have IUDs inserted into their bodies and (b) women's own desires and choices in the realm of fertility control. At a different analytical level, the focus on agency includes considerations of the ways women may actively employ reproductive technologies like the IUD to accomplish social purposes in everyday life. As we shall see, IUDs may be viewed as much more than devices for fertility control: they may be seen as 'weapons of the weak' (Scott 1985), as tools used by women to manage and negotiate everyday social relations. In this sense, reproductive technologies not only act upon women's bodies, but are also used by women themselves actively to affect their social surroundings.

Human physiology

The second premise of the study concerns human physiology. At issue here are the complex interchanges taking place between human bodies and technologies. In the context of the present study, the question is: how are we to understand the experiences that Vietnamese women have with their IUDs, the feelings of weakness and pain which are associated with the presence of this device inside their bodies? This question is linked to a more general question of how we understand human experiences of physical pain and disease.

In line with most medical anthropologists, I see pain and physical distress as not merely physiological phenomena, but as experiences that are deeply integrated within our social and existential being (e.g., Desjarlais 1992; Csordas 1994; Kleinman 1995). I place this idea at the centre of my analysis in an attempt to overcome the Cartesian body–mind split which still dominates much of both scientific and everyday thinking. Where we are most used to thinking of the body as a separate entity, distinct from both mind and the social world, I have drawn inspiration from phenomenology in order to conceptualize the body as not just an object among other objects, but as the living centre of all our being and acting in the world (cf. Merleau-Ponty 1962). Through our bodies,

we are engaged in the world prior to reflection; and all consciousness and action ultimately derive from this bodily and pre-
reflexive inhering in the world.

Such a phenomenological understanding of the interweavings of
bodies, minds and social worlds happens to be very much in line with
the thinking of the women I met in Vietnam, to whom it is an obvious
fact that aching bodies are inseparable from stressful thoughts and
burdensome social lives. As we shall see in later chapters, the
symptoms which Vietnamese women associate with the IUD cannot
be understood apart from the wider contexts of their lives: as lived by
women, physical symptoms are closely integrated with thoughts and
worries and with the stresses and demands of everyday lives. This also
means that rather than being just things in themselves, reproductive
technologies are always part of life as it is lived, enmeshed in already
existing networks of meanings and relationships and engaging core
concerns and experiences in women's lives (cf. Rapp 1991; Ginsburg
and Rapp 1995).

Epistemology

The third theoretical premise of this study concerns epistemology.
Like other forms of ethnographic knowledge, the knowledge
produced in this study is based on the fieldwork experiences of
the ethnographer and thus grounded in personal experience and
engagement. In this sense it is a very personal and subjective
account which does not strive to meet classic criteria of reliability
and objectivity.

This raises questions concerning the value of ethnographic
knowledge of reproductive technologies *vis-à-vis* more 'hard'
biomedical knowledge which is based on controlled clinical trials
and on standardized scientific procedures. Is ethnographic knowledge relevant at all to biomedicine and to medical practice? Or are
the two forms of knowledge so fundamentally different from each
other that they are unable to engage in productive ways? Do
biomedical and ethnographic knowledges represent 'two cultures'
in C. P. Snow's sense? Posing the question this way presumes that
biomedical knowledge is actually 'objective', detached from the
observer and her social world. As recent science and technology
studies have convincingly argued, however, 'objective' scientific
knowledge is also subjective and value laden, reflecting the modes
of thinking and the social structures of its time (e.g., Latour and

Woolgar 1979; Haraway 1991; Strathern 1995). In other words, as Kirsten Hastrup has put it, 'the hardness of facts is an expression of social agreement rather than a quality of the facts themselves' (Hastrup 1993: 734). The real epistemological challenge therefore becomes one of recognizing and reflecting on the grounds on which science is produced and of trying to integrate differing partial perspectives in ways that provide us with better ways of organizing our worlds and living together in them (see Rorty 1991).

In the context of the present study the question therefore is: What are the implications of this study – which illustrates and maintains that physiological reactions are deeply socially grounded – for biomedical understandings of contraception and contraceptive side-effects? How may the links between physiologies and social worlds, which are relatively easily discernible through an ethnographic lens, be translated into knowledge that is useful also in the context of biomedicine, contraceptive development, or family planning programmatic improvements? The study starts from the assumption that 'soft' ethnographic knowledge and 'hard' biomedical knowledge are not as fundamentally different as often assumed, and that an engagement between the two forms of knowledge is not only possible, but required if we are to create more liveable social worlds.

I shall now briefly describe the social and political context in which IUDs are inserted into the bodies of Vietnamese women, a context that is set by an ambitious national family planning policy.

Family planning in Vietnam

'How many children do you have?' I asked a 42-year old commune woman.

'Six', she said, looking slightly embarrassed: 'At that time I did not yet understand about family planning. Now I understand and if I were to have children today I would not have had six children. At that time we were still feudal, you see, valuing many children.'

Over the past decade the national family planning policy has fundamentally affected the ways fertility control is perceived and practised in Vietnam, changing the daily lives of men and women all over the country. From the perspective of the Vietnamese government, a successful implementation of the family planning policy is an important precondition for continued social and economic development. Today population pressures are urgently felt in many areas of Vietnam and population growth is a source of considerable concern to both government and people. Vietnam's population of 77 million people (VNA 1997) is growing at a rate of 1.88 per cent annually, and the government hopes to stabilize the population at 120–125 million people by the middle of the twenty-first century. Even though fertility levels have fallen drastically, from a total fertility rate of 6.1 children per woman in 1960 to a rate of 2.8 children today (GSO 1995), population growth remains a serious problem, not least because of the age structure of the population: 57 per cent of the Vietnamese population is under 25 years of age (UNFPA 1997).

In order to control and curb population growth, a one- or two-child policy was issued in 1988.[3] This policy is modelled on the Chinese family planning policy, yet it is less rigid in both design and implementation (cf. Goodkind 1995). The policy sets a family planning norm of one to two children per couple,[4] spaced with an interval of three to five years (JPRS 1989).[5] Since the failure to overcome 'psychological barriers and old customs' (NCPFP 1993a) is considered as one of the main reasons for continued population growth, the policy strongly emphasizes mass mobilization and IEC (information–education–communication) as the means to reach demographic targets.[6]

Rather than economic means of persuasion, official policy strategies consider *normative change* as the core of family planning activities. The goal of the IEC programme is to 'create a substantial change in perception and action of the entire society as well as of each member of the society,' and to promote the 'small, happy, and prosperous family as a social norm' (NCPFP 1992). Family planning messages are widely communicated through radio, television, newspapers, magazines, loudspeaker announcements, and the out-reach work of family planning cadres. In cities and along rural roads large billboard posters depict the happy one- or two-child family, declaring family planning to be the direct road to 'a stable population; a wealthy country; a happy family', or encouraging people to 'stop at two children in order to take good care of them.' Loudspeaker announcements in the late afternoon remind people of the necessity of family planning for both individual families and the nation. Family planning booklets and messages in radio and television depict population growth as the

5.ĐÔNG CON LÀM GIẢM HẠNH PHÚC GIA ĐÌNH

Mọi ước mơ về một cuộc sống tốt lành sẽ khó thực hiện được
đối với những gia đình đông con.

Vậy ta nên làm gì để biến những ước mơ đó thành sự thật ?

Fig. 1: *Many children reduce family happines* (NCPFP/UNFPA, VIE/
93/P08)
Top: *'All dreams about a good life will be difficult to realize for families
with many children.'*
Bottom: *'What should we do to make such dreams come true?'*

root cause of poverty and misery, hindering social progress and causing serious environmental problems.

In these messages, large families are associated with the past, with backwardness, feudalism, poverty, and ignorance, while small families are associated with modernity, wealth, progress, enlightenment, civilization, and the future. It is made clear that only uneducated and backward people believe that 'Heaven gives birth to elephants, so heaven will make grass for them' (*Trời sinh voi, Trời sinh cỏ*) – today, all enlightened people should be aware that there is not enough grass for the elephants.

Both the 1989 Health Law and the 1993 Population and Family Planning Strategy (NCPFP 1993b) explicitly emphasize the voluntary nature of family planning and contraceptive use. At the same time, and somewhat contradictorily, the 1987 Law on Marriage and the Family, the 1988 Council of Ministers decision which forms the basis for the family planning policy, and paragraph 40 in the 1992 Constitution all stress the obligation of citizens to plan their families (cf. Banister 1993). In practice, local authorities may use a range of measures to convince people of the benefits of family planning. The 1988 Council of Ministers decision states that couples who do not comply with the policy will be 'penalized by their immediate management agencies' and must contribute economically to a social support fund (JPRS 1989), while a 1993 Resolution on Population and Family Planning outlines a wide range of means to be used to create favourable conditions for the small family, including cash incentives for contraceptive use, tax exemptions, access to low-interest loans, and exemptions from public labour (NCPFP 1993a). In addition to this, local family planning cadres often try to persuade women to plan their families through repeated home visits and explanatory lectures, which point out the health and economic benefits to women themselves of limiting the size of their families (see Chapter 3).

The general guidelines outlined in national family planning strategies leave much scope for interpretation, and local implementations of the policy vary considerably (cf. Jain *et al.* 1993; Goodkind 1995). In some provinces and communes fines are levied on couples who exceed the family planning limits, while in others no financial penalties are applied.[7] Also the amount of

4. ẢNH HƯỞNG ĐẾN ĐỜI SỐNG HÀNG NGÀY

Thu nhập của gia đình không đủ đáp ứng nhu cầu cuộc sống.

Gia đình đông con làm cho điều kiện sinh hoạt khó khăn.

Fig. 2: *Many children and everyday life'* (NCPFP/UNFPA, VIE/93/P08)
Top: *'The family's income cannot cover daily needs.'*
Bottom: *'Having many children makes living conditions difficult for families.'*

normative pressure put on people seems to vary. Research carried out in the Red River delta's Thái Bình province – one of the country's most densely populated provinces – suggests that strong persuasion is being used here to motivate women to adopt a modern method of contraception (Lê Thị Nhâm Tuyết *et al.* 1994). As we shall see, however, even in areas where little direct pressure is placed on people to conform to national family planning norms, the population policy and the normative standards it sets strongly affect women's bodies, health, and daily lives.

While family planning is in principle voluntary, in practice – and usually for economic reasons – many people feel obligated to have no more than two or three children. This throws into doubt the question of the voluntary nature of the programme. Even though I have neither experienced nor heard reported cases of the use of direct force or violence (as has happened in Chinese family planning), the economic and normative disincentives to 'excessive' childbearing are often overwhelming. The power of the Vietnamese family planning policy therefore seems to lie more in subtle manipulation of personal motivations and desires than in the use of brute or direct force (cf. Gammeltoft 1996).

One important effect of the family planning policy has been the increasing availability of modern contraceptive methods in Vietnam. Today the national family planning programme provides IUDs, condoms, contraceptive pills, male and female sterilizations, and in some areas implants and injectables are being introduced on an experimental basis. Also 'menstrual regulations' and abortions are readily available and are very commonly used methods of fertility regulation: in 1992 the official total abortion rate was 2.5 per woman (Goodkind 1994a).[8]

Despite a 1988 government decree to diversify contraceptive methods and despite the variety of contraceptive methods which are in principle available throughout the country today, the IUD is still by far the most commonly used modern method of contraception. According to the 1994 Intercensal Demographic Survey, the contraceptive prevalence rate for women in Vietnam is 65 per cent. Among contraceptive users, 33 per cent use an IUD, 21 per cent use safe periods/withdrawal, 4 per cent condoms, 4 per cent female sterilization, 3 per cent contraceptive pills and 0.2 per cent male sterilization (GSO 1995). The family planning policy is popularly known as the 'IUD insertion policy' (*chính sách đặt vòng*); local family planning campaigns are known as 'IUD insertion campaigns' (*chiến dịch đặt vòng*); and a woman who wants to stop or postpone childbearing is most likely to go to her local health clinic or hospital and ask for an IUD without even considering other methods (cf. Jain *et al.* 1993). Given women's perceptions of the IUD as a dangerous and harmful device, this seems paradoxical – yet as we shall see in the following chapters, there are very good reasons for the prevalent use of the IUD by women in Vietnam.

But how did it happen that the IUD came to be the most favoured method of contraception in the Vietnamese family planning programme? Interestingly, there has been a major shift in the contraceptive method mix in Vietnam during the 1980s, from condoms and pills to the IUD. In 1980, 62 per cent of modern method users used either condoms or pills while only 36 per cent used the IUD. By 1988, however, 87 per cent of modern method users were IUD users (World Bank 1992). As the World Bank notes, this shift in the method mix does not reflect an increasing preference among contraceptive users for the IUD, but stems from the limited supplies of other contraceptives and the preference of health and family planning workers for long-acting provider-controlled methods (World Bank 1992: 16). According to the World Bank, the reasons for the current emphasis on the IUD in Vietnamese family planning are

> its low cost, the provision of free supplies from the Eastern European countries, the non-availability of imported supplies of pills and condoms due to lack of foreign exchange, and its appeal among health workers because of its durability of protection and easier monitoring (World Bank 1992: 16).

In other words, global politics and local family planning programme dynamics interact to create the heavy reliance on the IUD we see today. Trade embargoes and the Western world's isolation of Vietnam after the wars, a strained national budget, and a distrust among health care providers of people's ability to control their own fertility all work together to produce a situation where many Vietnamese women are forced to use the IUD for contraception whether this device suits them or not.

The intrauterine device

Intrauterine devices represent one of the most commonly used methods of fertility regulation in the world. Today more than 100 million women worldwide use an IUD for fertility control (Petta *et al.* 1996). For many years it has been unclear how IUDs prevent pregnancy, but recent research indicates that IUDs are not abortifacients, as was assumed for some time, but work by creating a foreign-body response in the uterus which leads to a damaging of sperm and eggs so that fertilization is impossible (Treiman *et al.* 1995). The idea of placing an object within the uterus to prevent pregnancy is an old one, reportedly first practised by Arabs, who placed an object in the womb of female camels in order to prevent them from getting pregnant on long journeys (Petta *et al.* 1996).

Modern IUDs have been developed in the twentieth century, and particularly since the early 1960s. In order to improve the effectiveness and reduce the side-effects of the devices, researchers have developed and tested a large number of different IUD models. The first IUDs were made of polyethylene, but in the 1960s and 1970s it was discovered that adding copper to the IUD increased its effectiveness. Then in the 1970s IUDs which release a hormone in the uterus were developed. Hormone-releasing IUDs often reduce menstrual bleeding, while copper IUDs may increase it. Today a copper-bearing IUD, the TCu380A,[9] is the most widely available IUD in the world (Treiman *et al.* 1995).

Clinical studies testing and comparing different IUD models usually employ relatively uniform study designs and evaluation criteria. In most studies, IUDs are evaluated in terms of contraceptive effectiveness, continuation, and rates of removal due to side-effects and complications (bleeding and pain, perforation, expulsion, and infection). The use of clinical trials for the testing of contraceptive methods has been criticized by women's health advocates for providing inadequate information on the safety of contraceptive technologies. Anita Hardon (1992: 755) sums up the problems in clinical trials from a women's health perspective:

- trials are conducted in controlled settings;
- the variety of potential users are not represented in the trial;
- researchers determine which effects of a technology are relevant to take into consideration and which are not;

- long-term health effects cannot be assessed;
- and rare side-effects cannot be identified.

A central underlying assumption of clinical IUD studies is that the physical effects of technologies such as the IUD can be standardized and generalized; that an IUD tested in one population of women will have similar effects in other populations of women (cf. Oudshoorn 1996). In other words, it is assumed that human biology is identical across different populations and that physical reactions to a foreign element like the IUD will be relatively similar in all women. An important question one may ask, however, is whether such universalizing assumptions hold. Can we safely assume that physical reactions to contraceptive devices will be identical across different populations of women? Recent clinical studies suggest that we cannot. Clinical IUD studies often encounter serious difficulties explaining the widely varying effects of the same device in different populations of women (Chi 1993; Treiman *et al.* 1995). For instance, clinical trials of one IUD, the TCu380A, have shown significantly different rates of discontinuation, ranging from 10 per cent to 30 per cent after twelve months of use, of which rates of expulsion swing from 2.4 per cent to 7.1 per cent, contraceptive failure from 0.3 per cent to 1 per cent, and removal due to bleeding/pain from 3.6 per cent to 14.2 per cent (Treiman *et al.* 1995). This seems to suggest that the effects of technologies on human bodies cannot be easily generalized and that there are no simple links between technologies and physiologies. Yet, as Rachel Snow (1994) has pointed out, the state of science is largely speculative on why this is so.

In order to understand how technologies like the IUD interact with human bodies, it may be necessary to consider the broader social context in which both bodies and technologies are embedded. In his review of recent research on IUDs, Chi concludes:

> In general, previous IUD studies have placed more emphasis on the IUDs per se than on the characteristics or history of the women who desire and/or use them. ... Future studies need to widen the scope, and examine IUD use in a greater sociocultural context, with the primary study goal being to improve women's health and their welfare. (Chi 1993: 99)

Moreover, as suggested above, it may be necessary to reconsider the very notions of technology and physiology. Can we be sure about the invariability of human biology and can we be sure that technologies have the same effects on human bodies across cultures?

Not only the characteristics of the device itself, however, but also the quality of family planning services are essential elements for the safety and effectiveness of IUD use. As noted by Sivin (1994: 47), 'Regardless of technological advances in IUDs, if health care providers cannot deliver them properly, the advances will be cancelled out.' On the service side it is important to ensure

- careful screening of potential IUD users,
- careful insertion, carried out under sterile conditions with disinfected instruments,
- informative and empathetic counselling,
- regular follow-up plus quick access to medical care (Treiman and Liskin 1988).

In many service delivery points, and particularly in developing countries such as Vietnam, these quality of care standards are not adequately met.

Besides the quality of family planning care, also the health of IUD users affects IUD performance. Among the contra-indications to IUD use are existing reproductive tract infections (RTIs), a high risk of sexually transmitted diseases (STDs), and severe anaemia (Angle *et al*. 1993). Since IUDs often cause menstrual blood loss to increase, for women with anaemia or weak nutritional status, IUD use may be contra-indicated (Hagenfeldt 1994, Sundström 1994). Reproductive tract infections and high STD risks are contraindications to IUD use due to the risk of pelvic inflammatory disease (PID). The risk of contracting pelvic inflammatory disease has been a major concern in relation to the IUD. Studies conducted in the 1970s and 1980s pointed to much higher rates of PID among IUD users than among other women, and for some time it was suspected that the IUD might cause PID (Chi 1993). Today, however, the dominant view is that the risk of PID associated with IUD use is primarily related to the time of insertion, while after insertion, risk of PID is associated with exposure to STDs (Sivin *et al*. 1992; Chi 1993; Burkman 1996). Importantly, however, already existing reproductive tract infections may be aggravated by the insertion of an IUD (Sundström 1994; Treiman *et al*. 1995). In other words, if a woman has a reproductive tract infection at the time of IUD insertion, IUD use is not safe. Again, this may have severe implications in third-world countries, where RTI rates are often high and where women's access to adequate diagnosis and treatment is often limited (Dixon-Mueller and Wasserheit 1991).

IUDs in Vietnam

In the history of Vietnamese family planning, several different types of intrauterine devices have been provided, including the Chinese 'Ota'; the Czech 'Dana'; a locally produced copy of the 'Dana', 'Vina'; the TCu200; the TCu380A; and the Multiload 375 (UN 1989; UNFPA 1994). Since the early 1990s, UNFPA has imported the TCu380A. At the time of this study, the TCu380A and the Multiload 375 were the IUDs most commonly provided within the Vietnamese family planning programme. As a background for the investigation of women's experiences with the IUD which the following chapters present, I shall now briefly consider the aspects of family planning services and of Vietnamese women's reproductive health which are relevant for an assessment of IUD use in Vietnam.

Few systematic studies of the quality of care in Vietnamese family planning have been conducted, but existing studies point to considerable weaknesses in the delivery of family planning services. First, the *technical skills* of providers are often inadequate, not least due to insufficient training (Jain *et al*. 1993). Đỗ Trọng Hiếu *et al*. (1993a) suggest that the high rates of IUD expulsion in Vietnam may be due to problems of technical competence.[10] A UNFPA evaluation of the quality of care in Vietnamese family planning services found the screening of new contraceptive recipients with regard to medical and gynaecological history to be weak, resulting in the possible oversight of contraindications to contraceptive methods. The evaluation also found infection control procedures to be highly variable; many providers did not wash hands between clients and did not use gloves for pelvic examinations (Jain *et al*. 1993). While the UNFPA evaluation found that providers did check for infections which would be treated before the insertion of an IUD, other studies have found that only minimal care was provided for reproductive tract infections and that providers' understanding of the aetiology, diagnosis, and treatment of RTIs was limited (IPAS 1995; WHO 1995). Second, *counselling* is still a novel idea in Vietnam (Jain *et al.* 1993; IPAS 1995; WHO 1995). The UNFPA evaluation found counselling to be practically non-existent; in the observed family planning consultations the total consultation time lasted from 2 to 6 minutes. Several studies have noted that information on contraceptive methods tends to be strongly biased towards the IUD, with providers either ignoring or directly discouraging the use of alternative methods such as the contraceptive pill. Sometimes they even promote the IUD in cases where another method might be more appropriate (Jain *et al.* 1993; UNFPA 1993; Knodel *et al.* 1995; WHO 1995). This may be due partly to the bias towards the IUD in the training of providers, partly to the many years of acquaintance with the IUD in Vietnamese family planning, and partly to providers receiving a bonus for new acceptors of IUDs and sterilizations but not for new acceptors of other methods (Jain *et al.* 1993; Knodel *et al.* 1995; WHO 1995). A third weakness in the provision of family planning services lies in the lack of *follow-up*, with clients returning for follow-up visits only if they have a problem with their method of contraception (Jain *et al.* 1993; WHO 1995).

Also the state of health of IUD users affects contraceptive experiences. As noted above, both anaemia and reproductive tract infections may be problematic with regard to IUD use. UNICEF Vietnam states that anaemia linked to iron deficiency is a major problem among women in Vietnam. Iron deficiency anaemia is found to affect 40 to 50 per cent of pregnant women in the cities of Hanoi and Hải Phòng and in the provinces of Hà Tây and Nam Hà (UNICEF 1994: 73). Reliable data on reproductive tract infections among women in Vietnam are scarce, but existing studies indicate that reproductive tract infections are very common (Desai 1995; Samuelson *et al.* 1995). The National Institute of Venereology and Dermatology states that 20–40 per cent of rural women have a reproductive tract infection (WHO 1995). A study carried out among 600 women in Hà Bắc and Sông Bé provinces in 1994 found the prevalence rate of RTIs to be 69 per cent (AFPC-UNFPA 1995),[11] while a 1996 study among 609 women in Thái Bình province found the RTI prevalence rate to be 33 per cent (Tran Hung Minh *et al.*1997). In another study, family planning providers estimated that 80 per cent of women who come for an abortion have an RTI (IPAS 1995).

In short, there appear to be several potential problems associated with the use of IUDs in Vietnam, including both the weaknesses of family planning care and women's state of health. But how do Vietnamese women themselves experience the effects of IUD use on their bodies? As the WHO (1995) has noted, relatively little is known about women's own perspectives on contraceptive use or about the effects of method choice on the lives of women in Vietnam. Yet a few studies do exist which investigate Vietnamese women's IUD experiences. A retrospective study conducted in 1991–92 among 1,697 urban IUD users found that 46 per cent suffered from side-effects (Phạm Bích San 1993). 80 per cent of the women reported that their state of health was worse now than previously and 90 per cent of these women attributed their worsened state of health to the IUD. The study concluded that 'it may be the case that the side-effects of IUD insertion were the main problem that has prevented the acceptance of the IUD TCu380A among Vietnamese women'. The side-effects reported were mainly irregular menstrual bleedings, stomach-ache, back-ache, 'light sickness' and weight loss. In a retrospective study conducted in 1992 among 206 women in Thái Bình province, almost two-thirds of current IUD users experienced side-effects (Lê Thị Nhâm Tuyết *et al.* 1994; Johansson *et al.* 1996a). Weakness, abdominal pain, backache, headache, and irregular, prolonged or heavy bleedings were commonly reported side-effects. Finally, in a retrospective study carried out in 1994 among 1,511 current or previous IUD users in Nam Hà, Thái Bình, and Hải Hưng provinces, 44 per cent of the women reported side-effects – mainly pain, bleeding, discharge, pelvic heaviness, menstrual irregularity and headaches. Twenty-three per cent of the women said that the IUD had affected their ability to do farmwork (Đỗ Trọng Hiếu *et al.* 1995b).

In short, existing studies document considerable health problems associated with the IUD, as experienced by women themselves. In general, however, these studies do not provide in-depth examinations of the health problems at issue. The meanings and implications of symptoms in the wider social contexts of women's daily lives are largely ignored, as are the local concepts of health and physiology by which the experience of symptoms is mediated.[12] In contrast, my intention with the present study is to provide an account of women's problems with the IUD which examines such problems in the light of local cultural concepts of the body and health, while also emphasizing the wider social, moral, and political contexts in which physical symptoms are produced and experienced.

Outline of the study

Chapter 2 introduces Vải Sơn commune and the livelihoods of its people, and describes the methodologies and processes of research.

Chapter 3 discusses the Vietnamese family planning policy and its implementation in Vải Sơn commune, paying particular attention to the notion of the 'happy family' which is both a central tenet of family planning messages and a prime aim and ambition in people's lives.

Chapter 4 provides a more detailed description and analysis of IUD side-effects as lived and experienced by women themselves, demonstrating how IUD side-effects are always experienced within networks of other kinds of stressful social and somatic experience.

Chapter 5 considers IUD symptoms in the context of local concepts of health and physiology and examines the ways such concepts engage wider social forms and cultural meanings, focusing on the ways physical ailments are closely associated with social stresses and tensions, and particularly with tensions within the family.

Chapter 6 considers 'local moral worlds' as sites for the generation and distribution of physical pain and weakness, analysing the moral complexities which seem to generate both social and physical tensions in women's lives and their embeddedness in cultural and historical traditions.

Chapter 7 discusses the meanings and implications of emotional expression and considers somatic expressions as one among many ways of expressing distress; and finally chapter 8 sums up results, discusses anthropological interpretations of human pain and suffering, and reflects upon the possible implications of this study for future research on reproductive technologies.

Notes

1. An IUD is a plastic or metal device which is inserted into a woman's uterus to prevent pregnancy.

2. The Vietnam Women's Union is a mass organization working to attain gender equality and to educate women to participate actively in the building of Vietnamese society. The Women's Union has branches at all administrative levels, from the central to provincial, district, commune, and hamlet levels.

3. North Vietnam has had a family planning policy since 1963 and in 1975 the policy was extended to the South. It was only with the introduction of the 1988 policy, however, that family planning was pursued with the vigour we see today. For overviews of the history of family planning policies in Vietnam, see Vũ Quý Nhân (1994); Goodkind (1995); NCPFP (1996).

4. Ethnic minorities are allowed to have three children per couple (JPRS 1989).

5. The policy also sets the minimum age at first birth at 22 for women and 24 for men in urban areas, government service and industry, and 19 for women and 21 for men in other areas.

6. In official discourse, the family planning programme is represented as a broad-based mass movement in which 'all forces are mobilized' (NCPFP 1992). In this sense, family planning activities correspond to previous 'mass mobilizing' efforts which have been central to political life in socialist Vietnam (cf. Turley 1993).

7. Goodkind (1995) notes that the fine system seems to be used only in the North, where population pressures are strongest and where there is a tradition of socialist mobilization campaigns.

8. Menstrual regulations are pregnancy terminations carried out within the first six weeks of pregnancy. As noted by several observers, the high abortion rates in Vietnam seem to be related to a lack of contraceptive choice and to inadequate contraceptive services (e.g., Goodkind 1994a; Johansson *et al.* 1996b).

9. Some studies have found that the TCu380A, while being more effective than most other IUDs, also seems to create more problems with pain and bleeding than other IUDs (e.g., Farr and Amatya 1994). Other studies, however, do not find differences between the TCu380A and other IUDs in terms of bleeding and pain problems (Chi 1993).

10. Đỗ Trọng Hiếu et al. (1993a) found twice as high rates of IUD expulsion in Thái Bình province than in Hanoi, and suggested that this finding may reflect a difference in the quality of IUD insertions in the two sites.

11. The methodologies and results of this study have been questioned by Jamie Uhrig, who suggests that the true prevalence of RTIs in the study is no higher than 21.3 per cent (Uhrig 1995).

12. Of these studies, only Johansson *et al.* (1996a) investigate women's IUD experiences qualitatively and in the wider contexts of women's lives. They interpret IUD symptoms as an expression of the contradictory demands that are placed on women's fertility: Vietnamese women are caught between state pressures to limit births and family pressures for sons. The IUD therefore becomes a symbolic expression of a more general social conflict of which for women's bodies are the battleground.

CHAPTER 2

Fieldwork

It is a warm and bright day in June just after the rice has been harvested. Inside the car the air-conditioning is on. Still red-faced from the beers he drank at lunch, the driver tells us funny stories with sexual innuendoes while miraculously managing to stay on the road, steering clear of children, dogs, and bicycles. Where a sign says *uốn tóc* (hairdresser), he turns off the main road and down a red, dusty dirt road. This is Vải Sơn, he informs us. Women working in the vegetable fields along the road look up from under their conical hats, and wide-eyed boys on the backs of their buffalos stare after the two white cars.

This is my first visit to Vải Sơn commune. I am accompanied today by three researchers from Hanoi, two representatives of the provincial Women's Union, and two members of the provincial Population and Family Planning Committee. The cars stop in front of a faded yellow building with *Uỷ Ban Nhân Dân* in large red letters along the front. This is the People's Committee, Phương from the Women's Union tells me, checking her hair in the mirror before she gets out of the car. The view from here is amazing. Patches of green paddy fields stretch before us, cut into smaller pieces by streams of golden afternoon sun. Everywhere people are working, weeding between vegetables, tending animals, carrying crops in big baskets on their bicycles.

'Come on in,' Phương says, pulling my arm. Inside the building a long table is ready, with nicely arranged piles of mandarins, blue grapes, white rice cakes and *Halida* beer. The walls are decorated with certificates and red banners, and Uncle Hồ watches the scene sedately from his pedestal. We are seated at the table and welcomed by the People's Committee Chairman, Hiếu. Having spent most of my time in Hanoi, I am surprised to find that all those sitting at the table are men, all looking alike in their grey or green army-like clothes. The only local woman participating in the meeting stays modestly in background, serving tea and preparing snacks, and it is only later that I realize

that the woman is Lan, the Chairperson of the local Women's
Union. The Chairman begins his welcome talk, and soon the
afternoon dissolves into long wordy speeches and toasts of beer.

⚮

The account that I shall present in this study is mainly based upon
my experiences and observations during twelve months of
anthropological fieldwork in Vải Sơn, a rural Vietnamese
commune. From November 1993 to December 1994 I lived with a
commune family, working closely with the Women's Union and
participating as much as possible in local daily life. In April–May
1996 I returned for six weeks, this time living in Hanoi and taking
day trips to the commune. In this chapter I shall describe my work
and relations to people in Vải Sơn, outlining the background conditions to the findings presented in this study. I shall also describe
how my research interests developed and changed in the context
of my changing relations to people in the field.

Vải Sơn commune

Vải Sơn commune is located 27 kilometres from Hanoi, in Hà
Tây province in the Red River delta. This densely populated delta
is often described as one of Vietnam's two 'rice baskets', providing rich harvests two or three times a year. Yet in spite of the
fertility of the land, life in the delta is harsh. The climate is brutal,
with mercilessly hot summers and freezing winters, and typhoons
and floodings often make life here precarious. Since land is
limited and taxation tough, many farming families struggle to survive, constantly searching for secondary occupations to supplement meagre agricultural incomes. But as elsewhere in the
country, new signs of wealth are now emerging – a small café or
sugarcane juice stall here, a shop selling birds or toys there –
pointing to the newly-acquired prosperity of at least some of the
delta's people.

    A bumpy, dusty – or in the rainy season muddy – road connects
Vải Sơn commune to the province capital. The paddy fields along
the road fill the air with a warm, pleasant smell of plants and soil.
The road is lined with busy workshops and newly built concrete
houses and crowded with people on bicycles loaded with vegetables, chickens, or pigs; teenagers on their way to or from school;
rusty noisy Russian trucks whirling up the dust, looking as if they

might fall apart any minute; and shining new Honda Dream motorbikes transporting newly-rich Hanoi youngsters clad in jeans and sunglasses. Just before the road crosses a river and as sharp blue limestone mountains rise over the rice fields, one reaches Vải Sơn commune.

On the day of my first visit to the commune I was taken to Quyết Định hamlet, to be introduced to the family with whom I was going to stay during my fieldwork. On this day everyone was at home: Bà (grandmother) Chính, her son Chính, daughter-in-law Kiều, and their 8- and 14-year-old sons Thích and Tuệ. There was no doubt as to who was in charge in this house: sitting in the heavy dark furniture in front of the ancestors' altar, Bà spoke with great authority, welcoming me to the family, but emphasizing the rules that the authorities had laid down. I was not allowed to leave the house unless I was accompanied by either a family member or a Women's Union or People's Committee representative, and she would under no circumstances let me wander aimlessly (*lung tung*) around.

Like other Red River delta communes, Vải Sơn is densely populated. By the end of 1994, the commune comprised 1,935 households and 9,168 inhabitants living on 40.555 square kilometres of land. Coming to the commune, one is immediately struck by the large numbers of people filling the landscape. The green paddy fields in between hamlets are dotted with women under conical hats weeding or watering the rice; roads are full of people transporting crops and animals; and in the alleys, large groups of children are playing. Vải Sơn commune consists in eight hamlets (*thôn*) – the largest of which is also known as Vải Sơn – 'bamboo-hedged', as other Red River delta hamlets, with narrow alleys and walled courtyards which seem to close in upon themselves, turning strangers away. It is an ethnically homogenous commune, with all inhabitants belonging to the *kinh* ethnic majority group. As evident from the three big, French-built churches, which attract large crowds on Sundays, the commune has a large Catholic population: 40 per cent of commune people are Catholic while 60 per cent are Buddhist.

My work was concentrated in the hamlets of Quyết Định and Vải Sơn, which are both predominantly Buddhist.[1] With its 2,000 inhabitants, Vải Sơn is the commune's largest hamlet. It is also the political and administrative centre, with the People's Committee building, the local branch of the Agricultural Bank, the health centre, and the secondary school. Quyết Định is a hamlet of around 1,000 people. It is located on the main road, about one kilometer from Vải Sơn hamlet. Immediately visible from the road is the centrepiece and pride of the hamlet, the 500-year-old temple/communal house, the *đình*. Once the centre of power and decision-making, the *đình* is now mainly used for festivals and ceremonies, being a symbol of village unity and of common ancestry and identity. Feelings of local belonging and communal identity are nourished and expressed in yearly festivals in the *đình* celebrating the village guardian spirit.

Within hamlets the houses lie closely clustered, with family members often living near one another. The people here closely follow and participate in each other's lives. Marriages and friendships are usually forged within the confines of hamlets, and it is within hamlets that economic cooperation is organized and help and assistance can be found in times of crisis. Numerous sayings express the importance of close neighbourhood relations: 'Even at night without light we still have each other' (*Tối lửa tắt đèn có nhau*) or 'Selling far away brothers and sisters, buying nearby neighbours' (*Bán anh em xa, mua láng giềng gần*). Hamlets are administratively subdivided into smaller units (*đội*), the previous cooperative workteams. More importantly, though, they are subdivided into lineages (*họ*) of which there are 13 in Quyết Định. These lineages trace their ancestors in the village several generations back, and each has a lineage head (*trưởng họ*) who is responsible for remembering and worshipping ancestors five to seven generations back.

Kinship is patrilineal and patrilocal: family lines are continued through the men, and women normally join their husbands' households upon marriage.[2] Yet as both historical and contemporary studies of Vietnamese kinship have noted, along with patrilineality and patrilocality goes a strong emphasis on maternal kinship relations (cf. Whitmore 1984; Hy Văn Lương 1989; O'Harrow 1995). Whereas in death rituals, ancestor worship and inheritance matters, paternal bonds are significantly more important than maternal ones, in daily social life maternal family relations seem to be no less important. The everyday reliance on both maternal and paternal social bonds is enabled by the fact that marriages are usually endogamous within hamlets, i.e. women often marry within their natal hamlets and thus stay close to their natal family.[3] Most parents prefer their daughter to marry a man from the same hamlet, or at least from the same commune. This is expressed in numerous sayings, such as, 'If one's daughter marries nearby she will bring a bowl of vegetable soup to her parents when they need it' (*Con gái mà lấy chồng gần, có bát canh cần nó cũng đem cho*), or, 'Better get married to a village dog than to a noble out-sider' (*Lấy chó trong làng hơn lấy người sang thiên hà*). If a woman's parents oppose a marriage, the reason is very often that the marriage will take their daughter too far away from them. Even a distance of 10 kilometres may be considered too far away, since it renders everyday emotional and practical support difficult, especially if the daughter's parents-in-law are unsympathetic towards her visiting her natal parents. Most women also consider it a great advantage to live close to their natal families, thus having a double social network of both 'inside' (*nội*) (i.e. husband's) and 'outside' (*ngoại*) (i.e. wife's) family, and being able to turn to their natal family for help and support when needed.

Most families in Vải Sơn are either nuclear or extended.[4] Upon marriage, young couples usually live with the husband's parents for the first few years and only later set up a household of their own. Old parents may live with any one of their adult sons, but as I shall discuss in Chapter 3, it is very rare for daughters to support their parents in their old age. When they get married and leave their families, daughters usually take with them just a bicycle or some gold, whereas sons inherit their parents' property when the parents die. According to Vietnamese law, sons and daughters have equal rights to inheritance. In reality, however, if old people die without having any sons, the sons of the husband's brothers will usually inherit their property (*ăn thừa tự*) unless a daughter marries uxorilocally. In other words, in this as in many other respects, 'The writ of the Emperor bows to the customs of the village' (*Phép Vua thua lệ làng*).

Đổi mới and changing everyday lives

With the recent economic reforms there has been a return to the household as the basic unit of agricultural production in Vietnam. Whereas land was previously collectively and cooperatively farmed, land reforms in 1988 provided each household with the responsibility for land management. Today most cooperative functions in Vải Sơn – except the management of irrigation and electricity – have been dismantled, and since October 1993 families have rented their land on a 20-year basis. In October 1992 all land in the commune was distributed equally among its people, with one *sào* (360 m^2) of land allocated for each person, so that today most households have one *sào* of land for each household member born before October 1992.[5] Better-off families may buy some extra land from other families or rent the rights to a fish pond from the commune, while the poorest households risk having their land confiscated if they do not manage to pay their taxes. In 1993 a new Land Law was issued, allowing land to be distributed to households for a period of 20 years, or, for some crops, for 50 years. During this time, land use rights can be transferred within and between families, inherited, or sold. Land Use Right Certificates are issued by local authorities to each household. This had not yet happened in Vải Sơn when I was there in 1996, but according to commune authorities the process was under way.

Even though it is still too early to evaluate its effects, there seem to be risks that the 1993 Land Law may lead to an entrenchment of male authority in rural Vietnam and increase women's dependence on relations within their families for resource control (cf. Beresford 1994; Fong 1994; Allen et al 1995; McDonald 1995; Trần Thị Vân Anh 1995). First, there is a risk that only the male household head will be named on Land Use Right Certificates. This may have serious consequences for women's rights to land in the case of widowhood or divorce and for their access to secondary benefits such as credit or extension services which are closely related to ownership over land. Second, if a woman marries outside of her natal commune, she loses control over her land – unless, as in particular cases in Vải Sơn, she walks or bikes to her natal commune every day to farm her land. In other words, even though its actual effects still remain to be seen, there does seem to be a considerable risk that the new Land Law may have negative implications for women's social status and opportunities.

Nearly all families in Vải Sơn cultivate wet-rice as their main crop, together with some additional vegetables, such as corn, peanuts, cabbage, or sugarcane. There are two rice crops a year and one additional crop of vegetables. Many families also raise pigs and chicken, and some have vegetable or fruit gardens. Even though most of the land in the commune is very rich and fertile, it is difficult to survive on agriculture alone. Most families eat most of their agricultural products themselves, selling only a fairly modest surplus. Therefore, it is by now the rule rather than the exception that male household members find work outside of the commune, leaving agricultural work for their wives, sisters, and mothers. Some men work in Hanoi as construction workers, some drive motor-cycle taxis in and around Hanoi, and some find work in provinces in the North. Women stay at home, taking care of children, old parents, farming the land, and sometimes doing some small trade in nearby markets.

This shift of men into non-agricultural occupations – and women consequently being left with the double burden of agricultural and domestic work – seems to be a general tendency in areas close to cities in Vietnam at the moment (Beresford 1994). An important effect of this gender division of labour is that women's economic contribution to the household becomes more invisible than men's, since the products of women's labour are literally 'eaten up' by the family. Women's agricultural work and small trade usually produce a very modest monetary income for the family, and whether a family is able to advance economically or not often depends on the husband's income. It is usually with the money earned by the husband (or adult children) that investmests are made or that houses are built. In other words, current gender divisions of labour contribute to the image of the husband as the person who is most important to the family's economic survival, thus reinforcing the image of the man as the family's 'pillar' (*trụ cột*) and household-head (*chủ nhà*).[6]

One obvious effect of the *đổi mới* policy is the increasing disparity in wealth among people in rural areas such as Vải Sơn.[7] While some families are building large new brick houses, others still live in bamboo huts which are freezingly cold in winter and which leak during the summer rains. While a few families eat plentiful and varied meals every day, most still live on a diet consisting of only rice, supplemented by fish sauce and some vegetables. A few parents are able to buy computer games for their children to play with, but most struggle hard to be able to pay school fees and buy pens and books. According to commune leaders, Vải Sơn is a poor commune, since its people do not have any really profitable secondary occupations (*nghè phụ*).

In a poverty survey carried out of all households in 1996, 10 per cent of commune households were categorized as 'hungry' or 'poor'. The category 'hungry' comprises households that suffer from food shortages for more than six months each year (60 households), and the category 'poor' covers households suffering from food shortages between one and six months a year (132 households). In the survey which I carried out among 200 women in Vải Sơn, 33 per cent characterized themselves as poor or very poor, 65 per cent as average, and only 2 per cent considered themselves to be well off. According to commune people, a major hindrance to local economic development is the limited access to credit. Bank loans are difficult for poor people to obtain and private lenders usually demand very high rates of interest, 8 to 10 per cent a month is not unusual. But as a new initiative the commune Women's Union may now act as guarantor for women's bank loans, providing women with loans at an interest rate of 2.3 per cent. In 1996, 42 women had obtained bank loans through the Women's Union. In addition to this, women in several hamlets have now organized their own savings and loan groups.

Current social and economic changes also seem to have important implications for women's daily work. Even though it is difficult to make direct comparisons between women's pre- and post-*đổi mới* work loads, several studies have noted that women seem to work longer hours as a consequence of the economic reforms (Allen 1990; Beresford 1994; UNICEF 1994). The dismantling of collective welfare systems tends to increase women's reproductive work burdens, and since more effort devoted to productive work now brings higher incomes, women seem to be inclined to work harder in the productive sphere than they did before. Many women in Vải Sơn say they work harder today than in the cooperative system, where there was more time to rest and talk to each other and it was more *vui* (happy, joyful) to go to work since everyone worked together. Now women feel they have more freedom to organize work as they want to and the economy is better, but workdays are also more demanding. There is less free time now and less time to attend Women's Union and other meetings.

The increasing personal responsibility for their families seems to weigh very heavily on women's shoulders and compels them to work as hard as they are physically able. As Women's Union cadres in Vải Sơn would often complain, there seems to be a tendency now for women to concentrate all their efforts on their families and their economic survival, leaving little time and energy for other activities such as training, meetings, or community work. This tendency has also been observed by Melanie Beresford:

> Women's retreat into the household also means that they have less social contact, an increased burden of productive and repro-ductive labour and fewer opportunities to improve their skills and decision-making capacity (Beresford 1994: 2).

In general, women's workdays are extremely demanding.[8] As women themselves often point out, the hardships of their working lives are directly associated with their being responsible for both agricultural and domestic work. In most families, the mother gets up early in the morning before everyone else, lights the fire in the kitchen and starts cooking breakfast for the family. She wakes the children, gets them washed and dressed, serves breakfast, sends the children to school or brings them to the creche or to grand-parents, feeds pigs and chicken, sweeps the yard, and does the washing of any dirty clothes. On market days she goes to the market to buy food and household necessities for the family. She then goes to work her fields, sowing, transplanting, harrowing, weeding, or doing other kinds of land preparation, crop tending, or harvesting. The only exclusively male task in agriculture is ploughing, while nearly all other tasks are undertaken by women.[9] The tools used in agriculture are very simple and almost all stages of agricultural production, from soil preparation to harvesting, are done by hand. A normal workday is physically very demanding, often involving hours of work in bent-over positions in the rice fields and the carrying of heavy shoulder-poles to transport water, seedlings, fertilizer, etc.

At midday women return to their families to prepare lunch. In some families other female family members – a daughter or a grandmother – may cook the lunch, but often this also falls to the mother. In most families, cooking food for the pigs is also normally the mother's job, while children sometimes collect grass and leaves to help feed the pigs. In the afternoons most women work in their fields for a few more hours and return home in the late afternoon to wash and take care of children, cook dinner and do other household chores such as mending clothes, sweeping floors, etc.

If children are ill, it is usually their mother who brings them to the health centre, goes to buy medicine for them, and stays awake to take care of them at night. In most families, the mother goes to bed last and sleeps least, often staying awake to breastfeed and care for children.

It is therefore hardly surprising that many women perceive sexual activity as just another physical burden on top of all the other exigencies of a normal work day; indeed, one of many terms for 'having sex' is *làm việc*, to work. In addition to this, when assessing the work women do every day, the underlying and invisible daily fears and anxieties should also be borne in mind. Not only do women work hard, but most of the women I knew in Vải Sơn were also constantly worried about whether they would manage to provide well enough for their families during the coming months. These fears and anxieties seem to add considerably to the burdens of everyday chores.

The current era is perceived by commune women as one of both risks and opportunities. Almost everyone agrees that in most respects life is easier now than it was before, with larger varieties of food and consumer goods available and a rising standard of living for most people. On the other hand, with the cut-backs in state subsidies and the introduction of fees for health care and education, the ability to cover such expenses has become a major concern to many families. Whereas previously everyone was equally poor, today both dreams of wealth and fear of economic failure loom large in many women's minds. Economic success or failure has now largely become a personal responsibility determined by individual talent and effort rather than by social circumstances or party policies. Most people seem to feel that with effort and talent, one can considerably improve one's lot in life, while those who are weak or lazy soon get left behind. 'The strong get rich' (*Ai mạnh thì giàu*) was how one woman described today's social world. In other words, with more scope for private initiatives, new social and economic opportunities now exist, but the current era also seems in many ways to be one of greater uncertainties and greater stress than previous times.

Poverty is usually understood as not just a question of economic income and material living standards, but as a moral issue as well. People who are lazy and 'don't know how to work' (*không biết làm*) are looked down upon, while there is social and moral prestige to be gained by working hard and with ambition. There is a considerable concern (not to say obsession) with economy in everyday lives. When I met people for the first time, the conversation would somehow always start out with economic issues. A standard opening remark which I heard ad nauseam was, 'Vietnam is very poor, isn't it?' People seem to bring up poverty as the first theme of conversations, partly to excuse themselves and their homes for being poor and simple, and partly because economic problems are simply very urgent problems in their lives. They compare their own standard of living to the Western one they see on television, and there seems to be a widespread feeling that poverty is a sign of not only personal but also national inferiority; it expresses a failure to organize the society effectively, and a failure to manage the resources available. Even though the wars are partly to blame for today's poverty, many people also feel that the wars are long over and that it is time for Vietnam to divest itself of its poverty and misery.

Women's health

Since a main theme of the present study is women's own perceptions of their bodies and health, a few words need to be said about common health problems among women in Vải Sơn as biomedically perceived. In common with the female population elsewhere in Vietnam, women in Vải Sơn suffer from nutritional deficiences, from intestinal parasites due to the lack of clean water and the use of human faeces as fertilizer, and from reproductive tract infections (cf. UNICEF 1994; Desai 1995; Samuelson et al 1995). In Vải Sơn, basic sanitation and clean water supplies are practically non-existent and most families get their water from shallow wells or ponds. Diets are often poor and inadequate and in many families women eat last and least. In addition to this, as already mentioned, women's daily work is physically demanding and apparently increasingly so in the current era of reform. With the introduction of charges for health services, women may also be more reluctant than before to seek professional help. UNICEF describes the effect of economic reforms on women's health as follows: 'Women's health is expected to suffer from a combination of increased workload and the increased costs of health care' (1994: 33).

As summed up by Susan Allen , the main health problems faced by women in Vietnam are varied:

• backache, joint problems, headaches and accidents occasioned by heavy physical work and stress;

• anaemia brought on by poor diet and insufficient nutrition. This is a particular problem during and after pregnancy and is often made worse by repeated abortions and heavy bleeding caused by IUDs;

• gynaecological problems due to lack of antenatal care and poor or nonexistent care during childbirth;[10]

• complications and side-effects of the various methods of family planning available to Vietnamese women. (Allen 1990: 11)

In short then, as we shall see throughout this study, poverty, hard work, and experiences related to reproduction all seem to adversely affect women's health.

The family of Bà Chính

The family I lived with during my year of fieldwork in Vải Sơn was known as Bà Chính's family (*gia đình nhà Bà Chính*). Bà's son Chính is an engineer and works in Hanoi, his wife Kiều teaches at a nearby secondary school, and Bà Chính cultivates and sells bananas and peanuts. Bà Chính's family differs from most other families in Vải Sơn by not having economic problems: everyone in the family is well-fed and dressed and their house is one of the roomiest and nicest in the commune. In addition to this, Bà Chính is a woman who is respected for her high morality. A former Chairperson of the local Women's Union, she is known as being morally upright and knowledgeable.

Her husband died fighting the French less than a year after their marriage and thus never got to see his son Chính, with whom Bà was seven months pregnant when he died. Bà Chính did the morally correct thing: she never remarried, but stayed and took care of her son and her late husband's old parents. Bà often talks about the poverty and hardship of the years when she was raising

Chính: the hunger; how they did not even have rice to eat but had to eat manioc; and the hard work she had to do to keep her son and her parents-in-law alive. Even though her neighbours laughed at her for it, Bà insisted that her son should go to school and have a proper education, and today Bà enjoys her large and rich house and her perspicacity for insisting on an education for her son. While often envied for their wealth, however, the family of Bà Chính is far from envied for the atmosphere in the family. Everyone in the commune knows that relations between Kiều and her mother-in-law are extremely strained and often erupt in loud quarrels.[11]

Ông (grandfather) Quý, who is the elder brother of Bà Chính's husband, lives in the house next door to Bà Chính, and he often states that 'the two houses are one'. Ông Quý's first wife died when their only son Quảng was just 1 year old, and Ông Quý later married a woman 16 years younger than himself, Bà Quý, with whom he had six children. He says with a grin that seven of his brothers and sisters died during the war, so he had to put seven new people into the world, didn't he? Next door to Ông and Bà Quý lives his eldest son Quảng with his wife Bình and their two sons who are aged 6 and 8. Quảng has a very quick temper; he sometimes gets so touchy (literally 'hot' in Vietnamese) that nobody dares come near him. Bình's and Quảng's income is very unstable, and Bình often has to work as a day labourer for a salary of 10,000 *đồng* (US$1) a day.

A few houses away lives Lý, a daughter of Ông Quý. Lý and I became very good friends during my stay in Vải Sơn. She is a strong and upright woman, living with her husband Kha, their three children, Kha's mother Bà Báu, and her very old and blind mother, Cụ. Another woman I got to know well was Bà Chính's 48-year-old sister-in-law, Mơ. She married Bà Chính's younger brother as his second wife (*vợ lẽ*), and together they had five children. Today Mơ is a widow and lives with her eldest son and daughter-in-law, their 1-year-old son, and her own two youngest children in a small house near Bà Chính. Also some of the neighbourhood women, particularly Lai, Loan, and Hoà, became my good friends.

Both Lai's and Loan's families are among the poorest in Quyết Định. Lai and her husband have five children, and their eldest daughter suffers from a disease which is costly in terms of both medication and hospitalizations. Loan and her husband have three young children today, and since her husband works outside the commune Loan both farms their land and takes care of the children. Hoà and her husband Sản are relatively well off; Sản is very industrious and their three children are better fed and dressed than most other children in Vải Sơn.

Fieldwork under supervision and control

Between 1954 and the early 1990s, very few Western anthropologists were able to conduct field studies in Vietnam,[12] and in 1992–93 when I lived in Hanoi and prepared this study, travel permits were still required for all journeys out of Hanoi. At that time, as today, permissions to do field research were not easily obtained. As David Craig notes:

> For any outsider – and especially a foreigner – to move around and inspect or research unaccompanied in a village is a very rare thing, achievable only after central and local authorities are made fully aware of the outsider's goals, and after a thorough period of getting to know and trust them. (Craig 1997, p. 77).

Prior to my twelve months of fieldwork in Vải Sơn there had been three months of preparatory paper work and a lot of effort to obtain all the necessary permissions, with numerous meetings, innumerable phone calls, and an endless transit of papers hither and thither. My project was presented as a study focusing on family planning and women's health, and as such it fitted well with national priorities. Still, at the time when I sought permission to do fieldwork, my request to stay in a commune and do ethnographic research for a year was far from a standard request, and took a considerable amount of time to get through the system of central, provincial, district, and commune authorities.[13]

Permission to do fieldwork requires close cooperation with a Vietnamese social science institution, and acceptance of the project from authorities at all levels. Key persons and institutions in the process of preparing my fieldwork were Professor Lê Thị Nhâm Tuyết, who is the Director of the Research Centre of Gender, Family and Environment in Development (CGFED) in Hanoi, and the Committee for Population and Family Planning (CPFP) in Hà Tây province. Professor Lê Thị Nhâm Tuyết introduced me to the provincial Population and Family Planning Committee, and the committee introduced me to Vải Sơn commune and to Bà Chính's family.

From my very first day in Vải Sơn, the preconditions for my working and living there were clearly spelled out. I was only allowed to leave the house in the company of either a family member or a representative of commune authorities or the Women's Union, and at the beginning of each week I was to present a detailed working plan to the commune People's Committee, with a precise plan of my activities for the coming week. At the end of each week I was to present a report of my activities of the previous week to the provincial Committee for Population and Family Planning. In addition to this, a policeman was placed in the commune during the time I was there. All these precautions were taken only in order to protect me, I was told. Since the commune in general and Bà Chính's family in particular had assumed responsibility for me, they had to make sure nothing bad happened to me. As a Westerner and thus by definition rich, I was also a potential target of economic abuse, Bà Chính often said and forbade me to lend money to anyone.

In practice, the person who was assigned the daily responsi-bility for assisting and supervising my work in Vải Sơn was Lan, the 34-year old Chairperson of the commune Women's Union. Even though neither of us had chosen the arrangement from the be-ginning, we both gradually came to appreciate working together. Since my knowledge of Vietnamese was limited to begin with, Lan would function as my 'interpreter', translating from the local dialect into a simpler and more understandable Vietnamese. She also became a 'role model' and teacher to me in several respects. The more time we spent together, the more my respect grew for her commitment to her community and her work, her honesty and selflessness, and her grace in social relations. Lan's husband is in the army and works in the South, usually coming home only once a year. It is therefore Lan who farms their 4 *sào* land and takes care of their two children and her 88-year-old father-in-law who is very weak and requires special care. In addition to this, she has the overall responsibility for all Women's Union activities and family planning work in the commune.

Another important person in my fieldwork was Liên, the Women's Union Vice-Chairperson. When Lan could not assist me, Liên would do so instead. Liên's husband also works in the South, and she, too, has not only young children but also elderly parents to take care of. She has three children and lives with her husband's parents who are both in their early eighties. In contrast to Lan's father-in-law, however, Liên's parents-in-law are still strong and healthy, and it is not least their assistance in childcare and cooking which enables her to be both a member of the People's Committee and an active member in the commune Women's Union.

Phases in fieldwork

When I think of my fieldwork today I see it as falling into three different phases.

The first phase was in winter/spring when I felt I was hardly considered as a real human being,[14] and when I was quite closely supervised and watched over. At this stage my research agenda was fairly open and I was enquiring into all kinds of issues related to fertility, family planning, and family life.

The next phase was in summer when I was becoming more of a real person to people and was gradually allowed more freedom to move and to participate in normal, everyday life. I now started to focus specifically on women's health problems and their connections to social stress, beginning to carve out the contours of the argument that I pursue in this study.

The last fieldwork phase was in autumn when we did a survey of reproductive histories and contraceptive experiences, when I conducted several series of relatively structured interviews with a small group of women focusing specifically on the issues of health and family tension, and when my relationships to some of the women in Vải Sơn developed into what I feel certain will be lifelong friendships.

Winter and spring: supervision and control

During my initial months of fieldwork, the close supervision by authorities and the pre-planning of all activities created some very specific and not always pleasant working conditions. Except for interactions with family members and immediate neighbours of Bà Chính, when I met and talked to people during these first months, it was almost always in situations that were 'set up' and prearranged. In my weekly workplan I was expected to present a list of people whom I would like to meet and talk to in the coming week. Later I realized that in order to make arrangements for such interviews with women, Lan or Liên would simply go to their houses and basically order them to be at home the following day at a set time. Women who for one reason or another preferred not to participate were given the option of declining, and a few did, saying that they were too busy to take part. However, it was probably not easy to avoid an interview for women who did not want it.[15] During the interview the next day, either Lan or Liên would usually be present assisting with note-taking and 'translation'. Since they both belong to the local moral-political elite, their presence, along with my being a stranger and a foreigner, sometimes lent the whole occasion a fairly formal atmosphere. This was mainly so, however, when we met women whom Lan or Liên did not know very well. In other cases, when the women interviewed were family members or neighbours of Lan or Liên, as they often were, the atmosphere was considerably more relaxed.[16]

The issues I was interested in during these first months of fieldwork were mainly family planning, contraceptive experiences, reproductive histories, and notions of reproductive physiology. It was already at this early stage of fieldwork that my attention was drawn to the overwhelming problems that women experienced with the IUD. These problems are very difficult to ignore as soon as one talks to women about health, contraception, or reproduction. Fairly soon it also became clear to me that IUD problems are closely interlinked with other health problems. This was quite obvious during interviews and conversations, where an initial focus on the IUD and reproductive health would inevitably slide into talk about weakness in general, backaches and overwork, social and economic distress, etc. But while I did learn a lot about health problems, ideas about the body and physiology and a range of other issues during this stage of research, I also had to realize that there are limits to what one can learn through an interview, particularly as a stranger and a foreigner. As Margery Wolf writes about her fieldwork in China: 'If the loss of autonomy is the most frustrating aspect of doing research in China, the pervasive influence of politics is the most awesome' (Wolf 1985: 32).

Not least due to the continuous influence of mass education and mass mobilization campaigns, nearly all aspects of everyday life in Vietnam are politicized. In fields as diverse as diet, marriage, religion, and pregnancy, there are politically right and wrong answers to any question, and everyone knows precisely what is politically correct and what is not. This is particularly true for family planning issues, which have been accorded a very high priority on the government agenda at the moment. Obviously, then, people often provide a strange and foreign researcher with the politically correct answers only, while keeping alternative perspectives and experiences to themselves.[17] Many people prefer to stay in a jargon of generalized statements, and only reluctantly talk about their personal feelings and experiences to persons they do not know well. In China studies, such 'politically correct' statements are often understood either as 'false facades' which cover people's 'real ideas' (Mosher 1983), or as a mindless parroting of Party slogans (Wolf 1985), or as a deep imprint of state norms on to individuals (Greenhalgh 1994). I shall argue in Chapter 3, however, that I think there is reason to be careful about seeing politically correct statements as less valuable or 'true' than other kinds of information.

During this first phase of fieldwork Bà Chính strongly insisted on her right and duty to monitor my daily work plan and to put in a veto if I was intending to be with people whom she deemed it inappropriate to be with.[18] 'Some people are good and some people are bad', Bà said, 'and you will not be able to distinguish the good from the bad.' But Bà Chính obviously had firm ideas on who was good and bad. Her monitoring of my acquaintances seemed to have several good reasons; besides her well-intentioned wish to protect me, there was undoubtedly also an element of wanting to censor my impressions of life in Vải Sơn. Bà wanted me to socialize only with 'good' people; i.e. people who behaved in morally appropriate ways and whose families were known to live up to certain moral standards. Her son Chính often tried to explain to her that to conduct my study I might need to talk to people whom Bà Chính thought were not 'good', but such arguments did not make any impression on Bà. As long as I was with members of the family, i.e. women like Lý or Bình, or with Women's Union cadres such as Lan and Liên, Bà was happy and content. But Hương, a woman I got to know well and very much enjoyed being with, belonged to the category of 'bad' people, according to Bà Chính.

Since Hương's small house was located on the way between Quyết Định and Vải Sơn, we would often meet and chat for a few minutes when I was on my way between the two hamlets. Hương is a very outspoken woman and easy to be with. She speaks quite frankly of things which many other people would keep to themselves, and this is probably one of the reasons why Bà Chính does not like her. Hương's husband drives a motorcycle taxi and thus spends most of his time in Hanoi, while Hương does the farming and takes care of their sons Mạnh and Cường. My friendship with Hương became an issue of conflict between Bà Chính and me, since I appreciated Hương's company too much to give it up for no good reason. At this stage of fieldwork there were not many other women with whom I felt as relaxed as with Hương; the afternoons when we were lying on her bed, small-talking and laughing were too valuable in the life of the lonely ethnographer to give up because of the vague 'bad moralities' which Bà Chính insisted on but refused to give a proper explanation of.

But it was not only Bà Chính who did her best to monitor my acquaintances and impressions. Later I learned that before I came to the commune, Lan had carefully instructed Bà Chính and Kiều to avoid quarrelling while I was present in the home. Instead, they should try to give me an impression of a happy and harmonious family life, even though everyone knew that their family was probably as far from harmonious as a family could be. When I later asked Lan why she had told them this, she said that she had felt uncertain about what I would write about Vietnamese people and Vietnamese families. She did not want me to get a wrong impression or let the world think negatively about people in Vietnam. Similarly, one day when Lan and I were talking about ghosts and their interference in people's lives, she suddenly interrupted herself and asked, 'What will you write now about people in Vietnam? Will you write that they are superstititous and feudal?'

During fieldwork I often regretted my interest in family relations and family morality, since troubled family relations are clearly not a field to which foreigners and strangers are easily allowed access. It is generally held that 'family issues should be discussed behind closed doors,' and most people do their best to cultivate the impression of their family they wish to present to the outside world. Ideally, families should be conflict-free, happy, and harmonious, and it is clearly important to people to convey an impression of a family and community life abundant in *tình cảm* (mutual sympathy/feeling). As we shall see in Chapter 7, *tình cảm* is considered to be a core characteristic of social life in rural Vietnam. A life rich in *tình cảm* implies that people care about and support one another, family members are loyal, loving, and under-standing towards each other; and neighbours help each other out whenever it is needed. Unless I knew people well, therefore, they would usually avoid elaborating on personal experiences of disturbed feelings or morally flawed social relations, preferring to stay within the safe realm of abstract statements and explanations of how things generally are or ought to be.

Summer: social and moral education

My insights into everyday life in general and into women's ex-periences of their bodies and health in particular grew considerably during the summer, when Lan became preoccupied with other kinds of work and had less time to assist me in interviewing. This allowed me to talk to women alone and to let conversations develop more spontaneously and in directions which the previous and somewhat more rigid interviews had not allowed for. Also, my language skills were now at a level where I was able to manage without Lan's assist-ance and patient explanations. At this stage, I started to enquire into the problems of 'lack of blood' and 'weak nerves', which seemed fairly prevalent among women and clearly related to IUD problems.

I was now also given permission to participate in work in the fields and started working together with Lý. Since Lý is both a member of Bà Chính's family and a respected community mem-ber, my working together with her was apparently considered acceptable. During this period I spent most of my time with the women from Bà Chính's family: Lý, Bình, or Mơ, assisting with work in the fields. I also spent some time at the health centre, observing family planning service delivery, or talking to Mỹ, the health station midwife. Mỹ and I had gotten along from the first day we met and I often visited her and her family. She lives with her husband, their two children, and her husband's parents, and works as both a midwife and a farmer. Her father used to be the head of the health station and in 1968 her mother was the first woman in Vải Sơn to have an IUD inserted.

During the summer, my relations to many people in the com-mune changed in important ways. By taking part in everyday activities, I came to understand and experience facets of life other than those I had learnt about during the previous interview phase. Whereas during interviews I had improved my language skills and learnt a lot about what social relations should ideally be like, I now started to learn more about how social relations were experienced and practised. Being present when events take place is obviously different from listening to people's accounts of past events. During my time in Vải Sơn, many important events took place in the lives of the people I knew: Lý and her husband were very close to getting divorced; Kiều and Bà Chính had several serious disagreements which nearly split up the house; Hương was seriously ill and hospitalized following a spontaneous abortion; Lý's mother-in-law moved back and forth between her children, each trying to place her in the other's house; and Lan's brother-in-law died after a long period of illness. My being there and experiencing these events as they happened taught me a lot about what morality and social relations are like when they are lived. Also, it takes time to get to know people and to build up trust, and I was only gradually allowed to share experiences which involved exposures of 'moral flaws' of families or expressions of politically 'incor-rect' values and knowledges.

During this period, people were also increasingly concerned with my social and moral education. While in the first months of fieldwork my manners or behaviour were rarely commented upon, people would now say, 'The one you love you strike; the one you hate you let play around' (*Yêu thì cho đòn, ghét thì cho chơi*). Particularly Bà Chính and Lan made an effort with my education. Bà Chính would do all she could to explain to me the difference between 'good' and 'bad' people. Good people are hard-working and uncomplaining, they know their place socially, recognizing 'who is above and who is below', and they are modest, always aware of the debt of gratitude they owe to others, most notably their own parents. Lan would teach me simple manners like greeting people properly or handing a bowl of rice to another person in a polite way, and she would carefully explain to me whenever I did something wrong. But Lan was a teacher to me not least through her own exemplary manners. I learnt a lot from observing her ways of being with other people: her attention to and care for the old people who might be present when we entered a house, her polite way of addressing others, and her smooth and tactful way of exercising authority.

It was also during this period that I accepted that my initial intention of trying to understand both men's and women's perspectives on health and family planning was not likely to succeed: the worlds of women were open to me in a way that the worlds of men were not. When talking about health, reproductive physiology, and family relations, I often had experiences in common with women; despite the obvious differences between our lives, there was common ground as well. There was an immediate place for me in the women's worlds, helping with cooking, washing, and work in the fields, taking care of children, and talking about husbands, love, and jealousy. In the men's world, however, I did not fit in at all; their communities of beer drinking, smoking and gambling were fairly closed to women. I had great trouble and rarely succeeded in establishing rapport with men, and they always seemed to talk in a tiring and lecturing jargon of moral-political truths. There were a few exceptions to this, though: Chính, Ông Quý and the neighbour Sản were men with whom I could reasonably 'connect'. In general, though, I preferred being with women, who also seemed much more relaxed in my company than did men. My living in a women's world during my time in Vải Sơn has obviously had fairly important consequences for the results that I shall present in the following pages. The insights I have been given are clearly insights from a women's point of view, conveying women's experiences of community and family life.

Moreover, they are the insights and experiences of a particular group of women: when I talk about 'women' in the following pages, I mean women in their early or mid-thirties. Social divisions based on age have had quite important implications for my fieldwork in the sense that the women with whom I spent most of my time and established the closest relations were women of my own age; i.e. women who were in their early thirties during my fieldwork. The life situations and experiences of both older and younger women would undoubtedly differ from the experiences of this particular group. As elsewhere in Vietnam, age is an important factor of social division in Vải Sơn. A person's age has implications for her position in family and community, for her relationship to others, and for the ways in which she is addressed and addresses others. People born in the same year often feel tied together by special bonds and they usually participate in important events and celebrations in each other's lives. There are special associations of people born in the same year (*hội đồng niên*) that sometimes organize credit groups for mutual help and support. Given this emphasis on similarities in age, it is probably no co-incidence that three of my closest friends in the commune, Lý, Hương, and Mỹ were born in the same year as I.

Autumn: focusing on the socio-somatics of IUD symptoms

During autumn I enquired more systematically into women's IUD problems and into the experiences of '*lack of blood*' and '*nerves*' to which IUD experiences seemed closely related. In order to get a larger and more systematic picture of IUD and other contraceptive experiences, I conducted a survey of reproductive histories and con-traceptive experiences among women in the commune. The survey covered all hamlets in the commune and comprised 200 female and 100 male respondents who were selected randomly from a commune list of all people and households.[19] Male respondents were included in the survey and in focus group discussions owing to my initial intention of highlighting both male and female perspectives on family planning and contraceptive use. However, since this study has become one with a principal emphasis on women's perspectives, in the present account I shall draw primarily on the answers provided by female respondents. Eligible as respondents were married women with at least one child, and the husbands of 100 of the 200 women selected were also interviewed. The average age of female survey respondents was 32 years and the women had an average of three children each. For a profile of female survey respondents, see Table 1 overleaf.

The survey included questions on socio-economic characteristics of the household, contraceptive knowledge, fertility preferences, re-productive and contraceptive history, and experiences of contra-ceptive side effects. During the summer Lan and I had worked out the survey questionnaire and pilot-tested it. A team of seven assistants – six women and one man (i.e. Lan and Liên, two other Women's Union cadres, two local teachers, and a health station nurse) – was set up in order to collect the data. The interviews were conducted over a period of three weeks and the respondents were interviewed in their homes. Each day I joined different interviewers on their rounds and in the afternoon I collected the survey questionnaries and reviewed them, checking for internal consistency. Every day we had morning and afternoon meetings in the survey team and discussed problems and issues that had come up during interviews.

Table 1: Profile of female survey respondents

Respondents	% of women
Age:	
18–25	21
26–32	30
33–39	34
40–49	15
Occupation:	
Farmer	99
Teacher	1
Education:	
0–3 years	8
4–6 years	43
7–9 years	43
10–12 years	6
Religion:	
Buddhist	76
Catholic	23
Atheist	1
Family form:	
Nuclear	72
Extended	28
Number of children:	
1	13
2	28
3	25
4	22
5+	12

These discussions were often very heated and lively, covering a range of issues – from sexuality, gender and family relations, through household economy to life after death.

Immediately following the survey, we conducted six focus group discussions, two with men aged 30–35 and four with women aged 25–30 and 30–35. Lan, Liên, and two male assistants, Tiến and Hùng, functioned as moderators and referees. The group discussions were tape-recorded and I took part in the groups with women but not in those with men. Participants in the groups were men and women who volunteered when the idea of focus group discussions was introduced to them by Lan, Liên, Tiến, or Hùng. The main themes of the group discussions were the benefits and drawbacks of different contraceptive methods, and discussions therefore included the topics of sexuality, gender relations, work and health. Some of the groups were not particularly successful; people were reluctant to say very much and seemed to feel that the whole situation was fairly awkward. Other groups, however, were dynamic and intense, provoking heated discussions and many good laughs. I was surprised at the openness with which sexuality and gender relations were often discussed in these groups; in some respects group discussions turned out to be much better ways of researching personal and sensitive issues than individual interviews.

After the series of focus group discussions was conducted, I did qualitative follow-up interviews with some of the survey respondents who had reported health problems with their IUDs. Of the 106 women who said they had suffered from side effects of their IUDs, I interviewed the 21 women who lived in Quyết Định or Vải Sơn hamlets. Some were neighbours or acquaintances whom I already knew, while others were women I had never talked to before. I met and interviewed each of these women between one and five times, depending on how well the initial interview went and how interested the woman was in doing another one. During interviews we talked about the health issues that were of importance to each woman, and particularly about *lack of blood* and *nerves*. We talked about social stress and worries, about families, family planning, happiness, and economy. I did some of these interviews alone, and others with the assistance of Lan or Liên. Whereas I had started to make connections between IUD side effects, other health problems, and everyday concerns through my conversations and work with women during the summer, it was not until this last phase of research that I systematically followed up these connections, substantiating my ideas and building up case histories. The five women I shall present as cases in later chapters (Hảo, Ngọc, Quế, Hạnh, and Tuyết) were all women I met during this phase of interviewing.

Besides the five women who are presented as case studies, I established fairly close relations to several other women during this phase of research. Since the insights and experiences of three of these women have been particularly important for the analyses presented in later chapters, I shall briefly introduce them here:

Mai is a 34-year-old neighbour of Liên who lives with her husband and their seven children. While I was in Vải Sơn she was pregnant with her seventh child, a child that neither she nor her husband had wanted. Her husband is reliable and hard-working, but he comes home only once a month so Mai's days are very busy with the dual tasks of agricultural work and childcare.

Nhị is 36 years old and married to a lazy, quick-tempered, and unpredictable husband with whom she has four children. She is a very outspoken woman and very critical of existing gender and family structures.

Như is 34 years old and lives with her husband and their two children. Như did not know her husband well before she married him and when she did get to know him she realized he was very moody and difficult to live with.

During some of the interviews with the above women I used a tape recorder and during others I did not.[20] While in some situations I was still mainly met with standardized and generalized statements, many of these later interviews and conversations with women took on a different and more personal character than had surfaced during my first interactions with people. This probably had to do with my being less of a stranger by this time (even if still a foreigner), in combination with my greater familiarity with the women's world and better skills in communicating. In this last stage of fieldwork I drew upon all my previous experiences, spanning and pulling together different strands of women's lives in my comprehension of the events and experiences they related. In this sense, my understanding of what is at stake in women's lives has been built up slowly and over time, gradually allowing me to place feelings, events, and experiences within wider social frameworks of understanding.

Representing women's experience

The account that I shall present in the following pages is mainly based on two groups of commune women: (a) the above women whom I got to know and interviewed during the autumn, and (b) the women who were my assistants, family members, or neighbours. The second group of women comprises Women's Union cadres like Lan and Liên; health workers like Mỹ; members of Bà Chính's family such as Kiều, Bình, Lý, and Mơ; and the neighbours Hoà, Loan, Lai, and Hương. Even though most of the women in the

second group were too close friends to be turned into case studies, I
have learnt a lot from them and their experiences play an important
part in the account that follows.

The women are all very different in terms of personality, character, and personal life histories, but they also share a fairly broad
range of living conditions and life experiences. Most of them are
in their early or mid-thirties. They were nearly all born and
brought up in Vải Sơn, in the hamlets in which they currently live.
They all grew up in the wake of socialist mobilization, war, and
post-war scarcity and poverty. They married in the years following
the war and most of them have two or three children today. With
the exceptions of Kiều and Mỹ all the women live mainly by
farming their land, doing hard physical work every day and
fighting hard to keep their children clothed and fed. They are all
fairly articulate and critical; most of them are more outspoken than
the average 30–35-year-old woman in Vải Sơn. They either live
in nuclear or extended families and some bear the sole burden of
responsibilities for children and parents since their husbands are
working elsewhere. Many of them are IUD users; they all suffer
from physical weakness, exhaustion, or pain in some form, and as
we shall see, they all relate such health pwoblems to their social
and economic conditions of life.

Since the account I shall present here lays weight on women's
own experiences and perceptions of their lives, some reflections
on the ways in which social scientists represent the experience of
other people seem called for. Obviously, we can only know other
people's experiences through their own expressions of them.
Therefore, as Kirsten Hastrup writes, what we are concerned with
is 'not the unmediated world of the "others", but the worlds
between ourselves and the others' (Hastrup 1992:117).

Given the socially sensitive and 'private' character of the issues
under study, the experiences that I have been able to share with
women are largely those that they have wanted to share with me.
My account is based on the feelings and experiences of invisible
social pain and physical discomfort which women in Vải Sơn
have told me about, while my chances to observe actual social
practices have often been fairly limited. It is almost as impossible
to observe the handling of family conflicts as it is to observe sexual
and contraceptive practices. Therefore it is only in 'my own'

family that I have directly observed and participated in conflicts, while otherwise relying on women's own accounts of problems and tensions in their families. In other words, this is largely an account of accounts, based on women's representations of themselves and their lives. This raises two somewhat contradictory problems. First, have I been loyal enough to women's own experiences and self-understandings? Second, have I stayed too close to women's own self-representations?

The first problem has to do with the fact that experience as experienced is indeterminant, contradictory, and always in the making (Kleinman & Kleinman 1991). But in the account that follows, I have imposed an order and fixity upon these chaotic and open-ended experiences, carving out cultural themes and contradictions and making generalizations which cut across individual experiences. I have tried my best, however, to convey as much as possible of the personal experiences upon which my generalizations are based; and we obviously have to live with the fact that it is impossible to do science without some degree of generalization and abstraction of more general themes and patterns out of the complexities of lived life.

The second problem has to do with my strong reliance on women's own accounts of their lives. The question here is: why have these women represented themselves to me in the ways they have? It is interesting to compare Stephen O'Harrow's (1995) article on gender relations in Vietnam with the perspectives I shall present here: O'Harrow describes women as strong, powerful and dominating lionesses, whereas the women I knew would most often represent themselves as weak physically and socially, silently enduring hardships, bending and yielding like willows. Even though O'Harrow's account also points to female subordination and weakness, and even though my account also points to forms of female strength and power, there is a distinct difference in emphasis which seems to call for explanation. Why did the women I worked with in Vải Sơn describe themselves as so weak?

I have asked myself whether I have simply been caught in dominant gender stereotypes: have women represented themselves to me as weak, yielding, and subordinate because these are the dominant gender ideals of femininity and because it is more virtuous and woman-like to bend and yield than to dominate?

Another suggestion could be that women implicitly compare their own lives to what they assume are the realities of life of the privileged Western anthropologist, and find their own hardships enormous in comparison? I do not think any of these are the most important explanations. Rather, my impressions of women's lives and experiences should be considered in light of the social contexts through which they were produced. Since women's health problems and the social stresses with which such problems are associated have been the main fields of investigation and interest, the attention of the study is turned towards experiences of social and physical stress and exhaustion rather than towards joys and happiness. In spite of this overall focus on hardship and distress, however, I do hope that the strengths and self-certainties which women possess come through as well.

But before looking more closely at the health problems that women experience with the IUD, we need first to consider the social and political context in which it is used. The following chapter therefore examines the implementation of the national family planning policy in Vải Sơn commune, paying particular attention to women's reactions to the policy and to the local social and cultural meanings of family planning. An important issue to be highlighted here is the paradoxical question of why women continue using IUDs for fertility control if these devices cause them such great health problems.

Notes

1. Since I worked mainly in two Buddhist hamlets, this study does not examine the possible differences in perspectives on fertility control of Buddhists and Catholics respectively.

2. In the survey that I conducted among 200 commune women as a part of this study, 189 women had married patrilocally, 10 women had married neolocally (i.e. setting up a new household), and one woman had married uxorilocally (i.e. the husband moving in with the wife's family).

3. Of the 200 female respondents, 147 women had married a man from their own hamlet, 21 women had married a man from another hamlet but within the commune, 23 women came from a different commune but less than 10 kilometers from Vải Sơn, and only nine women had grown up more than 10 kilometers from Vải Sơn.

4. Of the 200 female survey respondents, 28 per cent lived in extended families and 72 per cent in nuclear families. These numbers are very

similar to those for Vietnam as a whole, where 72 per cent of families are nuclear, 23 per cent extended, and 5 per cent 'other' (Desai 1995).

5. Land policies play an important role in relation to fertility and family planning. As we shall see in Chapter 3, the fact that no additional land is being allocated for children born after October 1992 seems to be an important, indirect incentive to limit births.

6. Several recent studies have pointed out that men's work has more prestige than women's. Despite the fact that women work longer hours than men, men's work is perceived as more important and husbands are seen as playing the dominant economic role in the family (Đặng Nguyễn Anh 1989; Vũ Mạnh Lợi 1991; UNICEF 1994; Phạm Văn Bích 1997).

7. On poverty and social inequality in Vietnam see UNICEF (1994), Allen et al (1995), United Nations (1995).

8. Several studies have noted that women tend to bear the major share of the workload in agricultural families (e.g., Đặng Nguyễn Anh 1989; Vũ Mạnh Lợi 1991).

9. A study conducted in two rural communes notes that the main occupation of men between the peak labour times of the agricultural cycle was sitting around the tea-table chatting and attending ceremonies as representatives of their families (Đặng Nguyễn Anh 1989).

10. As officially reported, maternal mortality is 115/100,000 births (Samuelson *et al* 1995).

11. When I returned in 1996, Kiều, Chính, and their eldest son had moved to a new house near Kiều's school, 5 kilometres from Vải Sơn.

12. Exceptions are Gerald Hickey's *Village in Vietnam* (1964) about a village in the South, and Georges Condominas' *We Have Eaten the Forest* (1957/1977) about a Mnong Gar village in the Central Highlands. Due to the scarcity of field studies of social life in Vietnam, I shall draw fairly extensively on China studies for comparisons and discussions of my own findings. Vietnam was under Chinese rule for nearly a thousand years, from the second to the tenth century AD, and Vietnamese society and culture have been strongly influenced by the 'Chinese model' (Woodside 1971).

13. In the light of the historical relations between foreign research and foreign domination in Vietnam (cf. Salemink 1991), the fairly close supervision and control of foreign researchers is understandable to some extent. However, quite a lot of 'bureaucratic inertia' seems to be at issue as well. For similar experiences with research in China, see Wolf (1985).

14. As a provincial family planning cadre said to Bà Chính, 'She is a foreigner, but she is still a human being.' This initial status changed gradually, though. Contributing factors to this seemed to be the frequent visits of my partner Rolf, who worked in Hanoi, and the visits of my mother and brother in the spring.

15. This points to the need to be very ethically conscious when doing fieldwork in Vietnam and very careful about how 'consent' is constructed. Apparently, people often do not have much real choice of whether to participate or not.

16. As I shall discuss in Chapter 3, in common with other local cadres, Lan and Liên are not only party and authority representatives, but also ordinary community members: the sisters, cousins, daughters, and neighbours of other women.

17. Kleinman and Kleinman (1991: 288) cite the Chinese professor Yang Kuo-shu for his assertion that the Chinese 'compartmentalize' their social relations, distinguishing between an inner circle of family and close friends, more distant family and friends, and strangers. While trust is unconditional in the inner circle, it is conditional in the next, and there is an absolute lack of trust in total strangers. In other words, while personal experience may be shared with family and close friends, it is definitely not shared with strangers.

18. The provincial Committee for Population and Family Planning supported her in this, emphasizing that Bà Chính acted as their representative while I was in Vải Sơn.

19. In order to balance the religious composition of the survey population with that of the country as a whole, 15 per cent of the survey population was drawn from hamlets that are predominantly Catholic and 85 per cent from hamlets that are mainly Buddhist.

20. In general, I used a tape recorder sporadically throughout my fieldwork. In all, I have 69 tape-recorded interviews of varying duration. Even though I draw fairly heavily on these interviews for quotations, they are obviously only a minimal part of the total sum of knowledge which constitutes this study.

CHAPTER 3

Planning Happy Families

It is a Saturday afternoon in July. It is hot and the sun is unbearably sharp, so for the first few hours after lunch the health station is just as empty as the paddy fields around it, standing quiet and deserted with its yellow faded walls and dried-out herb garden. But now in the late afternoon, as the sun hangs low in the sky, losing a bit of its power, women start arriving and sit waiting on the porch outside the room for gynaecological examinations. The health station does not have running water, so a water container with a tap is placed outside the examination room for the staff to wash their hands in between clients.

As usual on Saturday afternoons, a nurse and a nursing assistant from the district have come to perform IUD insertions and menstrual regulations. Their talking and laughing and rattling with tools can be heard out on the porch where the women are waiting. I sit down next to the woman at the end of the queue. She is crushing the faded blue band of her conical hat in her hand, looking nervous and uneasy. I ask her how many children she has:

'Thank you, four, I am very afraid of having another pregnancy, our finances cannot bear any more children, four are already too many. Last time I had an IUD I could not bear it, it made me very weak and sick, but now I have come to have an IUD again, because I am so afraid of having more children, and menstrual regulations are also very harmful to one's health.'

We talk for a while about her family's financial situation and about her health, and I ask her if she has ever considered contraceptive pills as an alternative to the IUD. She looks interested, but says she does not really know what these pills are or how to use them.

At this point her turn has come and she is called into the examination room. She takes off her trousers and climbs onto the examination bed, placing her legs in the stirrups. As she is lying there, the nurse asks her what her name is, which hamlet she is from, and how many children she has, notes, 'So you have come to have an IUD, have you?' and inserts the IUD without any further questions. A few minutes later, the woman picks up her clothes and leaves.

❧

Family planning efforts are intensive in Vải Sơn today. Slogans painted on the walls of houses and pagodas announce, 'You should have only one or two children in order to be able to care for them', or 'Vải Sơn is determined to promote planned births'. At the commune health station, walls and cupboards are decorated with family planning posters; loudspeaker announcements throughout the commune remind people of the importance of family planning; and television and radio often broadcast programmes about population growth or documentation about hard-working family planning cadres.[1] But the most important family planning activities in the commune are probably the campaigns (*chiến dịch*) which are now carried out four times a year, and run for three days at a time. During the campaign conducted when I was in Vải Sơn in 1996, the loudspeaker message ran as follows:

> Dear People of Vải Sơn. Currently population control and family planning are issues of concern in all countries of the world. Population increase causes land shortages, the draining of natural resources, social insecurity, lack of food, unemployment, malnourishment in children, and school drop-outs due to a lack of educational materials. Against this background, our commune, under the leadership of the Party, the People's Committee, and the Population Committee, has made important progress in family planning. Many couples have already chosen a suitable and modern contraceptive method and accepted the model of the small family with few children, thus contributing to reducing birth rates and rates of third children every year.

> In order to improve family planning efforts, the commune Family Planning Committee asks all couples of reproductive age who do not yet use a method of contraception – for your family's happiness, your children's future, and for the prosperity of the nation – to go to the commune health station to sign up and start using a method of contraception during the days of May 6–8, 1996.

During campaigns, health staff from the district hospital carry out IUD insertions and menstrual regulations at the commune health station. Furthermore, the district Women's Union sometimes arranges public meetings where women are told about the social and economic consequences of rapid population growth and about the advantages to their health and their family's economy of having only a few, well-spaced pregnancies. Family planning cadres visit the homes of women who are not yet using a modern method of contraception, informing them about family planning and trying to persuade them to accept an IUD or another method of contraception. Women who are difficult to persuade will be visited again and again. As one family planning worker described it:

> Some people do not agree [to have an IUD]. So one has to persuade them. If one does not succeed this time, then the next. If not the next, then the next again. After three times they will accept. But there are also some cases, no matter how much one calls them, they don't go [to get it].

But efforts to promote family planning have not always been this intensive. As a Women's Union cadre, Lan has been involved in family planning work for more than a decade now, and as the Chairperson of the Women's Union she is today in charge of population and family planning activities in Vải Sơn. In order to get an overview of previous family planning efforts, I asked Lan to tell me about the history of family planning in the commune.

The history of family planning in Vải Sơn

Lan and I are sitting in the People's Committee building on a quiet and sunny mid-afternoon, just before office hours begin. Outside in the sun women are bending down to do their weeding after the lunch break and children are playing in the shade of the eucalyptus trees. It is the fifth of the month, the day when all family planning cadres in the commune meet to report the results of this month's work. The meeting is set to begin at three, but since no one is likely to show up much before four, Lan and I have time to talk. In the following, I shall paraphrase from my fieldnotes what she told me about the history of family planning work in the commune.

Family planning activities have changed considerably over the years, Lan says. IUDs were first made available to women in the commune in the late 1960s and early 1970s, but were not systematically promoted. In the early 1980s, family planning efforts intensified; incentives were introduced and women who accepted an

IUD were rewarded with 20–30 kilos of rice. However, many women had their IUDs removed as soon as they had received their ration of rice, so this policy proved too expensive and was abandoned.

In the mid-1980s, a family planning norm of 1–2 children was set in the commune and efforts to persuade and educate people on the benefits of family planning increased. During biannual campaigns, district health staff came to the commune to insert IUDs and to inform women about family planning. In these campaigns, the names of married women with children who were not yet using an IUD were read out over the loudspeakers, in an attempt to persuade these women to go to the health station and have an IUD inserted.

In 1989, following the introduction of the national one- or two-child policy in 1988, a system of levies for three or more children was introduced. Couples having a third child now had to pay a sum of 100,000 dong (US$10) to commune authorities; couples having a fourth child had to pay 150,000 dong, etc. Lan emphasized, however, that this was not to be considered as a fine, but only as payment for the extra land the family would be allocated for the newborn child. People could refuse to pay, and some did; but most parents would rather pay the money and receive an extra plot of land.[2] After a few years, this system was abandoned, and today no payments are levied from parents who exceed the two-child limit.[3] 'Does this mean that no incentives or disincentives are used any more?' I ask. Lan replies that today the only extra financial burden placed on parents who 'break the plan' is a slightly higher charge for deliveries at the commune health station: for first and second births the cost of a delivery is 10,000 dong (US$1), for third births it is 20,000 dong, for fourth births 30,000 dong, etc. The only incentive used is for sterilizations: each person who is sterilized receives a bonus of 120,000 dong (US$12).[4]

In Lan's eyes, family planning work in the commune has improved considerably since the early 1990s. In 1991, a Family Planning Committee was established in Vải Sơn, consisting of the chairmen of local mass organizations and of the People's Committee.[5] The Family Planning Committee is responsible for meeting the yearly family planning targets handed down to the commune from district and provincial authorities. Targets are set for numbers of births, IUD insertions, new condom- and pill-users, and male and female sterilizations. At the end of each year, a representative from the district visits the commune, either praising or reprimanding the Family Planning Committee for the current year's performance. Being reprimanded is very embarrassing, says Lan, and something she very much wants to avoid. With the establishment of the Family Planning Committee, and with better funding for family planning activities in the 1990s, family planning work has become much more effective than before: now record-keeping is more detailed and comprehensive, and couples who do not use modern contraception are directly targeted.

In 1993, a network of family planning workers (*cộng tác viên*) was established in Vải Sơn.[6] The sixteen workers – two for each hamlet – are responsible for day-to-day family planning efforts. They inform and educate people on the benefits of family planning, distribute condoms, and keep track of vital statistics. For this they receive a small salary of 10,000 đồng (US$1) a month, plus a bonus of 2,000 đồng for each new IUD-user they 'mobilize'. At regular meetings, the family planning workers evaluate their own and each other's work. Those who have registered many new IUD users receive a cash bonus, and those who have done particularly badly have to offer a 'self-criticism' (*kiểm điểm*), explaining the reasons for their low performance. Lan tells me that at one meeting the 'top scorer' reported that the key to her success was that she would use any occasion to inform women about family planning: during work, in the market, in the creche, or wherever she met other women, she would take up the issue of family planning.

'So how would you compare family planning work today to say, ten years ago?' I ask Lan.

She answers that being a family planning cadre is much easier today than when she first started working as a Women's Union cadre in 1984. People have become much more 'conscious' and aware of the benefits of family planning than they were previously, and most people now plan their families voluntarily. But she also finds that even though people need less persuasion today, consciousness-raising efforts are still important and necessary.

Vải Sơn does not do particularly well with regard to family planning; the commune has one of the highest rates of third and higher-order births in the district. In 1995, 30 per cent of births in Vải Sơn were to women who already had two or three children. **Even though this number has dropped from 32 per cent in 1994**

and 45 per cent in 1993, it is still considered by Lan and other commune leaders to be far too high. So even though people have become more conscious of the need for family planning, there is still
much to be done, Lan says. But she feels confident that things are
going in the right direction, and ends by saying,

> 'In the future, as society gets more civilized, the policy will not be
> necessary any more. People will be more aware and society will
> have progressed. As soon as people become aware, they voluntarily
> have fewer children, one does not have to go to mobilize them any
> more.'

From a human rights perspective, the massive efforts to promote
modern methods of fertility control and the targeting of women in
their homes through repeated visits by family planning workers
appear questionable. These methods do not seem to give women the
opportunity of freely deciding when to have children and whether to
use contraception or not (cf. Gammeltoft and Hernø 1998). But what
do women themselves think of the family planning policy and the
methods that are being used to implement it? How do the 'targets'
of family planning activities feel about being cornered in their
homes by eager family planning cadres? Do women object to such
outside intervention in their reproductive decisions, or to the
existence of a family planning policy as such?

Women's views of the family planning policy

At first, I was surprised to find that the majority of women in Vải
Sơn expressed appreciation of the family planning policy. People
feel that there are 'too many people, too little land' and many say
that the shortage of land makes life more difficult now than it was
earlier, forcing people to use poisonous and dangerous pesticides.
When I asked women what they thought of the family planning
policy, most would repeat national family planning messages,
either pointing to the demographic situation of the country and
the dangers of continued population growth, or – most often –
emphasizing the benefits to the family's economy or to their own
health and life of having only a few children. I never heard
anyone directly criticize the principle of having a policy setting
norms for births. The closest anyone came to a critique was when
women said: 'The policy is not necessary any more'. Bình, for
instance, did not disagree with the small-size family ideal of the

policy as such, but considered that the policy had been rendered unnecessary by people's own desires to limit fertility:

> Today everyone is aware of the benefits of family planning. There is no need for encouragement any more, people are already aware. The policy is really not necessary, today nobody wants to have many children anyway.

But women's publicly-declared support of the policy is very often contradicted by their actual fertility practices: many women have more children than the one or two that the policy advocates. Of 178 children born in Vải Sơn in 1995, 124 were first or second births, while 27 were third, 16 were fourth, 8 were fifth, and 3 were sixth births. So how are we to account for such discrepancies between women's fertility preferences and practices? Are people lying when they say that they agree with the policy, while their real views are expressed in their actions?

Such questions have often been pondered in studies of China, where the discrepancies between people's words and deeds, or between norms and behaviour, are often difficult for researchers to handle (e.g., Wolf 1985; Milwertz 1997). In her study of family planning in China, Greenhalgh (1994) suggests that people's desires are deeply imprinted by state norms for fertility and that people are being 'moulded' by powerful state policies into the very core of their beings. Anagnost (1994) suggests that people are play-acting, parroting party slogans in order to be left in peace, while Mosher (1983) writes that people simply reproduce state rhetoric out of fear.[7] But are people really being terrorized into reproducing state propaganda or passively moulded to conform with the policies of the state? Let us take a closer look at the relations between women's attitudes and practices in the field of fertility control.

First, since family planning has only recently become a burning issue, many women in Vải Sơn had their children before the idea of fertility limitation gained ground. Therefore, when mothers of four or five children say that two children is their ideal, they may mean that it is their ideal today, even though it was not the ideal when they had their children. Women who had their children in the 1970s or early 1980s would often agree with the mother of six we met in Chapter 1, that with hindsight, they would not have opted for such a large family. But women who had their children in the period of intensive family planning efforts, from the late 1980s onwards, rarely cite a lack of knowledge as explanation for their having more than the two children the policy advocates. For these women, it is usually either contraceptive failure or the particular fertility needs of the family which caused them to 'break the plan'. Loan, who recently gave birth to her son Đạt as her third child, is a typical example of the ambiguities and tensions between state norms and family needs. When I asked her if she thought the family planning policy was necessary, she said, repeating propaganda statements:

'Of course! There is too little land and it is not good for the economy of families to have too many children.'

'But you have just violated the policy yourself?'

'Yes, but you know, there is also the tradition of the family. According to the tradition of the family,you have to have a son, even if it takes nine children to have him.'

Like Loan, people may in principle agree with state norms, while in practice state demands are overridden by the family's needs of additional children. But why do people not adjust their expressed fertility desires to their actual practices then? Why insist on a verbal compliance with the two-child norm, knowing that one will not or has not acted in accordance with it? First, by expressing recognition of the two-child ideal, women demonstrate that they have 'understood' the family planning messages, i.e. that they are educated, civilized, and forward-looking. In this sense, people's declared adherence to state norms can be seen as a strategy through which they create an image of themselves as educated, modern, and enlightened. Second, I believe that women actually *do* agree with the policy – in principle. When it comes to practice, however, the needs of one's family are, not surprisingly, always more concrete, urgent, and immediate than the generalized fertility norms of the state.

In other words, the apparent contradictions between women's attitudes and practices do not necessarily represent a split between a 'false facade' and 'true views'. Nor are fertility norms being simply 'imprinted' on to people by 'the molding power of two decades of forceful state policy on reproduction' (Greenhalgh 1994). Rather, what we have here are two different sets of ideals which are both equally real, but one of which carries more weight than the other when it comes to everyday practice. Women agree in principle that the policy is a good and necessary measure, but they *also* think that the immediate needs of their own families come first. A double set of ethics seems to be at play: one abstract and general, the other concrete and specific.

In her work on the gift economy in China, Mayfair Yang (1988) identifies a similar double ethics, which she refers to as a *universalistic* vs. *relational ethics*. The universalistic ethics operates with fixed norms and standards, clearly defined rights and wrongs, and fixed categories of relationships and roles, while the relational ethics is much more flexible and adaptable to particular situations and needs, forming the basis of personal and specific relationships such as friendship and kinship. The universalistic ethic is often an ethic of the state: it goes together with universal goals, norms and standards and with efforts to educate and mobilize people. The relational ethic, on the other hand, forms the basis of concrete, and flexible everyday social interactions and works 'be-neath' state norms and policies.

In my opinion it makes a lot of sense to see the Vietnamese family planning policy in the light of such a 'double ethics'. As Loan's statements above exemplify, people may feel a serious commitment to universal state norms, seeing the national policy as good and necessary, while at the same time basing their everyday actions on the much more concrete and specific relational ethics. Underlying people's verbal agreement with the policy, then, is the precondition of 'family needs first': the policy is accepted on the premise that one follows it only as far as the specific conditions of one's family allow one to. In other words, people do not uncritically absorb or parrot state propaganda. They may accept state norms as overall and general guidelines, but they also adjust such guidelines to the specific needs and demands of their own situation.[8]

But does the recognition of the need for fertility control also include an acceptance of the methods that are used to implement the policy in Vải Sơn?

Women's views of policy implementation

During my stay in Vải Sơn, I regularly joined family planning workers on their rounds. Initially, I was very surprised to find that no women seemed to object to the visits of family planning workers. On the contrary, the conversations I observed were usually very relaxed and friendly, and it was quite obvious that family planning workers were just as much ordinary community members as representatives of commune authorities – they were the neighbours, cousins, and aunts of the women they targeted.⁹

During a typical visit, the cadre would first small-talk for a while with the woman about whatever came up. Then she would adopt a more formal tone, informing the woman that these days there is a campaign going on and encouraging her to go to the health station and have an IUD fitted. In her explanations of why the woman should have an IUD, she would emphasize the economic benefits of having only a few children, the importance of being able to raise and care well for one's children, and the benefits of family planning to the health of mother and children. Some women would then immediately accept, or say they were already planning to go. (This, however, was in some cases clearly a strategy used in order to get rid of the family planning worker as soon as possible.) Other women would say they were using 'their own method', a euphemism for withdrawal, and did not intend to use other methods. Many women said they were afraid of the IUD or that they had already had one, but they could not 'bear' it and had to have it removed. If a woman responded negatively to the suggestion of having an IUD, or said she was satisfied with the traditional method she already used, this would always be respected by the family planning worker without further argument. If she said she wanted another child, the family planning worker would accept this, but advise her to at least space the children. If a woman had only daughters, it was quite obvious that the family planning worker fully sympathized with her desire to try again for a son. In these cases, the family planning worker would say, as it is her duty to do, that 'any child is as good as the other', 'girls are all right as well' – but everyone would know that in reality, this is not the case.

Family planning workers' understanding of the wishes of other women is exemplified by an episode when Hương, who already had two sons, became pregnant for the third time. She told me that when she met a leading Women's Union cadre in the market and told her she was pregnant, she just laughed and joked that Hương would be punished. Obviously, neither Hương herself nor the family planning worker took her breaking the plan very seriously, both seeing the wish to have a daughter as quite understandable and legitimate.

When talking to women about the visits of family planning workers, I met many different reactions, ranging from appreciation, to resigned acceptance, to dislike or anger. The majority of the women I talked to expressed appreciation of the family planning workers, saying: 'They only come to help and support, they are concerned about one's family, one's economy.' Since these home visits seemed fairly intrusive in my opinion, I had difficulties in understanding these positive reactions at first. But I gradually came to understand some of the positive connotations which home visits also have. When family planning workers do house-to-house visits to inform women of the benefits of family planning, it is called to *vận động* (mobilize) or *động viên* (encourage). The term *vận động* is used also about cadres visiting people in order to inform them about a vaccination campaign, to collect money for the victims of a natural disaster somewhere else in Vietnam, to organize meetings where new agricultural techniques are taught, etc. – i.e. social activities which most people would agree are good and important. The term *động viên* is used about family planning workers encouraging women to have an IUD; but it is also used about visiting a person who is sick, encouraging him to get well, or about encouraging a sad person to cheer up again. In other words, what is implied in the practice of 'encouraging' other women to have an IUD is not only a state-controlled intervention into people's most private lives, but also an expression of care and concern for other people in one's community.[10] One family planning worker explained to me:

> To go 'mobilizing' women to have an IUD is an example of women helping each other. We help each other to build the economy, build a happy family.

But not all women adopt an equally positive attitude towards the family planning workers. Many seem to take a more pragmatic attitude, considering the family planning policy as a necessary measure which the family planning workers are duty-bound to carry out – but which is also relatively futile, since in the end, fertility decisions are made in the family. An example of this attitude is provided by 34-year-old Vinh. Even though she had been repeatedly targeted by family planning workers, she did not resent them coming to her house.

'After all, they are only doing their duty. There is no reason not to receive them and listen to what they have to say, they are only trying to help you overcome your poverty.'

Quế took a similar view:

'If you want to go and have an IUD, you go; if not, you don't go. Nobody forces you. I just let them talk and keep quiet, and do as I want to do myself.'

Paraphrasing party slogans, another woman said:

'In the end, the people are the master (*dân làm chủ*). They encourage, but it is only oneself that can decide.'

But other women were much less tolerant of the family planning campaigns, criticizing this intervention into people's private lives, and insisting on the rights of families and individuals to choose and decide for themselves without outside intervention. For instance, when she was pregnant with her third child, Hương said:

'It is people's right, if they want children, they will have children. It is a question of individual freedom. They themselves take care of their family's finances, it is not people outside who take care of it. Whether they can manage their finances or not is their own responsibility. If they are well off, they can have many children; if not, they can't. They themselves have to protect the happiness of their children. If people come to "encourage", they will say to them: "Why don't you take care of your own affairs, and I will take care of mine?" So they don't dare to come to one's house any more, they will only call on the loudspeakers, "each couple should have only one or two children"'.[11]

When I asked Lan whether she and other family planning workers were always received in a friendly manner, she said no – that sometimes people get angry, abuse her and tell her to mind her own business. But there are fewer cases like that today. Today, Lan said, the strategy of people who want to avoid more visits from the family planning workers is often simply to sign up for condoms; it is obviously very difficult for authorities to control whether they actually use them or not.

In short, even though some women see family planning campaigns and cadre visits as illegitimate violations of their rights to privacy and self-determination, most 'sympathize' with the policy and the means used to implement it, and most people seem to agree with the government that small families are happier than large ones. But the question still remains as to what constitutes a small family in practice? Is the state norm of one or two children accepted by people, or may three, four, or even five children still qualify as a small family?

How many children do people want to have?

The 1995 Intercensal Demographic Survey (ICDS) clearly indicates that few Vietnamese women want to have many children.[12] When asked if they wanted more children, 74 per cent of Vietnamese women with two children said no, and in the Red River delta 90 per cent of women with two children said they did not want more children (GSO 1995). In the survey that I conducted in Vải Sơn, 74 per cent of mothers of two children said they did not want more.[13] In the survey we also asked women how many children they had dreamt about having before getting married. To this question, 79 per cent of women in the youngest age group (18–25 years) said they had wanted two children, while in the oldest age group (40–45 years) no women had wanted only two children.[14] In other words, as the ICDS states, 'the "two-child family" norm promoted by the government is widely established, at least at the level of survey responses' (GSO 1995: 76).[15]

In common with many other women in Vietnam, then, women in Vải Sơn seem to agree with the government that two is the most desirable number of children. An obvious question to ask, however, is whether such survey results can be trusted? Given the moral and political sensitivity of the issue, it is not surprising if people provide politically correct answers to survey questions, and the problem of 'courtesy biases' has frustrated many a researcher in Vietnam (e.g., Allman *et al.* 1991; Goodkind 1995). Let us therefore consider what the women in Vải Sơn had to say about family size.

Some women say – and mean – that two children are enough. Bình, for instance, whose husband is unreliable and whose income is very unstable, is determined to have no more than the two sons she already has. When we talked about the possibility of her having another child, she said:

'You know, our finances are very limited, I don't want any more children. People have said to me, "Why don't you have the IUD removed and have another child?" but I can't. If I have another child, our finances will be even more limited, more restricted; we'll die!'

But not all women think like Bình. While many people say that a son and a daughter is the 'most beautiful' combination, others find that in rural areas, two children are still insufficient. When I returned to Vải Sơn in 1996, Hương was pregnant with her third child. When I teasingly asked her, 'So you don't think one or two children is the ideal, do you?', she replied:

'Everyone will tell you that two children are best and that they only want two children. But in reality, they will have an IUD after two children and wait some years until their income has become more stable and the children have grown, and then they will have a third child. In the cities, it is enough to have one or two children, but in rural areas three is best. Four is a little too many, but three is fine: two sons and one daughter.'

To make a broad generalization, then, I would say that among women of childbearing age in Vải Sơn today, the norm for the happy family is two or three children rather than one or two. Having only two children is acceptable, but three children – ideally two sons and one daughter – is better and more 'safe' (*chắc chắn*). The notion of 'safety' refers not only to the risk that a child may die, but also to the risk that children may be morally spoilt (*hư*) and not take proper care of their parents later in life. With three children, one balances the family's need to preserve the continuation of family line, the need of brothers and sisters for one's children, and the joy of having children against the demands of child-raising in the modern era. To have four children is, as Hương says, 'a little too many', and more than four is definitely too many. In other words, local norms for fertility are 'larger' than state norms, allowing for two, three, or sometimes four children. But there is one very important difference between state norms and local norms for fertility: in contrast to state norms, local norms also take the gender of children into consideration.

The importance of sons

Even though the government's family planning messages strongly emphasize the 'backward' character of son preference and even though everyone is aware that a preference for sons belongs to the category of 'feudal attitudes', the need for sons is still a basic fact of life for people in Vải Sơn as for many people elsewhere in Vietnam (cf. Mai Huy Bích 1991; Vương Xuân Tính 1994; Phạm Văn Bích 1997). I never met or heard of anyone in the commune who stopped having children before they had at least one son, and everyone knows that, sooner or later, a mother with only daughters will have to bear more children. Having at least one son is absolutely required and many people feel that to be without a son is almost equal to childlessness. This is expressed in numerous old sayings, such as: 'One son and you have a descendant, ten daughters and you can write nil' (*Nhất nam viết hữu, thập nữ viết vô*), or 'Daughters are the children of someone else, only daughters-in-law are your own since you have bought them home' (*Con gái là con người ta, con dâu mới thật mẹ cha mua về*).

Son preference is closely related to patrilineality and patrilocality, and, as people often explained, it is associated with the old and feudal attitude of 'respecting men, disregarding women' (*trọng nam khinh nữ*). Since only sons can continue the family line and undertake the practice of ancestor worship, to be without a son is the gravest form of 'unfiliality' (*bất hiếu*). By not having a son, one lets down the people – parents and ancestors – to whom one owes one's own life. Without a son to carry on the worship of ancestors, the entire realm in which one's ancestors live (*âm*) will be destroyed and the ancestors turned into restless and hungry wandering ghosts (*ma*) (cf. Chánh Công Phan 1993). Also one's own soul is likely to end up hungry and restless, without the care and provisions it needs. Therefore, not having a son means that 'When one dies, one is finished' (*Chết, mình là hết*). With a son, in contrast, life continues after death. As one woman said: 'Even though one dies, if one has a son who lives, one can still enjoy things up in the world. After this life there is another.' Or as a man who had four daughters before a son arrived said, 'I always thought about death and felt sad and depressed inside.'

Besides being responsible for funeral rites and ancestor worship, sons traditionally provide for their ageing parents. While daughters 'get married and disappear' into their husbands' families, sons continue being members of their natal families, providing for their parents in their old age, carrying out the required rituals when they die, and inheriting their property. Not having a son therefore means living with a high risk of ending one's days in poverty and destitution. Finally, the lack of a son has social implications: it often exposes both husband and wife to the ridicule and contempt of others and makes it more difficult for the wife to become accepted in her husband's family. Lai, who had four daughters before her son was born, said:

> 'If you don't have a son, people despise you. They look down on you and insult you. They don't come around to your house. [...] There is not equality as in your country. People despise you, they don't come to visit you. [...] Now that I have a boy, people like me, they are friendly to me. Also my husband's parents, they despised me before, they like me now. Not having a son – it is terrible, you know.

Couples without sons often say they feel inferior and worthless when they compare themselves to other people. By the time of my second stay in Vải Sơn in 1996, Loan, who had two daughters the first time I was there, had had a son in the meantime. She was a strikingly changed woman now: whereas before she used to be very timid and shy, she would now talk loudly and at length, with a totally new aura of self-assurance and self-worth about her. She named her son Đạt (to achieve), short for *đặt nguyện vọng* (to realize one's aspirations).

Despite all efforts, it sometimes happens that a couple fails to have a son. In such a case, one of their daughters may take over most of the functions for which a son would normally be responsible. Even though a daughter cannot continue the family line, she can still take care of her parents in their old age and of their souls after death. The problem is that whether a daughter will be able to support her old parents or not largely depends on her husband: if he is 'good', he may agree to support her parents; if not, he may refuse. The problem of the daughter's dependency on her husband is solved if she marries uxorilocally; she and her husband then provide for her parents in their old age, inherit their property, and worship their souls after death. But usually only men from very poor families agree to marry uxorilocally (*ở rể*; live as a son-in-law), since such men are often ridiculed and considered as 'not real men.' Another problem when daughters are responsible for ancestor worship is that there is a considerable risk that the worship will only last for one generation: the daughter's children may easily forget about their maternal grandparents and only worship their father's ancestors.

Not surprisingly, then, it is often the need for sons which makes people 'break the plan' (*vỡ kế hoạch*) and have more than the two children the family planning policy prescribes. When I was in Vải Sơn in 1996, Lan and I conducted a small survey of 'reasons for having more than two children' among the 67 women who had 'broken the plan' in 1994. The survey very clearly pointed to the need for sons as the major reason for having more than two children: 54 of the 67 women said they had another child because they wanted a son.[16] Of the 54 women, 25 had one or more sons already, but still wanted to try for another. In local perception, then, the norm of at least one son overrides the small-family norm; it is absolutely acceptable and even expected that people 'break the plan' in order to have a son. But along with this strong son preference goes a desire to have daughters as well, since daughters are considered more helpful and affectionate than sons.

In short, given that at least one child is a son, most people in Vải Sơn accept the small-size family ideal promoted by national family planning campaigns. The next question to be considered is therefore why this is so? What makes people embrace the small-size family ideal? What makes the family planning policy and its norms for childbearing acceptable to people? To understand this, we first need to consider women's dreams of creating a happy family.

Dreams about the 'happy family'

Most women in Vải Sơn work extremely hard every day, from early morning until late at night. The neighbour, Loan, for instance, I rarely saw rest or relax. While her husband was away driving *xe ôm* (motorcycle taxi) in Hanoi, Loan would always be busy, going to or from the fields heavily laden with tools or crops; preparing meals for her family; cooking large pots of food for the pig; washing clothes; or caring for her three young children. Another neighbour, Bình, works even harder than most women, getting up at three in the morning to walk 8 kilometres to work as

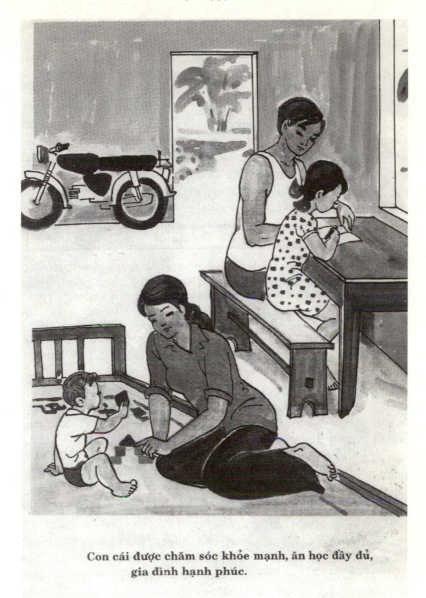

Con cái được chăm sóc khỏe mạnh, ăn học đầy đủ,
gia đình hạnh phúc.

Figure 3: *The children are well cared for and healthy, they have enough to eat and are given good education, the family is happy.* (NCPFP/UNFPA, VIE/93/P08)

a day labourer and earn some extra income for the family, before returning to take care of her own fields and family.

From the women's own perspective, the ultimate aim of all this hard daily work is the creation of a happy family. As Bình says, 'I have to work like this to be able to take care of my children and protect the happiness of my family.' Even though all women feel that working this hard saps their bodies and minds of energy and strength, most also feel that these everyday efforts are necessary, worthwhile, and meaningful, since they keep the children clothed and fed and contribute to the creation of a happy family. As mentioned in the previous chapter, with the dismantling of collective welfare systems, personal responsibility for the welfare of the family now seems to weigh more heavily on women than ever before. One woman said:

'Now it is up to you whether the family starves or not. Before we worked collectively, but now, if you want a good income, you have to work hard.'

In other words, while happy families have probably always been important, women today feel a very urgent personal responsibility for the creation of such families. But what does a 'happy family' (*gia đình hạnh phúc*) mean precisely to women?

A family (*gia đình*) is usually understood as parents, children, and possibly grandparents living together and sharing an income. In order to be happy, families should also have 'enough' (*đầy đủ*) and be orderly and stable (*ổn*). Most people see a sufficient income and a good atmosphere as very important and closely related preconditions for family happiness. A good income promotes good family relations, while poverty often causes discords and quarrels; and a family whose members know how to behave well towards each other and how to cooperate will also be better off economically. Family harmony and family finances are therefore closely associated. Reading through my notes one day, Hương put a circle around the sentence 'enough to eat, enough to spend – that is complete happiness,' and added with big letters, *quan trọng nhất!* (most important!). 'If the finances are good,' she said, 'there is nothing to think or worry about. Family relations will be good and others will praise the family.'

The everyday emphasis on the happy family among women in Vải Sơn goes along with a more general celebration of the 'happy family' in Vietnamese politics and popular culture (cf. Barry 1996). The emphasis on the family is not new in Vietnam: in Confucian doctrine the family is represented as a crucially important moral microcosm which forms the basis for larger national and macrocosmic orders. Moreover, in socialist Vietnam, Hồ Chí Minh's dictum, 'If society is good, the family will be good; if the family is good, society will be good. The family is the cell of society', has been an important cornerstone of political campaigns and movements over the years. But even though the celebration of the family is longstanding, the notion of the happy family does seem to be systematically and emphatically promoted in newspapers, magazines, television, and political slogans at the moment. In her article 'Women striving to build a family of "prosperity, equality, progress, happiness"', the Chairperson of the Vietnam Women's Union, Trương Mỹ Hoa, writes:

> In every society, the family has an important position. In Vietnam in this period of economic transition the family is even more important, it is an integrated part of and the very energy of development (NCPFP 1994: 5).

Government documents such as the 1987 Law on Marriage and the Family and the 1992 Constitution describe the family as the 'core' or 'basic cell' of society, as the fundamental basis for social and economic progress, and this is an idea that is being disseminated in newspapers, radio, and television all over the country. Several women's magazines, such as *Hạnh Phúc Gia Đình* (Family happiness) and *Gia Đình Ngày Nay* (The family today) are dedicated solely to issues concerning the happy family: how to create and maintain it. All women's magazines abound with advice on how to protect the happiness of the family: how to bring up one's children, how to talk to one's husband, how to treat one's parents-in-law, so that the happiness and the harmony of the family are preserved. Letter columns in women's magazines nearly always encourage readers to do whatever is best to 'protect the happiness of their families', and the Women's Union arranges competitions where people's knowledge of how to create a happy family is tested.

In short, the notion of a happy family, which is centrally placed in family planning messages, seems to be an element in a more general 'happy-family' theme, which exists semi-independently of family planning rhetoric. It is tempting to agree with Anagnost

(1995) that the family and reproduction, in Vietnam as in China, is becoming the new locus of state control in an era where control of other social fields has been reduced. Even though it may not be a deliberate political strategy, the emphasis on the happy family does seem to have socially and politically stabilizing effects: people appear to be too busy building their happy families to think about politics or political change. Kathleen Barry describes the current commitment to 'family happiness' in Vietnam:

> In the cultural ideology of the 1990s Vietnam, the balance and harmony of traditional Vietnamese belief is fitted with a compatible world view of socialist ideology that deemphasizes economic disparity and disequilibrium and like filial piety in family relations expects appropriate behaviour in relation to state law and policy (Barry 1996: 12).

While being an important theme in government discourse, however, family happiness is also an orienting theme in daily lives, and particularly important for the shaping of women's desires to control their fertility.

The moral economy of childbearing

As we have seen, a happy family is closely associated with an economically stable family; and one of the most direct and viable ways of creating a strong family economy is by limiting the number of one's children.[17] By noting this, I am not arguing that people necessarily make 'rational choices' about how many children to have, but simply that family size and family economy are experienced as closely associated phenomena. People in Vải Sơn clearly perceive children as an economic burden rather than an economic advantage; to the large majority of families children bring far more expenses than income.

Each family has so little land that there is hardly any agricultural work for children to do. As one woman said, 'Before there was plenty of land, but now there is so little land that one has to maintain one's family from nothing.' Children usually only engage in minor chores such as tending cows or buffaloes, cutting grass for animals, cooking, and sweeping. It is not until they become teenagers or adults that children are really economically useful to their parents: as teenagers they may work either in household handicraft production or in factories in Hanoi; as adults, they are extremely important providers of economic support for their parents in old age. Most people therefore seem to reason that having fewer children and caring for them well, both educationally and in other respects, is a better 'investment' than having a large number of children for whom one cannot provide adequately. Bà Chính is living proof of this: she had only one son, but he was well cared for and well educated and today her family is among the wealthiest in Vải Sơn.

The economic demands placed on child-raising also seem to be increasing at the moment. During conversations, women often kept returning to the fact that today it is not enough to give birth to children; one also has to be able to care for them properly. A 67-year old woman said that a generation or two ago, childbearing was perceived very differently from today:

> 'Before, to get pregnant was to give birth, we did not know how to avoid pregnancies. We gave birth until we did not have any more eggs. We did not think about children in the same way as people do today.'

Today, privatization of responsibility for the family's economic survival also includes privatization of child-raising responsibilities; nowadays also health care, day care, and education represent major expenses to parents. The beginning of each new school year – with school fees to be paid and new books, pens, and notebooks to be bought – generates a considerable amount of stress in many homes. Children going to secondary school may need a bicycle to get there and few mothers want their children to be more poorly dressed than the other children at school. Women often say that their children should be 'like their friends' (*bằng bạn bằng bè*); if they are not as well dressed and well equipped as other children, they may be teased and looked down upon by others. As one woman said: 'If my children go to school without being properly dressed I feel embarrassed and uneasy, my conscience feels tormented.'

Another major expense of having children, particularly for parents with many sons, is the arrangement of children's marriages and the setting up of new homes for sons and daughters-in-law. The marriage arrangements for both sons and daughters can be costly, but marriage celebrations arranged for sons are usually larger and more expensive than those for daughters. In sum, one woman said:

'A mother has a responsibility towards her children, she has to care about food, education, so that the child will become a person. It is my responsibility that the children are like their friends, that they can eat and study like others. When they grow up we have to pay for their marriages and build houses for them. That is the responsibility parents have towards their children.'

While education, food, clothes, and healthcare are the minimum requirements of proper childcare, most of the women I knew in Vải Sơn were also dreaming about modern and well-equipped houses for their children to grow up in, with a television and nice furniture. These wishes seem similar to Chinese women's strivings to 'cultivate the perfect only child' (Milwertz 1997): people have fewer children, but invest more in each child. But the raising of children also seems to be inscribed in more general aspirations to wealth and economic progress in Vietnam today. Children are sometimes compared to commodities, as when a woman told me that 'a child more is a television less'. After many years of poverty, people's wishes and expectations for an economically brighter future are high, and this is very clearly felt in the expectations surrounding child-raising. The standard reply, therefore, if one asks a young woman how many children she wants, is: 'Two, otherwise I cannot take care of them.' On the prospect of having four or five children, young women often laugh and say: 'It is death!' (*Chết!*).

While obviously springing from love, concern, and ambition, women's wishes to care well for their children also spring from another important concern: the question of what will happen to them as mothers in their old age. Many mothers fear that if they do not treat their children well while they are young, the children may fail to take proper care of them later on. In the worst-case scenario, children may 'forget' their parents and not worship their souls after death. When a person dies, his soul lives on in the underworld (*dưới Âm*) (cf. Chánh Công Phan 1993). There is usually a relationship of mutual help and assistance between living and dead family members; the souls *(linh hồn)* of the deceased help and protect the living, and the living remember and care for the dead. If a family forgets a dead family member, he may return and cause trouble (*quấy đảo*) in the lives of the living. This happens particularly often with the souls of spinsters, who are easily forgotten since they do not have children to take care of them.

The idea of one's soul being forgotten, flickering around hungry and lonely and with no one to take care of it, is very unsettling and frightening to most people. One woman tormented by such thoughts was Mai, who had six children and was pregnant with her seventh while I was in Vải Sơn. Her first five children were daughters, her sixth child was a son, and the seventh pregnancy was unintended. Her family's economy was very strained and Mai was clearly tired and worn out from hard work and caring for her children. She was worried about her own health and the immediate day-to-day survival of her family, but the fears that tormented her most were whether her children would grow up to resent her for being such a bad mother who did not know how to care properly for the children she had brought into the world.

When I was in Vải Sơn in 1996, Mai's two eldest daughters, aged 14 and 17, had started living and working in a factory in Hanoi. This had improved the family's finances considerably, but again, Mai was tormented by worries about how her girls were doing and whether they would later reproach her for being sent away to work. She said,

'If parents do not take responsibility for their children, the children will not respect their parents. To be without responsibility ... People say that you only know how to give birth but not how to take care of children, that you do not take responsibility. So the children will not respect you. The children may say: "What did you give birth to me for? You gave birth to me but you cannot take care of me, you should not have given birth to me." It happens. [...] In life, there is endless worry. For instance, giving birth to children and not being able to maintain responsibility towards them, your conscience is tormented and you never feel relaxed.'

Mai is not only tormented by thoughts about how her children will treat her in the future. She is also tormented here and now by other people laughing at her for having too many children. In Vải Sơn as elsewhere, the economic values associated with given family sizes are embedded in wider systems of social and moral meaning (cf. Whyte 1984). Women's dreams of happy families exist within a moral climate in which large families are associated with backwardness, poverty, and the past, while small families are associated with modernity, wealth, and progress. As in the government's family planning messages, among people in Vải Sơn the ability to limit family size is associated with modernity and enlightenment, while large families are associated with backwardness and a lack of knowledge and education. Educated and knowledgeable people know how to limit their fertility and establish a small and happy family, while uneducated people do not know how to manage and control their lives.

Apparently, fertility norms[18] have changed considerably in recent years. One or two decades ago women with only two children would be ridiculed for 'not knowing how to give birth' (*không biết đẻ*), while today mothers of many children are ridiculed for 'knowing how to give birth but not how to take care of children' (*biết đẻ, không biết nuôi*). Mai therefore felt terribly ashamed of having so many children and now being pregnant with her seventh:

'I feel very ashamed for being pregnant again now. People are laughing, mocking, saying I don't know how to take care of my children. Now we live under the system of having only a few children, and so you are laughed at for having too many.'

When women in Vải Sơn talk about other women who have many children, they often turn their eyes to the sky, saying, '*five* children, tut tut,' or '*seven* children, scary isn't it?!', half in condemnation, half in pity. When asked how many children they have, women are often obviously and visibly ashamed of having many children. Women who are now in their thirties and had their children in the late 1980s or early 1990s would often say, as for instance Quế did:

'I am hopelessly old-fashioned. I have four children now, but if I were to have children today I would definitely have only two.'

During my work with Lan, people would often ask her how many children she had. To her reply – a son and a daughter – people would say with appreciation: 'That's beautiful, and your economy is probably very stable, isn't that so?'

If the family's finances are strong it is acceptable to have many children, though. For instance, it was considered quite acceptable for a private entrepreneur couple in Vải Sơn to have six children since they were wealthy enough to be able to provide well for all six. If the family finances are weak, however, having too many children may easily expose one to the contempt and ridicule of others. In this sense, the field of fertility and childbearing is not only an economic but also a moral field; having few or many children clearly has both economic and moral consequences.

In sum, being able to build a happy family is of immense social, moral, economic, and existential importance to women in Vải Sơn. In the present social and economic climate, having a large number of children is neither economically viable nor morally acceptable. In everyday parlance, therefore, a happy family is equivalent to a small family: by keeping their families small, people strengthen their capacity to provide proper childcare while also cultivating an image of themselves as modern, educated, and enlightened. In other words, it is not only in state propaganda that the small, happy, civilized family exists as a social norm or that small families are associated with wealth and health. The distinctions made in state messager between the modern vs. the backwards, the educated vs. the uneducated, the wealthy vs. the poor, also exist in everyday life in Vải Sơn. They exist in people's evaluations of self and other and in everyday dreams and aspirations. In this sense, national family planning messages contribute to the creation of a specific normative atmosphere where the demands and expectations of parental care for children are high, and where large families are associated with ignorance, feudalism and backwardness. The most important conclusion to draw from this is that people in Vải Sơn, as people elsewhere in Vietnam, urgently need to be able to control their fertility safely and effectively (cf. Knodel *et al.* 1995). The next question therefore is: What means are available for people to control their fertility? What tools do women have to plan their happy families? To assess this, I shall consider first the provision of contraception in Vải Sơn and then the health concerns that are associated with contraceptive use.

Family planning services and contraception in *Vải Sơn*

Today a range of different contraceptive methods is available in Vải Sơn. The health station provides IUDs, sterilizations, condoms, and contraceptive pills for free; family planning workers distribute free condoms to couples who 'sign up' for them; and local pharmacies sell both pills and condoms. Given the variety of methods available, and given the health problems many women experience with their IUDs, the high rates of IUD use seem surprising. In 1994, 794 out of 1,550 couples of reproductive age in Våi So'n used a modern method of contraception. Of these, 690 women – or nearly 90 per cent of all modern-method users – were IUD users. When I returned to Våi So'n in 1996 this percentage was, to my surprise, unchanged. If women really experience such great health problems using IUDs, then why do they not try some of the alternative contraceptive methods that are available today? Why is the IUD still so widely used? To explain this, let us first consider contraceptive provision in Våi So'n.

As providers elsewhere in Vietnam, family planning providers in Våi So'n have a clear preference for the IUD (cf. Jain *et al.* 1993; UNFPA 1993; Knodel *et al.* 1995; WHO 1995). Both health station staff and family planning workers consider the IUD as the 'best and safest method' and strongly encourage women to use it. The idea that the IUD is the 'best method' is supported by a system of incentives in which family planning workers receive bonuses for IUDs but not for other methods, and by a system in which yearly targets for IUDs are much higher than for other methods. Although they do recognize that many women experience serious side effects from their IUDs, health- and family-planning workers also often say that women's health problems are imaginary rather than effects of physiological disturbances. As family planning workers see it, women tend to focus all their thoughts and worries on the IUD, attributing all sorts of problems to it, while the real problems often lie elsewhere. A provincial Women's Union cadre said, 'If I have a headache, I say it is because the weather changes. If these women have a headache, they say it is because of the IUD. It is a disease of the mind.'

During the family-planning house visits I observed, it was quite depressing to witness the inadequate counselling skills of the family-planning workers. Apparently, family-planning workers lack skills in anything but IUD promotion (cf. Jain *et al.* 1993); they have never received any training in counselling and often their knowledge of alternative contraceptive methods to the IUD is extremely limited. Women's worries about potential side effects of the IUD were most often ignored by the family planning worker, who – instead of advising the woman on alternatives to the IUD – would simply say, 'No, no, there is nothing to worry about. Why don't you just try the IUD, I will take the responsibility.'

Along with the IUD, also sterilizations are fairly actively promoted by family planning workers, but, as we shall see, with little effect. While strongly promoting the IUD and sterilizations, however, health- and family-planning workers hardly ever mention the contraceptive pill as an option – and if they do, they often discourage women from using it. As other studies have noted, provider dislike of the pill is common throughout Vietnam (UNFPA 1993a). I often discussed the inadequate promotion of the pill with health care providers and family planning workers, who would argue that rural women are too busy and cannot remember to take a pill every day, or that the pill is dangerous to women if they are not exceptionally strong and healthy. The pill may be a good method for urban women, they would say, but it is not suitable for rural women who are busy, work hard, and whose health is often weak. Moreover, it is a complicated and laborious process for health workers to obtain the pills which they have to get from the district hospital.

Condoms are more actively promoted than pills, but according to users there are often supply problems with the condoms: family planning workers sometimes do not receive new supplies on time, and the eight to ten condoms given to each couple per month are not always enough. In 1994 the condoms distributed by family planning workers in Vải Sơn were imported from Indonesia, whereas in 1996 the Vietnamese brand 'Happy Family' was used. There is widespread dissatisfaction with the 'Happy Family' condoms which are said to be of a poor quality and too thick, causing irritation in women and reducing sensitivity in men.

Finally, with regard to more 'natural' forms of contraception, safe periods and withdrawal are considered to be 'backward' and unsafe methods by health and family planning workers, who strongly try to dissuade women from adopting these methods.[19]

But there is more to contraceptive choice than simply the promotion and provision of contraceptives. In order to account for the continuing strong reliance on the IUD among women in Vải Sơn, we also need to consider the perceived health risks associated with contraceptive use, as well as the social context in which contraceptive decision-making takes place (cf. Nichter and Nichter 1989).

Contraception: health concerns and social constraints

Before looking more closely at alternatives to the IUD for women in Vải Sơn, let us briefly consider local concepts of reproductive physiology and of conception. Two different understandings of conception seem to co-exist in Vải Sơn. In the first – presumably older and now less common – explanation, conception takes place through the mixing in the uterus of the 'white blood' (*máu trắng*) of the man with the woman's blood. This understanding of conception has a parallel in Sino–Vietnamese medicine, where the existence of ovaries is not recognized, and conception is understood as the union in the uterus of the male (*yang*) and female (*yin*) principles in the form of the man's sperm and the woman's blood (see Coughlin 1965).

The second explanation of conception is much more common and seems to draw on biomedical ideas. As many women told me, they have learnt about reproductive physiology from health care and family planning providers or from posters at the hospital or health station. According to this viewpoint, conception takes place when the man's semen meets with the woman's egg. The egg 'falls' once a month and at this time the woman may get pregnant. Many women are familiar with biomedical perceptions of reproductive physiology and explain how the egg develops in the ovaries and moves through the ovarian tubes into the uterus.

In the first understanding of conception, fertility depends on the strength of the blood and may therefore be reduced by a weakening of the blood, while in the second understanding, conception may be prevented either by hindering egg and semen from meeting or by destroying the egg. Once conception has taken place, the foetus starts to develop and grow. In the beginning, it is only a 'blood clot' (*cục máu*) or a 'bean seed' (*hạt đậu*); after two or three months it looks like a little frog; and after four months it has the form of a human being. Therefore most of the women I talked to explained that it is not until it is four months old and starts to move that a foetus is really a human being. With this in mind, let us now consider each of the contraceptive methods that are available to women in Vải Sơn and which could be alternatives to the IUD. Women's perceptions of the IUD will be examined in detail in Chapter 4.

Contraceptive pill

This is not a popular method of contraception in Vietnam, where it is used by only 3 per cent of contraceptive users (GSO 1995). In Vải Sơn it is indicative that by the end of 1994 no women were using contraceptive pills. The pill is generally perceived as a 'harmful substance' (*chất độc*) which prevents pregnancy by destroying the woman's egg. Many women reason that if the pill destroys reproductive functions, it must be generally destructive to bodily functions and therefore harmful to health. The implicit idea, that no influence on the body works in isolation, is in line with traditional medical thinking, whereby all parts of the body are interrelated, in correspondence both with one another and with outside influences (see Chapter 5).

Some women fear that pill use might cause a permanent loss of fertility. Also the fact that very few women in Vải Sơn have ever used the pill makes it unattractive: women reason that if no one uses the pill, it cannot be a good method. The seven women in Vải Sơn who once tried using the pill have all discontinued use, finding that they could not tolerate the side effects. The three pill users I talked to had all experienced side effects of nausea, hot flushes, weakness, and headaches.[20]

Female sterilization

This method is understood to work by cutting the woman's ovarian tubes. In Vietnam tubectomy is used by only 4 per cent of contraceptive users (GSO 1995). By the end of 1994, only 19 women in Vải Sơn had undergone this operation. Sterilizations are unpopular methods of contraception because of the risks they pose:

There is risk involved in the operation itself which may cause blood-loss, infection or death. People in the commune say that one woman died from the sterilization procedure, and so other women 'learn from her experience' and avoid this method.

There is risk involved in the effects of the sterilization on both body and mind, since sterilizations are believed to interfere with the functioning of the nervous system, and so decrease the woman's strength, energy, intelligence, and sex drive.

There is a risk involved in the finality of never being able to have any more children, in case some accident or fatal illness should befall the children one has already.

For these reasons, both women themselves and their husbands often find that the risks of a sterilization far outweigh the potential benefits. An additional disincentive to sterilization is that few women in the commune have been sterilized, and this in itself makes sterilization an unattractive option.

Male sterilization

This is an even less popular method of contraception than female sterilization, used by only 0.2 per cent of contraceptive users in Vietnam (GSO 1995) and by just eight men in Vải Sơn. Vasectomy is understood as a method which works by cutting the semen-channelling tube. It is feared for more or less the same reasons as tubectomy: the operation may go wrong; the consequences for the man's health, intelligence, and sexual desires and capacities may be serious; and few men want to lose their ability to have more children in the future.

People would often tell me about a man in the commune who had undergone a sterilization a few years before and had to be hospitalized for three weeks afterwards. This was very unfortunate since he had wanted to keep the sterilization a secret. Since that time no men in the commune have been sterilized. Male sterilization is often equated with castration, and people fear that a sterilized man will become stupid and dull like a castrated chicken. For these reasons, sterilization is ruled out by most men, and few women want their husbands to be sterilized. Both women and men say they are too economically dependent on the husband's ability to work and perform normally to take the risks which a sterilization implies.

Condom

The condom is a relatively new method of contraception in Vải Sơn. In Vietnam, 4 per cent of contraceptive users were condom users in 1994 (GSO 1995), and by the end of 1994, 77 couples inVải Sơn received condoms from the commune family planning workers.

The condom is perceived as a barrier which hinders egg and sperm from meeting. Many older people feel that it is a method for the young and the urban, and many younger people feel shy to obtain and to use condoms. Condom use often influences sexual life negatively, causing embarrassment, inconvenience if the couple sleeps in a room with many people, and (particularly for men) reduced sexual pleasure. Even though condoms are often disliked by both women and men, many IUD-using women said they would have preferred a condom to the IUD, but that their husbands did not want to use condoms. From a woman's perspective there are several benefits to condom use: sexual intercourse is more 'clean' with a condom; condoms protect against diseases; and they do not have any adverse health effects.

Safe periods and withdrawal

Safe periods and withdrawal are the most commonly used alternatives to the IUD, both in Vietnam in general and in Vải Sơn in particular. In Vietnam as a whole, 21 per cent of contraceptive users rely on safe periods/withdrawal (GSO 1995). In the survey we conducted in Vải Sơn, 10 per cent of women said they were currently practising safe periods/withdrawal. For reasons of health, privacy, and prestige, many couples find traditional methods more attractive than any of the modern methods. They do not cause health problems, they do not require outside assistance or intervention, and there is considerable prestige to be gained by being able to practise safe periods/withdrawal successfully. The successful practice of these methods shows an ability on the part of the husband to control bodily urges through will and intellect, and indicates that the marriage is one of harmony and cooperation.

But there are also problems in the use of traditional methods. Both men and women often mention that withdrawal may be harmful to male health, causing weakness and discomfort, and many men find that the act of withdrawal reduces sexual pleasure. To women, the use of safe periods/withdrawal is often fairly stressful, being strongly dependent on male cooperation. In focus group discussions, women often talked about the trouble that they have in situations where the husband does not withdraw in time; the fights that may ensue as a result; and the worries of getting pregnant that are associated with such 'unsafe' sexual activity. In addition to this, safe periods and withdrawal are considered to be methods that are prone to failure, particularly if the woman has irregular menstruations.

In order to understand why safe periods/withdrawal often fail, people's perception of what a 'safe period' is needs closer scrutiny. Most of the women I talked to said that they would use withdrawal only during the days of the woman's cycle when she is able to conceive. But many people believe that a woman may conceive during the days immediately following menstruation, when the uterus is said to be open 'like a flower' and sperm therefore enters more easily. In the survey we conducted in Vải Sơn, 36 per cent of women believed conception takes place during the first ten days of the menstrual cycle, 49 per cent said it takes place mid-cycle, and 3 per cent said it takes place during the last ten days of the cycle. In other words, the middle and the end of the woman's cycle are considered by many to be 'safe periods', while only the days immediately following menstruation are perceived as being 'unsafe'.

Breastfeeding

Breastfeeding and postpartum taboo have traditionally been used to regulate fertility and are still used today. I was told that 'in the old days' there was a postpartum taboo of three months (which the parents ensured that the young couple maintained), but today the duration varies from couple to couple. Among survey respondents, duration varied from 1 to 24 months, with an average of four months.

Also breastfeeding is a commonly used method of fertility regulation. The fertility-inhibiting effects of breastfeeding are well known among women in Vải Sơn: 55 per cent of female survey respondents are convinced that a woman who is breastfeeding cannot conceive. Many women, however, are not aware that if breasteeding is non-continuous it may lose its contraceptive effects. Even though women generally breastfeed for quite long – the average duration of breastfeeding among Vietnamese women is eighteen months (GSO 1995), while seventeen months was the average among survey respondents in Vải Sơn – breastfeeding is rarely continuous. Most women start working again one month after delivery and breastfeed only about three times a day, while the rest of the day the child is fed supplementary foods, usually by grandparents or other relatives. This is probably the reason why many women have become involuntarily pregnant shortly after a previous delivery, when they thought they could not yet conceive (cf. Johansson *et al.* 1996b).

Menstrual regulation and abortion

These should be mentioned, since they are very commonly used methods of fertility control in Vải Sơn, as in Vietnam in general. It has been estimated that 40 per cent of all pregnancies in

Vietnam end in abortions (UNFPA 1997). In Vải Sơn probably at least half of all pregnancies ended in abortion in 1994: while 205 children were born, 181 menstrual regulations were performed at the commune health station. But total abortion rates are even higher than this, since abortions later than two weeks after a missed menstruation have to be performed in a hospital and are therefore not registered in the commune.

Women do not consider menstrual regulation and abortion as contraceptive methods, though, but as back-ups when other methods fail. Most women distinguish clearly between menstrual regulations (*hút điều hoà kinh nguyệt/điều hoà kinh nguyệt*; to draw out/regulate menstruation) and abortions (*nạo thai*; to scrape out the foetus).[21] Both menstrual regulations and abortions are considered as pregnancy terminations, but menstrual regulations are performed at such an early stage of pregnancy that the foetus is not yet formed, but is still considered to be only a 'blood clot' or a 'bean seed'. As commonly perceived by women, a menstrual regulation only sucks out blood (*hút máu*) and brings menstruation back to normal, in contrast to an abortion which destroys a foetus. In order to avoid an abortion, most women strive to go as early as possible for a menstrual regulation, and there may therefore be a risk that women who are not pregnant still have menstrual regulations performed (cf. WHO 1995).

Another term for menstrual regulation is *hút thai*, to suck out the foetus. If I used this term, however, I would often be corrected by women and told that it did not sound nice and that the proper term to use is *điều hoà kinh nguyệt*, to regulate menstruation. Menstrual regulations seem to be categorized with other methods of inducing or regulating menstruations, such as taking tonics or medicines, and they are considered to be much less harmful to women's health and well-being than abortions. Women often cite the old saying: 'One miscarriage/abortion is like three deliveries', meaning that the psychological stress of an abortion makes it harder to endure than a delivery, which is a happy event.

Many women also feel that abortions are morally wrong and feel very guilty about having them performed. Interrupting a pregnancy has traditionally been considered a sin (*tội*) (cf. Johansson *et al.* 1996b), and is still considered so by old people. Most younger women, however, distinguish between early and late pregnancy terminations, finding menstrual regulations acceptable and only late abortions really morally questionable. An abortion gets more sinful the later it takes place, and people say that with second trimester abortions there is considerable risk that the foetus will condemn (*oán*) its parents, bringing them misfortune and unhappiness. Talking about relatively early abortions, women often say that 'today the [family] economy determines everything'; i.e. it is better to have an abortion than a child which the economy does not allow one to take proper care of. One woman said:

> 'It is always better to avoid getting pregnant. But if you can't avoid it, of course you must take care of yourself and take care of your children, so you have to go [for an abortion]. You want to be financially secure, you want your children to be healthy and well provided for, so it is most important to take care of the children you have already. Don't you agree?'

Even though most women would clearly prefer not to have to resort to menstrual regulation or abortion, many women find that using traditional methods with menstrual regulation/abortion as a back-up poses much less of a risk to their health than an IUD which would be the likely alternative. Particularly women whose husbands work far away and only come home once in a while often find that resorting to menstrual regulations when they fear they are actually pregnant is far preferable to the daily suffering from an IUD.

Summing up: the rationality of IUD use

We have seen in this chapter that the field of family planning in Vietnam is a strategic site for the production of powerful normative standards for the quality and character of family life. Yet simply seeing the family planning policy as a top-down political strategy of the state or as a force working on people from the outside, constraining or inducing particular modes of acting, would be a very crude interpretation of the social dynamics at work in this field. State norms are clearly not merely imposed upon a passive and recipient population, but actively engage with a range of existing concerns in people's lives. Fertility control takes place within a social field that is tense with hopes, ambitions, and frustrations; it condenses a range of important economic and existential issues. Following Foucault (1977, 1978), we may therefore see the family planning policy as productive rather than re-pressive, as nourishing dreams and aspirations rather than simply forcing or oppressing people.

A core point of convergence between state discourses and individual dreams is the notion of the happy family. Happy families are at the center both of state family planning campaigns and of people's everyday strivings to get by and improve their lot. To most women, the creation of a happy family is the overall aim and meaning of life; and in a social climate where a 'happy family' is synonymous with a 'small family', fertility control becomes an important way for women to realize their dreams and create stability and safety in their lives. In order to be able to build the families and lives of their dreams, it is therefore crucially important for women to be able to decide for themselves if and when to get pregnant. But while women's motivations to control their fertility are strong, their means to do so are relatively limited. In the current context of family planning in Vietnam, women's contraceptive choices are strongly constrained, both by the inadequacy of contraceptive service provision, by the health problems associated with method use, and by male opposition to the use of certain methods.

Thus, in a situation where fertility control is urgently required, there are several good reasons for women to accept the IUD in spite of the fears attached to it. The IUD is strongly promoted by health-care providers and local officials. It is approved by most husbands – with the exception of those who are particularly concerned about their wives' health – since it does not interfere with sexual life or pose any threats to male health; it is reversible; and it is a more effective method than traditional methods or the condom. Moreover, it is 'normal' to have an IUD. WHO (1995) notes that there is a 'culture of IUD use' in Vietnam; by having an IUD women stay within the boundaries of what is normal and acceptable and so avoid being ridiculed or gossiped about for doing something no one else does. Yet many women also tend to see IUD use as a burden and a self-sacrifice, imposed on them by unequal divisions of responsibilities within families. As we shall see in later chapters, women's self-sacrifice for their husbands and families in relation to fertility control is but one element in a larger pattern of everyday social and moral relations where women often feel they have to submit and comply with their husbands and in-laws.

Having thus explored some elements of the social context in which IUD use takes place, we shall now scrutinize women's experiences with their IUDs in more depth, considering both their social contexts and the complex cultural meanings they engage.

Notes

1. In Vải Sơn, approximately one out of four households has a television. Televisions are widely shared: at night, or at noon when it is too hot to work outside, people often gather to watch television in the houses of wealthier neighbours. Television thus brings both state messages and images of life in other countries directly into most people's everyday lives.

2. Even though Lan emphasized that the payments due for third- and higher-order births were not fines, commune women clearly perceived them as such, seeing them as punishments for 'breaking the plan'. But this policy apparently gained some legitimacy from the fact that the money also brought in extra land for the family. For instance, a woman who had to pay 150,000 *đồng* when she had her fourth child in 1991 pointed to her daughter, saying, 'When I gave birth to this child, I was punished. [...] I got angry, it was difficult to find the money. But then I thought again. And I realized that I had to pay, but I also received land for my daughter, so I accepted.' But she also noted that the new land and family planning policies represented a reversal of previous practices. Before, the cooperative would provide each additional child with extra rations of everything, and in this sense parents were economically rewarded for having many children. Now, however, couples having many children felt they were being punished.

3. Today, however, limited access to land seems to be a very important, indirect incentive to limit births. As mentioned in Chapter 2, in October 1992 all land was distributed to families in the commune on a 20-year basis, with one *sào* of land per person. This means that no additional land is now allocated for new children; people simply have to survive on the land they were allocated in 1992. Even though Lan did not directly say so, my impression was that without the possibility of allocating additional land for new children born to a family, commune authorities simply did not have the power to maintain a system of economic disincentives for third- and higher-order births, even though they may have wanted to.

4. Officially, this sum is considered as a 'compensation' for lost working time and expenses to buy special foods rather than as an incentive.

5. Committees for Population and Family Planning now exist throughout Vietnam, at both commune, district, and provincial levels (NCPFP 1993b, 1996).

6. According to national strategies, networks of family planning 'collaborators' should be established in all communes and hamlets through-

out the country: 'Each of the collaborators is responsible for a number of households according to population grouping, for direct motivation and registration of an individual audience at reproductive age, and likewise, for provision of FP service such as distribution of condoms, pills; instructions and help to contraceptive acceptors' (NCPFP 1993b: 9).

7. Even though direct comparisons between Vietnam and China may be difficult in this area, since Vietnam has not experienced political terror and persecutions to the same degree as China, the discrepancies between verbal expressions and actual practices seem to be just as common in Vietnam as in China.

8. For similar points in relation to the Chinese family planning policy, see Greenhalgh (1994), Kaufman *et al.* (1989).

9. This 'intermediate' position of local-level cadres has often been noted in studies of China (e.g., Chan *et al.* 1984; Shue 1988; Oi 1989). For a detailed discussion of the role of local-level cadres in family planning in China, see Greenhalgh 1993.

10. Similarly, Milwertz (1997) writes that the urban Chinese women she interviewed experienced family planning activities as forms of *care* rather than control.

11. This statement may serve as a comment to those who assert that concepts of 'reproductive rights', 'individual freedom' etc. are alien to Asian women (see Corrêa 1994). Even though few women would express these views so clearly and cogently as Hương, there is no doubt that concepts of individual freedom, integrity, and rights do exist among women in Vải Sơn. The expectations and desires to be able to decide for oneself are difficult to overlook, which is also evident from Quế's statement.

12. As often noted (e.g., Greenhalgh 1995), the notion of fertility preferences is very questionable. It imposes fixity and certainty to questions that are more often experienced by people as uncertain and fluctuating. As other things in life, fertility desires change over time and even from moment to moment, under the impact of moods and life changes. However, asking people if they want more children probably does give a rough indication of general fertility preferences in a population.

13. Of the 59 women who had two children at the time of the survey, only 13 said they wanted more children. Of these women, nine had only daughters, two had only sons, and two had one son and one daughter.

14. In the group of 40–45-year-old women the most common wish was for four children (45 per cent of the women); in the group of 33–39-year-old women it was three or four children (32 per cent and 28 per cent respectively); among the 26–32-year-old women it was two children (63 per cent).

15. One study points out, however, that among some groups in the Vietnamese population, family size desires are still high (WHO 1995).

16. This, on the other hand, may also indicate that needing another son is a locally legitimate reason for 'breaking the plan', while simply wanting many children is not. Unless one has a very good economy, wanting many children places one in the category of the 'backwards and uneducated', whereas wanting another son is more understandable and legitimate. Of the 54 women, two also mentioned they felt pressured by their husbands' parents to have another child, and one mentioned she felt pressured by her husband. The remaining thirteen women gave the following reasons: contraceptive failure (six, of whom five used withdrawal, one the IUD); wanting to have more than two children (four); wanting a daughter (two); and accidental pregnancy soon after a previous birth (two).

17. Demographers often place 'the economics of childbearing' at the center of attempts to explain fertility changes in developing countries (e.g., Becker 1960; Easterlin and Crimmins 1985). In his flow-of-wealth theory, Caldwell (1982) argues that fertility declines when wealth starts to flow from older to younger generations rather than the other way around. This development – which seems to fit well with the current situation in Red River Delta communes like Vải Sơn – is closely connected with mass education and increasing costs of raising children. As pointed out by Whyte (1984), however, economic values are shaped in wider cultural contexts of meaning and significance. To understand 'the economics of childbearing,' therefore, we also need to consider the cultural and moral contexts in which economic values are generated.

18. I do not use the concept of norms in the traditional sociological sense of fixed structures of value which constrain and determine people's actions, but rather in the Vietnamese/Chinese sense: as *exemplary standards* which serve as guiding principles for conduct, but which may easily be overridden by more concrete and practical needs and considerations. On the concept of norms in China, see Anagnost (1991) and Bakken (1994, 1995).

19. Since many couples prefer using safe periods/withdrawal, a better strategy might be for health and family planning workers to inform people on the correct use of these methods.

20. In a study by Đỗ Trọng Hiếu *et al.* (1993a) of reasons for non-use of modern contraception among 2,088 women seeking abortion in Hanoi and Thái Bình, the majority of women either lack knowledge of the pill or believe that the pill is bad for women's health. A UNFPA study among 175 women found that only 26 per cent of contraceptive pill users did not experience any side effects (UNFPA 1993). The most common side effects were 'feeling hot', weight gain, headaches, menstrual pain, and nausea.

21. Second and third trimester abortions are called *phá thai*, to destroy the foetus. According to commune health staff, such late abortions are usually only performed on young, unmarried women for whom having a child would be socially devastating.

CHAPTER 4

The IUD and Women's Health

'Where were you yesterday?' Hùng asked with a grin, 'We were waiting for you.'

Yesterday had been a day of torrential rains, with alleys and roads flooded by red muddy water going nearly up to the waist of the few people who ventured outside.

Seeing me pulling on my raincoat and boots, Bà Chính firmly said, 'No, you do not go out in that weather. Besides, no one is working today. You haven't understood Vietnam yet, have you? Of course, no one would work on such a day.'

So I stayed at home, and the following day it turned out that everyone on the survey team of seven people had in fact come to work the day before, wading through the waters to the People's Committee building where our meetings usually took place. Today was the final day of preparations for the survey we were going to conduct on reproductive histories and contraceptive experiences among women and men in the commune. After weeks of preparation and deliberation on the wording of questions, piles of photocopied survey questionnaires were now lying ready in the cupboard in the corner, samplings had been done, lists of respondents prepared, and we were ready to start. This morning we finalized time plans and work schedules for the interviewers, and the following day they set out to start filling in the 300 questionnaires.

A survey of IUD side effects

In the survey we conducted, women's experiences with their IUDs were of central importance. The respondents were asked a series of questions concerning their current and previous IUD use: which type of IUD they used; reasons for IUD removals; what side effects they had experienced after the insertion of their last IUD; how long each of the side effects had continued; and what remedies they had tried to alleviate the symptoms. The survey questionnaire included a list of symptoms worked out on the basis of the qualitative interviews I had conducted with IUD users during the first months of fieldwork. In addition to this list of symptoms, the interviewers would write down any other IUD side effects reported by the women.[1] In other words, we registered the physical symptoms which women themselves perceived as side effects of the IUD and the side effects which women remembered at the time.[2]

Reviews of health interview surveys assert that with a recall period of more than a few weeks, results will be biased through errors due to memory decline (e.g., Kroeger 1983; Ross and Vaughan 1986). It is impossible to know, however, whether the symptoms reported by women in this study are objectively 'correct' or not, i.e. whether women actually did have the symptoms they remembered at the time of interview ot whether they would have reported something different had they been asked at a different time of their lives. So we have to be content with the fact that these statements indicate how women believed the IUD had affected their bodies. They are very subjective assessments, expressing women's own experiences of past or present IUD use as they recalled them later. But as long as we are primarily interested in women's own experiences of their bodies and health, these subjective assessments are of major importance in themselves. In this context, the question is not so much whether women's statements correspond to 'reality' or not: they *are* reality as subjectively experienced and remembered.

Among the 200 female respondents, 147 had used an IUD at some point in their lives and 102 were current IUD users.[3] Two IUD types were used; the 'Number 8' (*số 8*), i.e. the Czechoslovakian Dana or its locally produced Vietnamese copy Vina, and the 'Letter T' (*chữ T*), the copper-bearing TCu200 or TCu380. Nearly three out of four IUD users reported some kind of side effects of their IUDs. Of the 147 women who had ever had an IUD, 28 per cent (41) said they had experienced no side effect from their last IUD, while 72 per cent (106) had experienced side effects of varying duration and severity.[4] The IUD symptoms reported by the women were:

- backache (55 per cent of all IUD users)
- fatigue/weakness (50 per cent)
- menstrual disturbances (42 per cent)
- abdominal pain (41 per cent)
- vaginal discharge (29 per cent)
- weightloss (27 per cent)
- headache (22 per cent)
- bleedings (9 per cent)
- vaginal itching (7 per cent)
- dizziness (1 per cent).

The menstrual irregularities were most often heavier, prolonged, or irregular bleedings. Some women experienced only one of these symptoms, while most experienced several. There seems to be no systematic pattern in the way symptoms appeared; nearly all women experienced different combinations of symptoms.

But the fact that women report symptoms of backache, fatigue, menstrual problems, etc., does not give us much information about the severity of these symptoms. How much do they interfere with everyday activities? How much do women worry about them? How are they experienced? Even though questions concerning the experience of symptoms are better answered through qualitative research methods, some information may also be drawn from the survey on this issue.

First, 49 per cent (72) of all (current and previous) IUD users and 38 per cent (39) of current users said the IUD decreased their ability to work. Given the crucial importance of being able to work and take care of one's family, these are alarming numbers.

Second, many women seek remedial action for their symptoms: of the 106 women who suffered from side effects, 69 had sought some kind of health care at the time of the survey. A wide variety of remedial actions are taken, from consulting commune health station staff, district hospital staff or traditional healers, to buying Western or traditional medicines in the market. The place where women most often go for treatment is the commune health station. The fact that women, whose days are busy and whose incomes are meagre, spend time and money consulting a health practitioner indicates that they take their symptoms fairly seriously.[5]

Third, most women experience lasting side effects with the IUDs: nearly all had at least one symptom which lasted for more than three months and many women have had side effects during the entire time of IUD use. Of the 106 IUD users who experienced side effects, just 13 had suffered only from initial (i.e. less than 3 months) side effects.

Notably, however, many women continue to use the IUD despite the health problems they experience. More than two-thirds of the IUD users who find that the IUD decreases their ability to work had already had the IUD for more than 20 months at the time of the survey (27 out of 39 women). Furthermore, over a third of the women who had had their first or second IUDs removed because of health problems had had another IUD inserted later (14 out of 39). Does this mean that IUD side effects are not that severe after all, since many women either put up with them or have an IUD inserted again later? In clinical IUD studies it is often assumed that continued IUD use can be taken as an indication of the insignificance of symptoms. For instance, Farr and Amartya write:

> The increased incidence in reports of menstrual complaints among TCu380A IUD users did not result in an increased rate of removing this IUD for bleeding and/or pain [...]. Most likely these complaints were considered to be tolerable by these subjects since they continued use of their assigned IUD in spite of complaints about changes to their menstrual bleeding patterns. (Farr and Amartya 1994: 147)

The realities of women's lives, however, often seem to differ from the assumptions made by clinical researchers. In the remainder of this chapter, I shall try to show that the IUD symptoms which women experience are neither negligible nor tolerable, but that many women simply endure them for want of better alternatives.

To illustrate some of the different experiences women have with the IUDs, I shall now present five commune women: Hảo, Ngọc, Quế, Hạnh, and Tuyết. These five women were among the survey respondents with whom I later conducted in-depth interviews on contraceptive experiences, health, and daily life. Here, the presentations provided focus specifically on fertility control and experiences with the IUD, while in the next chapter I shall broaden the histories of the five women and describe the wider social contexts in which their lives unfold.

Case illustrations

Hảo, 44 years old

Hảo is a small woman who looks tired and worn out. She and her family – her husband Chên, their two sons aged 17 and 12 and their 15-year-old daughter – live in a simple one-room house with dirt floor, mud walls, and a thatched roof. As Liên and I reach the house, Hảo comes home from her fields, carrying a heavy load of sweet potatoes. She excuses herself for coming home so late, wipes her face with a towel from the clothes line strung across the yard, and invites us inside.

Pouring water from a thermos into a teapot, she apologizes for the poverty of her home, saying that the family's circumstances are very difficult, and even though she has always worked very hard they are still poor. Both her own, her husband's and her children's health are quite weak, and so life is not easy. I tell her that we have come today to talk more about her health and about her experiences with the IUD. Hảo looks a little worried, and says that we can talk about these issues, but we must bear with her for not knowing how to speak 'diligently'. She has only gone to school for a few years, she says, and does not know very much.

In brief, she then tells us the following story: When her youngest son was born in 1982, she had an IUD inserted. Since both her own and Chên's health was weak and their finances very strained, they agreed that they could not afford to raise more than three children. At that time it was still unusual to have an IUD, but Hảo decided to have one because she was determined not to have more children. After the insertion she often suffered from stomach pains, backaches, and dizziness, and she felt much weaker than before. During menstruation she lost more blood, her bleedings now continued for ten days each time and they were stronger than before. Still, she was very afraid of getting pregnant, so she did not have the IUD removed but instead took medicine to boost her blood supply and improve her health.

After six years, she went to the hospital where they told her to change the IUD and have a new one inserted. She had a new IUD, but her symptoms continued, and she still felt very weak. After another four years she had had enough; in 1992 she had the IUD removed and she and Chên agreed to practise withdrawal instead. But she almost immediately became pregnant and had to have a menstrual regulation.

To prevent this from happening again, Hảo had another IUD inserted, this time a 'T' IUD. However, the 'T' IUD was even worse than the two previous IUDs. Hảo had very strong and prolonged bleedings, continuing for nearly 30 days each month. She felt weak and tired and suffered from backaches and stomach aches. Once she felt so exhausted that she had to rest for a whole month and could not work. During this period, Hảo also suffered from itching and discharge due to an infection she thinks was caused by the IUD. After six months like this, she had the IUD removed in 1993, and since then she has been feeling much better.

When she had the IUD removed, the health station nurse suggested that she could use contraceptive pills instead of the IUD. She therefore tried taking pills for one month, but soon gave it up, since the pills made her feel very sick: she had headaches, felt dizzy and 'hot', and became tired and weak. I ask why they do not use condoms, but Hảo thinks condoms are for the young and for people in the cities, not for someone like her. So now she and Chên use only safe periods and withdrawal. But they rarely have sex anyway, Hảo says, they are already old and they work too hard to think about sex.

Ngọc, 42 years old

For the first few minutes of our conversation, Ngọc seems nervous and uneasy, fidgeting in her seat and casting frequent glances out into the yard where her husband is tending the buffalo. She lives with her husband and their five sons (who are today between 20 and 8 years old) in a relatively large and well-built house. Today only Ngọc and her husband are at home.

Ngọc tells us that she had her first IUD inserted back in 1982, after giving birth to her fourth son. This was before the 'family planning era', she says, when having an IUD was still unusual, but neither she nor her husband wanted more than four children. The IUD, however, made her very sick, particularly in the beginning. For the first six months she had irregular and prolonged periods, suffered from discharge, and lost a lot of weight. She went to the health station where they gave her some medicine which stopped the discharge. But she still felt very weak and often suffered from backaches and headaches, so after three years she decided to have the IUD removed.

However, since they did not know of any alternative method of contraception, Ngọc soon became pregnant again and gave birth to her fifth son. She then had another IUD inserted, and this IUD, too, made her sick. For the first ten months she had menstruation twice a month, continuing for a week each time. During menstruation she had very painful stomachaches and felt very

weak, and during the first months after IUD insertion she had
heavy discharge.

Still, she has kept the IUD, even though it makes her tired and
weak and causes frequent headaches and backaches. Every
month she suffers from headaches for about ten days and has to
stay at home and only do light work. I ask her why she does not
have the IUD removed, then? Because 'to insert is to insert,'
Ngọc says. Having an IUD means keeping it, and Ngọc is a
woman who knows how to endure. The only alternative she sees
to the IUD is sterilization – but the thought of undergoing an
operation scares her, so she prefers to keep the IUD.

Quế, 34 years old

'Here,' Quế says, handing me a red hairband, 'this is for you. I
have made it myself, it will look good in your blond hair.'

Quế and I have met and talked many times before. There is
something about her that I have liked from the first day I met her.
She is a tall and straightforward woman who talks more loudly
than most, voicing her opinion openly and directly. This has
given her a reputation of 'being like a man', of not knowing how
to behave in a properly feminine way. Quế has four children,
three daughters aged 12, 6, and 3, and a 9-year-old son. Her husband works in another province, and Quế does all the everyday
work of farming and childcare at home.

Today we are sitting in her dark little house while the rain is
pouring down outside, and I ask her if she can tell me again about
her experiences with the IUD. After her first daughter was born,
Quế says, she was often called over the commune loudspeakers
to have an IUD, but she and her husband Thá preferred to use
withdrawal to space their children. When her third child was born
in 1988, Quế did not want to have more children, she thought two
daughters and one son were fine. But her husband wanted another
son, since he is an only son and there are too few men in his
family. Also her husband's parents and her friends and neighbours encouraged her to have another child. She could not refuse,
Quế says; she was afraid that if she did not agree, her husband
would have a child with one of the women who could not find a
husband.

When the fourth child – another daughter – was born in 1991,
Quế and her husband had to pay a fine of 150,000 dong, and her
husband finally accepted that Quế should have an IUD. The IUD
made Quế's periods more painful, she had severe backache and
stomach ache during menstruation, when she was tired she felt

weaker than ever, and often dizzy. She did not consider these side effects to be unbearable, however, but thought she could easily live with them.

Besides the IUD, Quế and her husband now also practise withdrawal. 'Everyone knows that one cannot rely completely on the IUD,' she says, and since they are both afraid of having more children, it is better to use two methods at a time. Today Quế has only minor side effects from her IUD, mainly heavier and more painful menstruations, fatigue, and frequent backaches, particularly when she works hard. But as she says, she is more worried about the family finances than about the side-effects of the IUD.

Hạnh, 31 years old

It is early afternoon on a mild and sunny day when I meet Hạnh for the first time. She is washing her long hair by the well in the yard and combs it carefully while we are talking. We sit on the porch outside her house, in the shade, out of the earshot of her mother-in-law, but right under one of the commune loudspeakers which spews out production results and party policies at us.

With the exception of the loudspeaker announcements, it is a peaceful afternoon: Hạnh's three eldest children are away in school, her husband is away at work in another province, and her mother-in-law is playing with the youngest inside the house. The house is large and new and built of concrete, but has barely any furniture in it; just building it has probably taken all the family's savings. At the other side of the yard is the house of Hạnh's mother-in-law, a simple old house with thatched roof and mud walls. Hạnh and her husband Chuyên have four sons, of whom the eldest is 11 and the youngest 3 years old.

Hạnh tells me that when their third child was born in 1989, she and Chuyên had to pay a fine of 100,000 dong. After that they agreed that three children were enough and that Hạnh should have an IUD. Before she had the IUD fitted she was strong and healthy, Hạnh says, but after the IUD she felt weak and tired; she lost weight, her periods became irregular, she had pains in her back and stomach and a lot of discharge. After a year she had the IUD removed. She meant to have another IUD, but she soon realized that she was pregnant again. She was already five months along then, so it was too late for an abortion.

Even though it was not planned, Hạnh did not see this pregnancy as a disaster; she very much hoped that the fourth child might be a daughter. But she gave birth to another son, and then had another IUD. This IUD also causes her health problems: her menstruations are irregular, each period lasts nine to ten days, and sometimes she menstruates twice a month. When she works hard, she suffers from backaches, which she never did before she had the IUD. She has also lost weight and feels much weaker than before. Sometimes she is sick for three or four days, cannot eat, has a headache, feels dizzy, and has to stay home and rest. She has also had a lot of yellow and white discharge since she had the IUD. I ask her why she does not shift to another method, and Hạnh replies that she does not know what else to do. She is afraid of the pill and her husband does not want to use condoms. But she is very much afraid of 'breaking the plan' again, and so she keeps the IUD and takes vitamin B6 to strengthen her health.

Tuyết, 26 years old

When Lan and I arrive Tuyết is at the market, and we sit talking to her husband May for a while. The living-room is large and imposing with its tiled floor, newly painted green walls, and heavy furniture. May tells us about his trading, he buys and sells fruit at nearby markets. The couple seems to be among the people who know how to make the most of the economic reforms. Their house is large and new, built of bricks and with a tiled roof; in the yard there is a cow and a water buffalo; and in the pigsty there are four fat pigs. Tuyết and May have three children, two sons aged 8 and 1, and a 4-year-old daughter, and they definitely do not want any more children, May says. As Tuyết comes home, May politely disappears, leaving us to talk about 'women's matters'.

Tuyết is a pretty woman who looks strong and healthy with her round arms, round dimpled cheeks, lively eyes and frequent smiles. She had her first IUD inserted in 1989, she tells us, after her daughter was born. Both she and May agreed that to secure the family's economy they would stop at two children, one son and one daughter. But the first IUD was very soon expelled, and she had to have another IUD inserted. Before she had the IUD she felt weak already, but having the IUD made her feel even weaker, Tuyết says. The IUD caused headaches and fatigue, her back and stomach ached before menstruation, and it hurt when she urinated. Her periods became irregular and prolonged, she lost much more blood, and grew thinner and weaker. She grew dizzy more often than before, and it often happened that when she rose she could not see anything. When she worked hard and bent down, she had backache more often than she used to. If she went outside in the sunshine, she often had headaches and became very tired.

After four years of IUD use she got pregnant while still wearing the IUD and gave birth to their third child. In order to protect her health, her husband then agreed to use condoms. However, after a few months they gave up the condom, since they both found that it spoilt sexual pleasure and was difficult and complicated to use. Tuyết has instead had a third IUD inserted, which again causes tiredness, backache, stomach ache, headache, and dizziness, particularly when she works hard. Because of the IUD she tires easily and cannot work as long as she wants to. She thinks that the IUD affects her so much because her health is weak already. Still, she keeps the IUD since she is terrified af getting pregnant again and, after all, the IUD is the most effective method of contraception. To strengthen her health she sometimes takes tonics (*thuốc bổ*).

⚭

The five cases presented here illustrate how fertility control takes place in a social setting where both state policies and family considerations influence and set the framework for women's contraceptive decision-making. The cases also illustrate the fear and determination which characterize women's efforts to control their fertility: Hảo, Ngọc, Quế, Hạnh, and Tuyết all want to control their fertility, yet lack safe and effective means to do so. These are just five examples of the countless women who experience IUD side effects as detrimental to their health, everyday lives, work, and well-being, but who still accept the IUD since no better alternatives are available to them. In a situation where the IUD is practically the only modern contraceptive method available, women who can 'bear' the IUD therefore often praise themselves lucky. When we talked about her life-threatening experiences with unwanted pregnancies and abortions, Hương said:

'Those who can bear the IUD are the luckiest. If one cannot bear the IUD, one is forced into hardship, one has to bear the hardship.'

In short, in the current context of family planning in Vietnam there is a wide disparity between the strong moral and economic incentives to limit fertility and the limited means available for people to do so – and this is the dilemma in which Hảo, Ngọc, Quế, Hạnh, Tuyết, and many other women find themselves.

But how do commune women themselves explain the problems they experience with their IUDs? How do they perceive the IUD and its effects on the body?

Women's views of the IUD

In Vải Sơn, the IUD is almost universally perceived as a barrier which is placed inside the woman's uterus where it prevents the man's sperm from meeting the woman's egg.[6] In local opinion, the 'Number 8' and the 'T' IUD each has its strengths and drawbacks, but in general the 'T' seems to be preferred.[7] The 'Number 8' is said to break easily and to 'pulverize' inside the body, and it is more difficult to remove than the 'T'. While 'T' IUDs can be removed at the communal health station, removals of the 'Number 8' have to take place at the district hospital.

The two IUDs are understood as working in the same way, but being different in shape and material. Most women agree that the 'Number 8' is made of plastic, while some say the 'T' is made of plastic and others that it is made of copper.[8] Whether of plastic or copper, however, most women agree that the IUD is made of *chất hoá học* (chemical material).[9] One woman said that IUDs release *chất độc* (poisonous substance) which kills the sperm and therefore prevents pregnancy, thus associating the IUD (like the contraceptive pill) with toxicity and destructive capacities. Many women said that after some years of use, the IUD may rust (*bị rỉ*) inside the body and cause gynaecological infection.

Women's own explanations of IUD problems include physiological health and socio-economic factors.

First, women often point to possible *physiological* reasons for their problems with the IUD. To many it does not seem logical to apply one universal and uniform method to a population of different women. The women often emphasized that 'the structure of each person's body is different' – different women also have different physiologies, different states of health, and different needs. In this context the problem with the IUD is that it comes in only one standard size and therefore may be unsuitable for some women. Whereas one conclusion to draw from this could be that a greater variety of different contraceptive methods is needed, this was not what women in Vải Sơn expected. Rather, they would usually say that they wanted a greater variety of different IUDs –

a wish that makes sense in a social context where the IUD is almost synonymous with contraception and where limited knowledge of alternative methods exists.

Second, side effects of the IUD are considered by women themselves as being closely related to their *overall states of health*. Many women find that they cannot withstand the disruption and imbalance caused by the insertion of a foreign and 'chemical' thing into their body because they are already physically weak and overburdened. As the WHO (1995) notes, it is a common perception among people in Vietnam that one needs to be in good health to use contraceptive devices. Women particularly emphasize that the increased menstrual blood loss caused by the IUD may be a serious problem for women who are already weak and lacking blood. Another common concern is that the IUD 'influences thoughts': many women say that they think so much about the IUD that they get sick just from worrying about it.[10] Since many women have to have IUDs in spite of their fears, it is not surprising that these, once inserted, are surrounded by fears and tensions. As one woman said about her brief experience with the IUD,

'I had the IUD inserted, and I came home, and I thought about it all the time, I was afraid all the time, so it affected my health. I had a backache, and I thought about it all the time, I was afraid all the time, and after four months the IUD was expelled. [...] I was afraid because many people had told me one gets sick from the IUD.'

Third, IUD problems are perceived by women as being closely related to the *social and economic* circumstances of their lives. Whether perceived as a barrier or as a releaser of toxicity, the IUD is usually viewed as an artificial and 'chemical' object which is placed inside the body and which therefore creates some – at least initial – disturbance of bodily functions. Both health workers and IUD users usually say that the IUD needs some time after insertion to become 'stable' (*ổn định*) inside the body.[11] Early side effects are normal and to be expected, but in order for the IUD to 'stabilize' as soon as possible, women should avoid hard work and sexual activity for some time after insertion. But, as women would often emphasize, many women have to continue working immediately after the insertion of an IUD, or they come home to a husband who 'demands right away', without any concern for his wife's health. In other words, hard work in combination with demanding husbands often does not allow women the rest they need to give their bodies a chance to accommodate the IUD. In many cases the IUD therefore never has a chance to stabilize, which results in continous side effects.[12]

Many women also see direct links between their poverty and the IUD: it is because they are poor and unable to provide for more than a few children that they have to use IUDs. But ironically it is also often poverty – and women's ensuing physical weakness – which makes it impossible for them to 'tolerate' the IUD.

In short, among commune women the IUD is associated with poverty, hard work, and social submission. It is a device, in other words, which seems to engage more general problems and stresses in women's lives, and which forms a core point of intersection of important daily experiences. We shall now take a closer look at the social and cultural dynamics through which the IUD comes to take up this position. While the preceding presentation of the physical symptoms which women associate with the IUD has provided some insights into women's experiences, an overly narrow focus on symptoms also leaves important experiential aspects out of the picture. Asking women simply which symptoms they suffer from tends to isolate physical experiences from the social context of everyday life. For a more comprehensive and contextual understanding of what is at stake when women's bodies hurt, ache and bleed, a different analytical approach to the understanding of physical symptoms and complaints is therefore needed.

Analytical approaches to human experiences of pain

In a biomedical framework of understanding, physical symptoms are usually treated as signs which refer to an objective reality existing independently of its observers. It is assumed that the human body can be treated and understood as an objective entity, cut off from people's subjective experiences (cf. Gordon 1988; Good 1994). Such empiricist theories have been criticized by anthropologists who maintain that pain as a human experience is deeply imbricated with cultural categories and understandings, modes of perception and expression, and social relations and institutions (e.g., Good *et al.* 1992, Kleinman 1995). According to this viewpoint, physical symptoms are not simply objectively given signs which refer to an underlying layer of biological malfunctioning; rather, as part of human experience, pain and discomfort are by definition socially and culturally shaped. Therefore, in order to gain a more comprehensive understanding of the health problems which women experience with the IUDs, we need an approach that takes into account the social and cultural context of subjective experience.

Taking subjective experience seriously, however, does not mean that we have to deny the physiological character of women's IUD problems: these are clearly both physiological, existential, and social. However, if we reduce IUD side effects to questions of technology and raw physiology and ignore the social and existential experiences that are also involved when women's bodies hurt, ache and bleed, we risk a grave distortion of the problem at issue. In order to include the social and existential aspects of bodily experience in the analysis, we need a more phenomeno-logically oriented and 'experience-near' approach which attends closely to women's own understandings and perceptions of their bodies and lives.

While the notion of 'experience' is very often used in anthropology at the moment, it is not always clear what precisely is meant by the term. I have found the definition suggested by Kleinman and Kleinman useful:

> [Experience is] the intersubjective medium of social transactions in local moral worlds. It is the outcome of cultural categories and social structures interacting with psycho-physiological processes such that a mediating world is constituted. (Kleinman and Kleinman 1991: 277)

While Kleinman and Kleinman present their understanding of *intersubjective* experience as 'an elaboration of the Chinese paradigm', the intersubjectivity of experience is also a central idea in phenomenology. Phenomenologists attend closely to people's 'life-worlds', i.e. to the worlds of everyday lived experience. While being the worlds of individuals, 'life-worlds' are also social worlds of shared experience. Alfred Schutz writes,

> The world of my daily life is by no means my private world but is from the outset an intersubjective one, shared with my fellow-men, experienced and interpreted by Others; in brief, it is a world common to all of us (Schutz 1973: 312).

In the conduct of our lives, we are thrown into worlds of pre-existing 'textures of meaning' (Schutz 1973: 10), which were there before and will continue after us. In experiencing something – a moment of joy, a touch of sadness – I am not only engaged in my own private experience, but awash in meanings and relationships that extend far beyond my own singular being. Therefore, even though the experience of pain is in one sense a very personal and individual experience, it is also an experience created out of shared cultural 'textures of meaning' and located in webs of social significance and interaction. In this understanding, women's IUD symptoms are not just effects of biological imbalances, but also social experiences which come into being within much wider networks of meanings and social relationships. The question then is: How do we make the move from the mapping of symptoms to an understanding of the wider lifeworlds of which they are part?

A semantic network analysis of IUD symptoms

As a methodological approach to the understanding of such wider complexes of meanings and relationships, I have found Byron Good's *semantic network analysis* a useful point of departure. Good (1977) develops an approach to the understanding of illness which departs from both biomedical and ethnosemantic analyses. It is a methodological approach which combines a phenomenologic attention to lived experience with a Victor Turner-inspired analysis of core symbols in social life and interaction. Good replaces the idea of disease as a natural or biological occurrence with an understanding of disease as 'a "syndrome" of typical experiences, a set of words, experiences, and feelings which typically "run together" for the members of a society' (Good 1977: 27). Untangling such 'syndromes of experience' provides a means of studying illness contextually in relation to other everyday meanings and concerns, and gives methodological access to subjective experiences of pain and suffering.

A semantic network can be defined as 'a network of words, situations, symptoms, and feelings which are associated with an illness and give it meaning for the sufferer' (Good 1977: 39). The point in semantic illness analysis is to investigate the associations which people themselves make between various experiences in their lives, taking experienced physical symptoms as a point of departure and following them into the spheres of life which people associate with them. In these chains of associations, certain *core symbols* or *core categories* may be analytically distinguished.

Core symbols are particularly dense symbols which tie together a range of different experiences and spheres of life, connecting individual experiences with larger social and cultural themes. As Victor Turner notes, such symbols refer to central components of the social and moral orders of a society: 'Their essential quality consists in their juxtaposition of the grossly physical and the structurally normative, or the organic and the social' (Turner 1967: 29). Core symbols are often polysemic, i.e. they are very broad and general and carry multiple meanings, condensing a range of different life experiences. It is precisely this generality which enables them to bracket together various different ideas and phenomena and to span different spheres of life, providing a privileged point of departure for an investigation of the wider cultural meanings which experiences of weakness and ill health engage.

The force of semantic network analysis is that it enables one to tie together again the fields of experience which the pinning out of distinct symptoms has split up. This allows one to recontextualize symptoms, to retrace the networks of experiences in which symptoms are located when women live them. A semantic network analysis therefore provides a methodology for reconnecting symptoms to broader life-worlds; it creates a pathway from physical symptoms to wider fields of experience, allowing us to reach a more culturally and socially grounded understanding of health problems.

Inspired by Good's semantic network analysis, we shall now return to the problems that women in Vải Sơn experience with their IUDs. From my interviews and conversations with women it became very clear that IUD symptoms were closely related to other bodily and social experiences. What started as a talk about menstrual disturbances would very soon develop into a conversation about a violent husband, weakness experienced for years, or headaches which always turned up when the school year started and school fees had to be paid. Talking about backaches would soon lead the discussion to work, to bending too much and carrying too heavy loads. Talk about headaches would bring up thoughts and worries about the children, the household finances or a difficult mother-in-law. I take these 'slides' in the conversation as indications of the close connections that exist in women's experiences of physical symptoms and social distress. In experience several different domains of life are often united into one feeling – of pain, discomfort, dizziness, etc.

For the following analysis I divided the symptoms reported by women into two overlapping and closely related semantic fields (see Figures 4 and 5). It is important to point out that the semantic links I draw here are not links of cause and effect, but links of *association* which tie together different forms of experience. The first field comprises symptoms related to *sexuality and reproduction*, while the second field comprises symptoms related to the *social tensions of everyday life*.[13] In the field of sexuality and reproduction, *blood* is a core symbol, while in the field of everyday social tension, *nerves* are at the centre. The symptoms in each of these fields relate directly to central experiences in women's lives: experiences of being a wife and a mother and experiences of being responsible for the happiness and welfare of one's family. Together, the two fields represent the social and somatic context in which IUDs become a factor when they are inserted into a woman's body.

The field of sexuality and reproduction

The IUD symptoms that can be placed within the field of sexuality and reproduction are weakness, menstrual disturbances, abdominal pain, discharge and vaginal itching. As we shall see, a core category linking these symptoms is the category of *blood*. Blood – and the lack of it – is central both to women's physical weakness, to menstruation, and to gynaecological infections. I shall now consider each of the IUD symptoms in this field more closely and then draw up the links of associations which exist among symptoms and between symptoms and other life experiences.

Weakness/fatigue (yếu/mệt mỏi) is a symptom to which most other symptoms relate. Nearly all the women I knew in Vải Sơn felt fundamentally weak and exhausted physically, and IUD use only further aggravated these feelings of lacking strength and energy. The IUD often makes women feel weaker (*yếu*), tired/ exhausted (*mệt mỏi*), and depressed/sad (*chán/buồn*) than they would normally. Weakness is often described as a heaviness (*nặng*) in arms, legs, and body, as a feeling of being out of energy and strength (*hết sức/mất sức*), and as a feeling of bodily unease/ discomfort (*khó chịu trong người*). Weakness is usually accompanied by dizziness (*hoa mắt*) and disturbed vision (*chóng mặt*). When weak, women feel they lose their balance easily, they sometimes have to lean on the wall not to fall over, and they are often unable to see clearly. In Vải Sơn, even women who seemed to me to be physically strong and capable of shouldering enormous daily work tasks often felt their bodies were hopelessly weak and fragile. Most women seem to perceive physical weakness as simply a normal part of life and of being a woman. This is often expressed in sayings like, 'A weak buffalo is still stronger than a cow' (*Yếu trâu khoẻ hơn bò*); i.e., weak men are still stronger than women, or 'strong/healthy as a man' (*khoẻ như đàn ông*). Women usually see their weakness as closely related to female physiology and to women's role in reproduction: an important reason for women's weakness is their suffering from a *lack of blood* due to menstruation, abortions, and childbirths.[14]

Menstruation (*hành kinh*) is an experience which women have fairly ambiguous feelings about.[15] Most women see menstruation as something negative, as a tiring nuisance which makes bodies ache, turns tempers short, and creates more washing. Even though pre-packaged sanitary towels can be bought in the commune, most women use home-made menstrual cloths in order to save the 2,000 dong (20 cents) which a packet of sanitary napkins costs. The verb 'to menstruate', *bị hành kinh*, also indicates that menstruation is something negative: '*bị*' is used in the passive about negative events such as accidents and diseases. As perceived by women themselves, menstruation – particularly the stronger or prolonged bleedings caused by the IUD – contributes to physical weakness, further exhausting an already fragile body. Many women say that they feel more tired, angry and irritable prior to or during menstruation, they scold their children over trifles and answer their husbands back.

Menstruation is considered by women as a time when they are unclean (*bẩn*).[16] Most women feel proud if their menstrual periods are short, and many women say they would prefer not to menstruate but to be 'clean as men' (*sách như đàn ông*). The uncleanliness of menstruation, and hence of the female body, also seems to be the rationale behind the practice of washing women's clothes and/or underwear separately from men's. In the old days, women's clothes had to be dried separately from men's and underwear or menstrual cloths could not be dried in the open, but today many women see a hygienic rationale in drying menstrual cloths outside and in sunshine rather than in the dark corners of the house. Due to the polluting character of menstrual blood, menstruating women cannot go to the pagoda[17] and since women's bodies are more 'open' during menstruation, women generally avoid working with pesticides during their periods. Apart from this, I heard of no other menstrual taboos, and women say they live and work as usual during menstruation.

Even though menstruation has many negative connotations, women also see regular menstruations as indications of health, strength and fertility. Most women are very concerned about the quality and regularity of their menstruations, keeping track of dates every month and noticing the colour and smell of the blood. Irregular menstruation or dark and fetid blood are taken as indications of weakness and ill health, while regular menstruation and red, fresh blood indicate health and strength. Menstrual blood is considered to be 'dirty blood' of which the body needs to be cleansed every month, and women therefore consider regular menstruation important for the maintenance of good health.[18] Many women say that if menstruation does not start when it should, the dirty blood is collected inside the body, the stomach grows large, and the body does not feel well. In order to bring disturbed cycles back to normal again, women often take 'blood-regulating' medicine (*thuốc cao ích mẫu*). On the positive side, menstrual bleedings are indices of fertility and future security. To my question, 'Why do women have menstruation?', women would often answer, 'Because otherwise one has no future.'

Women's experiences of the IUD are often strongly influenced by the ways in which the IUD affects menstrual patterns. When the IUD causes stronger and prolonged bleedings, this is felt as a further draining of life forces which are already in short supply, and when the IUD causes periods to be irregular and changes the quality of menstrual blood, this is taken as an indication of more general harm done to the body by the IUD.

Discharge (*khí hư*) and *itching* (*ngứa*) are usually regarded as signs of *gynaecological infections* (*viêm*). While discharge in moderate amounts is considered a normal phenomenon, heavy discharge is regarded as abnormal and dirty. Infections are usually understood as being caused by any one of a number of factors: lack of hygiene; dirty water; dirty menstrual cloths; sexual activity during menstruation; work with pesticides during menstruation; sexual transmission of disease from one's husband; menstrual regulations or abortions; or use of the IUD. When talking about the causes of vaginal infections, women would nearly always stress lack of hygiene and say that they get infections because they work hard all day and do not take time off to wash themselves properly. Infections are therefore a health problem which most women feel very embarrassed about: they blame themselves for not keeping clean (cf. Tran Hung Minh *et al.* 1997).

Against this background, let us now look at the semantic links which can be drawn up in this field, connecting IUD symptoms with other health problems and life experiences (see figure 4).

- *Weakness – menstruation – lack of blood – poverty – IUD*: Women often ascribe their feelings of weakness and exhaustion to their blood loss from menstruation, abortions, or deliveries. Besides being related to their role in reproduction, lack of blood is perceived by women themselves as being closely related to poverty; to poor diet and insufficient rest. IUD use further aggravates the weakness women already suffer from, adding to their physical frailty and exhaustion.

- *IUD – menstruation – gynaecological infection*: The IUD often causes menstrual bleedings to be heavier or more pro-longed, thus making women feel more 'dirty' than normally. Menstrual blood is also linked to vaginal infections; infections are viewed as being caused by poor personal hygiene during menstruation, dirty menstrual cloths, sex during menstruation, or working with pesticides during menstruation.

- *Menstruation – pregnancy – childbirth – lack of blood*: Women lose blood throughout their lives, but particularly during childbirth. Pregnancies and childbirths, even though often desired, also exhaust women's bodies, causing weakness and blood loss. Pregnancy and, especially, postpartum are times when women's bodies are even more susceptible than normally to the disturbing influences of wind, temperature,

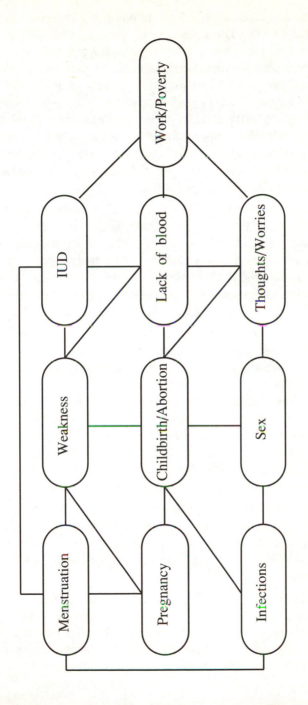

Fig. 4: *The field of sexuality and reproduction*

food, etc., and when women have to pay extra attention to the
care of their bodies. During pregnancy proper moral behaviour
is stressed more than usual; when pregnant, women should
ideally be occupied with good thoughts and behave well, since
both thoughts and behaviour may influence the child (cf.
Coughlin 1965). Also hard work is advocated during pregnancy,
since it is said to make delivery easier. Like menstrual blood, the
blood of childbirth is considered polluting and dirty. Childbirth,
like menstruation, is thus an ambiguous phenomenon, being
both positively associated with life and the future and negatively
associated with danger and pollution.[19]

- *Pregnancy – menstrual regulation/abortion – lack of blood –
  IUD – weakness*: Repeated menstrual regulations and
  abortions are considered a serious health risk, causing blood
  loss, weakness and an increased risk of gynaecological
  infections. Also the IUD increases menstrual blood loss, thus
  contributing to women's lack of blood and physical weakness.

- *Weakness – sex – gynaecological infection*: Sexual activity,
  even though a potential source of pleasure, is also a source of
  weakness, fatigue, and gynaecological infections. Particularly
  sex during menstruation is considered to be dirty and
  polluting.[20] In general, sex may drain both women's and
  men's bodies of energy, but men are said to become more
  weakened than women by sexual activity due to their loss of
  energy through semen loss.[21] On the other hand, men are also
  said to need sex more than women do; women often feel so
  tired and overburdened by everyday work and worries that sex
  becomes more of an additional burden than a pleasure.

- *IUD – thoughts/worries – weakness – lack of blood*: The IUD
  makes women think and worry about their state of health and
  their working capacities. Such thoughts and worries further
  weaken women's bodies and minds, draining them of blood
  and energy.

In sum, the field of sexuality and reproduction is full of para-
doxes: while pregnancy and childbearing are the most strongly
desired events of a woman's life, they are also events which are
potentially dangerous and drain women's bodies of energy and
strength. Liên put it in this way:

'You worry all the time. First you worry about whether you will get married, and about whether you can get pregnant, then about whether the child will be fine and healthy and the mother well (*mẹ tròn con vuông*; lit. the mother round the child square), then about whether you can take proper care of the child ... It is endless worrying.'

Ambiguity and anxiety are core features of all aspects of the reproductive process: *menstruation* is a sign of health, strength and fertility at the same time as it is polluting and dirty; *sexuality* is joyful, but also threatening and exhausting; *childbearing* brings risks and worries, but happiness, too. In short, the field of sexuality and reproduction carries promises of happiness and fulfilment together with threats of pollution and failure. It is a field that condenses the joys and stresses of womanhood, of being able to bear children and carry on life and of feeling exhausted and drained of blood and life. In the summary of his article 'Pregnancy and Birth in Vietnam', Richard Coughlin sees the entire field of sexuality and reproduction as creating immense anxieties in women's lives:

> The stresses and strains felt by women traditionally in Vietnam are persistent, recurring, never entirely relieved. What is felt in the mind is conceivably transferred to the body and acted out in ways that are not directly connected with the source of anxiety. [...] Many people in Vietnam [...] are faced with a gross imbalance between felt anxieties and known ways to get relief. Pregnancy and birth must rate high among the situations in which such imbalance is brought into sharp focus. (Coughlin 1965: 264–65)

The ambiguities and anxieties surrounding childbearing have probably become even more urgent in the current era of family planning, where the number and timing of children bring such crucial moral and economic consequences. In short, the effects of the IUD on women's bodies need to be seen in the light of this preexisting context of stress, worries, and ambiguities.

The other major field of symptoms and experiences within which side effects of the IUD are located is the field of *everyday social tensions*.

The field of everyday social tensions

The IUD symptoms belonging to this field are weakness, weight loss, and aches and pains in the head, stomach, and back. A core category which ties together the symptoms in this field is that of *nerves*. Both symptoms of weakness and diffuse aches and pains in the body are often associated with the functioning of nerves and linked up with 'disease of the nerves' (*bệnh thần kinh*). Even though both men and women may suffer from nerves, women are considered to be more prone to nervous diseases than men. As in the field of sexuality and reproduction, we shall now first consider each IUD symptom more closely and then link these to other life experiences.

Weakness is not only caused by women's role in reproduction, but also by work that is physically too demanding and by an over-abundance of worries. People in Vải Sơn generally agree that women work harder and speculate more over how to make ends meet than do their more 'carefree' (*vô tư*) husbands. Both hard work and troublesome thoughts weaken nerves and thus contribute to the exhaustion of women's bodies. Poverty is often considered a main cause of physical weakness: women's bodies are weak because they are provided with insufficient diets, because they have to work 'beyond their strength/energy' (*quá sức*), and because poverty forces them to worry endlessly about their ability to provide for their families. Poverty also makes it more difficult to preserve family harmony, causing frequent fights and quarrels.

Backache (*đau lưng*) is the most common side effect of the IUD. Many women suffer constantly from pains in their back and attribute such pains to hard work in combination with the IUD. Women often carry very heavy loads and work for long hours in bent positions, thus straining and weakening the nerves of the whole body and particularly of the back. For some women, backaches are mainly related to menstruation, such backaches are often considerably worsened by IUD use.

Weight loss (*gầy đi*) is seen as a core indicator of ill health, while fatness indicates health and strength. Difficulties in life often cause women to lose appetite, and thus to lose weight. Weight loss is therefore often associated with worries and troubles in life, with other health problems, such as 'nerves' or 'lack of blood', and with a general loss of strength and energy.

Headache (*đau đầu*) is a very common health problem among women. While headaches are often said to be caused by the wind or by sudden changes in the weather, women also often see headaches as being caused by the thoughts and worries that permeate daily lives. Such thoughts and worries mainly concern family finances or other domestic problems and tensions. Headaches are a core symptom of 'nerves', indicating a more general weakening of the nervous system.

Let us now look at the semantic networks which can be drawn up in this field (see Figure 5).

- *Backache – work – weakness – nerves – IUD – poverty*: Since most women work very hard in order to sustain themselves and their families, backaches are a frequent health problem. Backaches are often associated with a general weakening of the nervous system caused by over exertion and too little rest. Many women have found that having an IUD inserted aggravates already existing backaches.

- *IUD – headache – nerves – family problems – depression/ tension*: IUDs may either cause headaches or aggravate the headaches that women already suffer from. Women often see their headaches as being closely related to their thinking and worrying about the family's economic situation or about disobedient children, unfaithful husbands, or domineering mothers-in-law. Headaches are often considered as a symptom of a more general weakening of the nervous system. Weak nerves make people more susceptible to all kinds of outside influences and more prone to thoughts and worries. 'Nervous exhaustion' may therefore in some cases develop into feelings of sadness and depression, causing the sufferer to lose her ability and desire to live and work.

- *Family problems – lack of sleep – worries – nerves – weakness*: Lying awake at night, worrying about problems in the family exhausts the nerves and weakens the body. A 'happy family' is seen by many women as a precondition for health, and family problems are often considered major contributing factors to women's physical weakness, draining and exhausting their bodies of energy and vigour.

- *Poverty – thoughts/worries – nerves – weight loss – weakness*: Weak nerves – and ensuing fatigue, aches, pains, and dizziness – are often associated with poverty; with poor nutrition, hard work and little rest. Depriving one's body of energy through

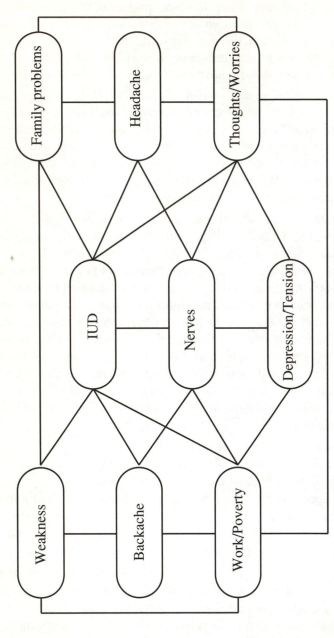

Fig. 5: *The field of everyday social tension*

hard work and worries while not nourishing it adequately causes weakness, weight loss and frail nerves.

• *Weakness – lack of blood – nerves – backache – IUD*: Weakness due to lack of blood also affects the nerves, causing even more weakness and various forms of aches and pains which are often aggravated by IUD use.

The most striking feature of the field of everyday tensions is the acknowledgement of the social context of bodily weakness which it reveals. Women clearly feel that social and economic problems fundamentally affect their bodies and health, and physical symptoms are often taken as indicators of social problems and tensions. Being poor directly affects the body, forcing women to work too hard, rest too little, and eat an inadequate diet. Poverty also often leads to marital and family conflicts, disrupting family harmony and causing fights and quarrels which wear out bodies and deprive them of energy and strength. It is important to emphasize that the two symptom groups outlined above do not reflect distinct and separate experiences, but are very closely interrelated. In women's experience, the weakness caused by increased menstrual blood loss may be perceived as closely related to the weight loss caused by worrying about the family. When a headache and a gynaecological infection are experienced at the same time, the result is one feeling of weakness and vulnerability, even though the sources of discomfort may be different.

The two semantic fields of sexuality/reproduction and of everyday social tensions have a core point of intersection in the social sphere of *the family*: both sexuality/reproduction and everyday social stresses are directly related to family life. As we saw in the previous chapter, creating a happy family is a core concern to most women in Vải Sơn; usually the family is both the setting and the center of women's lives. When women lie awake at night thinking and worrying, it is often family problems they are worrying about. Similarly, when women work long hours every day, exhausting their bodies, they do so in order to provide their children with food, clothes and education, and to build a family that is happy and respectable.

Summing up: the social context of IUD symptoms

As we have seen from the analysis of semantic illness networks, the symptoms which women associate with the IUD cannot be isolated from other bodily symptoms and from more general feelings of physical weakness and exhaustion. IUD symptoms are usually experienced within networks of other physical symptoms – of weakness, fatigue, aches, pains, and gynaecological problems. As Good *et al.* (1992: 8) write, the 'experience of pain is lived as a unified experience'. Many of the symptoms associated with the IUD – backaches, headaches, menstrual problems, fatigue, dizziness, etc. – are symptoms familiar to all women, whether they have an IUD or not. They are common female experiences, related to everyday life conditions which most women share. The insertion of an IUD, however, often either aggravates existing health problems or adds new ones to those already there. The IUD thus seems to cause further disturbance to bodies that are already destabilized by an overload of thoughts and worries, and to contribute to the weakening of bodies that are already frail, undernourished and overworked.

The analysis of semantic illness networks has also demonstrated that health problems cannot be separated from life problems. As Arthur Kleinman writes: 'Acting like a sponge, illness soaks up personal and social significance from the world of the sick person' (1988: 31). Experiences of pain seem to condense life experiences from widely differing domains, tying together stressful experiences from several different spheres of life into one feeling of discomfort and disease. In women's own understandings of their lives, it is an obvious fact that family disharmony causes headaches and sleeplessness and that poverty weakens one's body and health. In other words, social tensions and worries are not just 'mindful' but also bodily experiences. The experience of social stress is not just an artefact of thought and cognition but something that is lived by the body, prior to or concurrent with reflection (cf. Merleau-Ponty 1962). The IUD, then, draws together tensions and ambiguities surrounding sexuality and reproduction, everyday stresses of family life, and worries about economy and survival into one experience of physical pain and weakness. In this sense the IUD becomes a point of condensation for a whole range of stresses and tensions in women's lives which extend far beyond the field of family planning as such. This is not to say that IUD problems do not have a physiological basis or do not constitute urgently felt physical experiences for the sufferer – what I argue is simply that physical pain is often co-experienced with other forms of painful social experience.

In the following chapters I shall examine more closely the connections which women themselves see between the functioning of their bodies and their families. In women's perception, ill health has its origin in a range of everyday living conditions, from hygiene and work to diets and thoughts. However, most women also emphasize that the social matrix through which all such 'objective' conditions of life are filtered is the local community of the family. Family relations – whether balanced or not, tense or relaxed, harmonious or disharmonious – are perceived by most women as directly influencing their bodies and health. Given the strong ambitions and dreams surrounding the concept of the 'happy family', it is not surprising to find the family at the center of women's experiences of social stress and tension.

In the next chapter, starting from a discussion of local concepts of body and health, I shall examine more closely the categories of 'blood' and 'nerves' which emerged as core symbols from the analysis of semantic illness networks. As we shall see, such an analysis provides a privileged point of departure for an investigation of the wider cultural meanings which experiences of weakness and ill health engage, leading us towards some of the basic cultural orientations which inform social and physical experience.

Notes

1. The only additional symptom noted was dizziness.

2. Of the 147 IUD users in the survey, 54 had their last IUDs inserted more than five years before, 59 two to five years before, and 34 within the last two years.

3. The women who were currently using IUDs were on the average 33 years old and had 3.1 children at the time of the survey. There was a clear tendency for women not to use an IUD unless they had at least one son: among the 147 who had ever used an IUD, only two had no sons while 22 had no daughters at the time of the survey.

4. Two-thirds of current users (68) said they suffered from side effects of the IUDs while the remaining one-third (34) did not.

5. On the other hand, a considerable number of symptoms are not treated. For instance, only 22 out of the 81 women experiencing backaches and only 21 of the 60 women experiencing abdominal pain seek medical help. As I shall discuss later, this probably has to do with the fact that many IUD

symptoms are considered 'natural' for women; it is simply part of the female condition to bleed and to feel weak and exhausted.

6. One man in Vải Sơn said that having an IUD in one's body obstructs the flow of *khí*, vital energy, which is supposed to circulate freely in the body. Fears about obstruction of *khí* do not seem to figure greatly in the concerns of women in Vải Sơn, though. Studies of popular perceptions of the IUD in other countries have shown that many women think that something 'blocking' the woman is harmful to health, and many studies have noted fears that the IUD may 'travel' in the body and perforate lungs or brain (Nichter and Nichter 1989).

7. Johansson *et al.* (1996a) find in their study that women in Thái Bình province prefer the Dana/'Number 8' to the copper-T/'T' IUD and suggest that women's preference of the Dana is related to a less strict enforcement of the family planning policy during the years when this IUD was used.

8. Vietnamese social scientists joke about the copper T IUD: 'Do you know why women fear the IUD? – They are afraid of being struck by lightning!'

9. The category of 'chemical materials' seems to include both metals and everything synthetic and artificial such as rubber, plastic, chemicals and pesticides.

10. In the study by Johansson and her colleagues (1996a) women said that the IUD 'eats thoughts'.

11. Several of the women who experienced serious side effects of the IUD had it removed for some time in order to give their bodies a chance to regain stability before they tried again with another IUD.

12. The idea that the IUD has 'destabilizing' effects on the body seems to be in line with traditional medical thinking, where a key to health lies in maintaining bodily balances and where 'outside' influences on the body may disrupt the balance (cf. Chapter 5).

13. In his analysis of heart disease in Iran, Good (1977) distinguishes between two semantic fields: 'Female sexuality: potency and pollution,' and 'The oppression of everyday life.' The close associations between women's health problems and the fields of sexuality/reproduction and everyday social tensions are probably near-universal phenomena.

14. Also in traditional Chinese medicine, weakness is a key symptom, expressing loss or blockage in the flow of *chi* (vital 'matter-energy') (Kleinman 1982). As we shall see in the next chapter, traditional Chinese medical theories also draw parallels between women's role in reproduction and their inherent physical weakness.

15. This everyday ambiguity surrounding menstruation has parallels both in Chinese and Western medicine where menstruation is closely associated with health and fertility while also being considered an important source of weakness and vulnerability (Furth and Shu-Yueh 1992). Furth and Shu-

Yueh write: 'Both traditional and modern medical systems allow for a positive valuation of female powers of childbearing, while hinting at costs in an accompanying female bodily weakness' (1992: 28).

16. Several studies have noted that in China both menstrual blood and postpartum discharge are considered to be unclean substances. Women are therefore considered ritually polluting and unclean and are barred from certain activities (e.g., Wolf 1972; Ahern 1975; Seaman 1981; Furth 1987). The associations between womanhood and pollution apparently draw on a mixture of Buddhist ideas and folk beliefs. In *Purity and Danger* (1966), Mary Douglas hypothesizes that ideas about menstrual pollution are linked to women being potential threats to a male-dominated social order. This seems to fit well with the social realities described in studies of China, where ideas of women as ritual polluters go hand in hand with ideas of women as social disrupters who are potentially disturbing to the solidarity of male-centred groups (Ahern 1975). Ahern notes that things that the Chinese consider unclean are things that threaten the order of the two entities of the family and the human body, breaking their boundaries and bringing them into disorder.

17. In general, women under 50 rarely go to the pagoda; religious activities are mainly performed by older women.

18. Also in traditional Chinese medicine, regular and normal menses is understood as a sign of health, while variations in timing, consistency, colour or amount of menstrual blood flow are signs of internal disorder (Furth and Shu-Yueh 1982).

19. In her discussion of traditional Chinese medical views of pregnancy and birth Furth writes: 'Birth is a dangerous and dirty event, leaving the delivered mother weakened in vital energy' (1987: 12).

20. Ahern (1975) notes that popular notions in Chinese society consider sexual activity to be unclean and polluting, and Seaman (1981) writes that Buddhist teachings consider sexual intercourse unclean.

21. As we shall see in the next chapter, traditional Chinese medicine holds that men lose vital energy (*chi*) through semen loss while women mainly lose energy through blood loss. In local understandings in Vải Sơn, there are similar parallels between blood and semen; semen is sometimes referred to as a 'second blood' (*máu thứ hai*) or 'white blood' (*máu trắng*). People often joke that the reason why women live longer than men is that they do not lose anything from having sex, while men's lives are shortened by 0.1 per cent for each sexual intercourse.

CHAPTER 5

Body and Health

'Come,' Lai says, 'I am going to see Bà Hôm, are you coming along?'

It is a humid and mercilessly hot day in August. I am on my way home and already late for lunch. Lai is going in the other direction, heading towards the opposite end of the hamlet.

'Where is your hat?' she says with a stern look, pointing to her own worn-out conical hat, 'You are crazy to walk around in the sun without it.'

Curious to see where she wants to take me, I turn around and follow her down one of the narrow muddy alleys. 'Who is Bà Hôm?' I ask.

My aunt,' Lai replies, adding, 'she is very old and weak.'

At the end of the alley we enter a small house with thatched roof and dirt floor. It is dark inside, and the room is full of people sitting on the bed and on mats on the floor drinking tea, talking and laughing. On the bed a little old woman lies on her back with her eyes closed, a younger woman holding her hand and stroking her arm.

'She is dying,' a man informs me, 'I am her grandchild and,' – he points to the woman holding the old woman's hand – 'this is her youngest daughter.'

We sit there for a while, having tea and small-talking, until Lai says, 'Come, let's go home. You haven't had lunch yet.'

As we walk back, she says, 'You see. You asked about "nerves" the other day. This woman, she is now 82, but until this year she has been very strong and healthy. Me, I am just 38, but I am still much weaker than her. This is because I suffer from nerves, because my life is so difficult. I have to think a lot, about the economy, about my husband, about the children. It is endless worrying, endless thoughts, and therefore I am weak, weaker than Bà Hôm ever was.'

As we have seen in the previous chapter, it is widely recognized by women in Vải Sơn that bodily feelings and functions cannot be isolated from their social contexts. The feelings of weakness, dizziness and pain which are involved when women suffer from 'lack of blood' or 'nerves' are closely linked to daily social experiences of various kinds of stress and tension. In order to make sense of IUD symptoms, we therefore have to consider the already existing 'textures of meaning' through which the experience of such symptoms unfolds. When a woman feels her back aching or her bleedings become heavier after she has had an IUD inserted, these are bodily experiences which gain their meaning and urgency from wider webs of shared meanings and significances and from more general perceptions of the body, health and physiology.

In order to further explore the 'socio-somatic' linkages between the body and its social environment, this chapter will examine everyday perceptions of body, health and physiology and the social and cultural forms which such perceptions engage. This will include considerations of the medical and moral philosophies which everyday understandings of the body and health involve, as well as an extended analysis of the core categories *blood* and *nerves*.

Body and health: maintaining strength and balance

Health (*sức khoẻ*) is a central concern in the lives of women in Vải Sơn. Being in good health is vitally important; it is the foundation and precondition for women's ability to carry out their everyday chores, to keep family finances going, and their families together. In daily conversations, health advice is often exchanged, and the pool of common knowledge about health seems extensive and diverse (cf. Craig 1996, 1997).

From my first day in Vải Sơn, Bà Chính put a lot of effort into teaching me how to take proper care of my health, because she feared, she said, that her family's reputation would suffer if my health deteriorated while I was there. So Bà Chính taught me to avoid 'harmful winds' (*gió độc*); to be careful with the capricious Northern Vietnamese weather and protect myself from sun and cold; to avoid sudden shifts in temperature (i.e. never go straight to a cold bath after running); to eat a varied and protein-rich diet, to get my rest and sleep; and to avoid too much specu-lation over sad or strenuous things. The overall aim of these precautions, of which most people seem to be extremely aware, is to protect and build up bodily strength and balance.

In everyday life, the human body (*cơ thể; thân thể*) is usually perceived as a functionally integrated system of finely tuned inner balances, harmonious in health and disharmonious in sickness. The body is commonly understood as a united 'system' (*cơ chế*) or 'structure' (*câú tạo*), which is built up from many different and interlinked organs (*cơ quan*). While the 'insides' and 'outsides' of the body are usually clearly distinguished, it is also perceived as an open system, embedded in and interacting with its social and natural environments. The various organs inside the body are all closely interconnected and finely balanced. If one part of the body gets disturbed or brought out of balance, this imbalance cannot be isolated to the affected organ or body part but influences overall bodily functions.[1] Physical symptoms are usually considered in relationship to the whole body, and not just affecting part of it. As Kiều put it:

'Everything in the body is related, because human bodies are one united piece, they cannot be split up. For instance, if you have a toothache, your head also aches. Or if your back aches, it is not just a backache at all, but you also feel you cannot work, you feel tired and unwell, the food doesn't taste good and you can't sleep. Because your back influences the other parts of the body. All parts of the body are related.'

The body is usually understood as a hierarchical structure, with the brain (*não*) as the coordinating centre which governs and regulates the functioning of all other organs, ensuring their harmonious cooperation. Without the brain, the body would not be able to function at all. This emphasis on the brain and its ability to govern the rest of the body goes together with a relatively sharp distinction in everyday life between the human mind/heart (*tâm lý*) and body/physiology (*sinh lý*). 'Physiology' is the mechanical and mindless functions of the body, the simple animal- or plant-like urges to live, breathe and reproduce oneself. By contrast, it is the mind/heart which accommodates the specific human capacities for compassion, understanding, will and deliberation. People usually perceive minds and bodies, or feelings and physiologies, as closely interrelated, even though mental capacities are also distinct from and much more positively valued than 'raw' physiological functioning.

Health is most commonly understood in terms of the inter-related notions of strength (*sức khoẻ; khoẻ mạnh; sức lực*) and stability (*ổn định*). 'Strength' usually refers to the ability to work and carry out the tasks demanded by everyday life and to the capacity to withstand negative influences from without (cf. Craig 1996). 'Stability', on the other hand, refers to the stable and well-coordinated functioning of the various organs of the body. A person's appearance usually indicates his or her state of health: being fat and having rosy skin are signs of health while leanness and yellow skin indicate sickness.

The strength/stability of bodies is determined partly by each person's constitution (*thể trạng*) or 'capital' (*vốn*), and partly by the influence of various inside or outside forces on the body. The most commonly mentioned influences on the body are: food, sleep/rest, wind/weather, environmental influences, stressful thoughts and evil spirits. Sleep and rest are important for the maintenance of good health, since the overworking of one's body or mind (*làm quá sức*) may seriously deprive the body of energy and strength. Also 'harmful' winds, fierce sunshine (*nắng*), or rapid weather changes are considered harmful to health, disturbing the body's balances. Influences from the environment – pollution, pesticides, or other 'harmful substances' (*chất độc*) – may cause weakness and ill health. Furthermore negative thoughts and feelings of anger, sadness, and bitterness drain the body of energy and strength. In addition to all this, ill health may be caused by evil and revengeful spirits.

Particularly important for the building up of bodily strength is the daily regimen of food and drink (*ăn uống*). Diets rich in protein (*chất đạm*), i.e. containing meat or fish, are considered nourishing, while diets of only rice with vegetables and fish sauce are considered poor. Nourishing diets are rich in 'substance' (*chất*) and therefore also build up the body's 'substance', i.e. the stuff that 'feeds' the body and is transformed into strength and activity. Ideally, diets should also balance 'hot' and 'cold'[2] foods properly, depending on the season and on the character of each person's blood.[3]

Everyday medical ideas in Vietnam today draw upon a complex admixture of different medical traditions from both East and West. People usually distinguish between 'Western medicine' (*thuốc Tây*) and 'Eastern medicine' (*thuốc Y* or *thuốc ta*, 'our medicine'). There are two kinds of 'Eastern medicine'; *thuốc Nam* (Southern medicine), the indigenous Vietnamese medicine which is based on simple remedies and local herbs, and *thuốc Bắc* (Northern medicine), a Vietnamization of classical Chinese medicine (Ladinsky *et al.* 1987; Marr 1987). In addition to this, a third medical tradition focuses on the spiritual realm and on defence against evil spirits (Hickey 1964; Marr 1987). Western medicine was brought to Vietnam by the French colonizers in the 18th and 19th centuries (Marr 1987), and today Western medical ideas are clearly present in people's discussions about hygiene, nerves or hormones.[4] More importantly, though, the philosophy of Sino–Vietnamese medicine seems to be at the core of many daily health practices and philosophies.

Sino-Vietnamese medicine is based on the *correlative cosmology* which has been considered by some as the central stream of the entire Chinese 'structure of thought' (Schwartz 1985: 351). In this cosmology there are systematic correspondences between all of the world's different phenomena, from human bodies to social, natural, and cosmic worlds. As everything else in the world, human bodies are built up from the interacting dynamics of *yin* and *yang* (Vietnamese: *âm/dương*). Each of the body's organs is either predominantly *yin* or *yang*, and good health requires a balance between the body's *yin* and *yang* elements. Bodily *yin–yang* dynamics correspond and interact with the interacting *yin–yang* dynamics of social, natural, and cosmic worlds (Marr 1987; Hoàng Bảo Châu *et al.* 1993).[6] In this sense, the human body can be seen as a microcosm which reflects the balances or imbalances of much wider worlds (cf. Huard and Durand 1954).

Good health requires both 'internal' and 'external' bodily balances; it requires both a harmonious inner bodily functioning and an alignment of the body with the outside social and natural environment. In Sino-Vietnamese medical theories, ill health is therefore caused either by internal imbalances (*nội thương*) arising from emotional or physical strain, or by external forces (*ngoại cảm*) – wind, temperature, food, or drink – which disturb the body's balances (Marr 1987).[7] In the context of the present study, however, the most important aspect of both everyday health knowledge and traditional medical theories is their establishment of close connections – both literally and metaphorically – between social and bodily spaces.

Correspondences between social and bodily spaces

As correlative cosmology sees the human body as a microcosm of the wider social and cosmic universe, so everyday understandings draw close links between bodies and other social forms. In everyday perceptions the ideal of a healthy and balanced body extends analogically into the social and political spheres of the family, the village and the state.[8] Each of these social forms has an inside which needs protection from outside disturbing influences, and each can be seen as a hierarchical assemblage of several sub-units which need to work together harmoniously for the corporate whole to function.[9]

Imagery of the body is closely associated with imagery of the state and bureaucracy. As the organs of the body (*cơ quan*) are governed by the brain, so are state offices (*cơ quan*) coordinated and regulated by central governing offices (*trung ương*). In both cases, a higher placed centre governs and organizes lower placed sub-units, and so secures the coordinated and harmonious functioning of the whole. Hoàng Bảo Châu *et al.* (1993: 9) write about the concepts of physiology in Sino-Vietnamese medicine: 'The body functions like an administration with superior commanding organs [...] and inferior organs.' Another parallel between bodies and the nation is the idea that boundaries/borders may be attacked by outside aggressors – harmful winds or corrupt foreigners – and therefore need to be well secured and guarded. Also the village can be seen as a corporate body with clear distinctions between insiders and outsiders, with lineages as sub-units, and with sociopolitical hierarchies paralleling the body's internal divisions between governing and governed organs.

In the context of this study, however, the most important analogies are those between human bodies and families. As we have seen in the previous chapter, women often associate their feelings of bodily weakness and disease with disharmonious family functioning; thus seeing social and bodily tensions as immediately related. This view seems to draw some of its rationale from the close analogic relations that exist between bodies and families in everyday understandings. Symbolic anthropologists have often pointed to the close connections that exist between body and society – as Mary Douglas writes,

> The social body constrains the way the physical body is perceived. The physical experience of the body, always modified by the social

categories through which it is known, sustains a particular view of society. There is a continual exchange of meanings between the two kinds of bodily experience so that each reinforces the categories of the other (Douglas 1970: 93).

Body and society can be seen as models of each other's organization: particular images of the body help constitute particular experiences of social relations, just as images of society influence the ways bodies are perceived. Therefore, as Robert Desjarlais writes, 'The ways in which a given people build houses, conduct rituals, and tell stories influence the ways in which they experience their bodies' (Desjarlais 1992: 93). In Vải Sơn, both physiologies and families are understood as hierarchically organized social entities whose inner workings are important for their outward appearance and performance. Where bodies have brains which govern and regulate their functioning, families have household heads (*chủ nhà*) who organize and monitor daily activities. The close associations between body and family therefore seem to 'naturalize' the idea of the family as a hierarchically ordered structure.[10]

Just as bodies have insides which need protection from harmful winds and other outside pathogenic influences, families have insides which need protection from the public gaze and malicious gossip. As a person's state of health is indicated by the quality of his or her skin – whether it is yellow or rosy, bright or dull – the inner, moral qualities of a family are indicated by the outward manners and behaviour of its members. Just as bodies in health are stable, balanced and well coordinated, so are good families those of harmony (*hoà thuận*) and stability (*ổn*), which function as well-integrated wholes. A fear of families 'going to pieces' (*tan cửa nát nhà*) parallels the fear of bodily breakdown and decay. Ideal and respectable families are communities of balance and order where all family members know their proper places vis-à-vis the others and cooperate harmoniously in a mutual effort towards the attainment of shared goals. This, importantly, is the precondition for economic welfare and progress and so for the prospering of the family: as bodies need to be strong and balanced in order to work and perform well, so do families. Bodies and families mutually influence and depend upon each other: as strong and stable bodies are a precondition for the strength and stability of families, so do the health and strength of bodies depend on families being happy and harmonious.

By paying attention to the correspondence and interaction that exist between families as harmonious communities and bodies as well-organized wholes, we may gain a more comprehensive understanding of how women feel when their bodies are exhausted, aching, dizzy and 'unwell', and of the social contexts of these feelings. The interlinkages between good families and healthy bodies point us towards the inherently *moral* and *aesthetic* character of good health. To women in Vải Sơn, health is not only a question of 'raw' physiological functioning or 'natural' influences from wind or climate, but is also a state of the body which reflects the quality of social relations. For health to be optimal, social relations need to be orderly, balanced, and harmonious. Hạnh expressed a very widespread attitude when she said:

> 'If your parents-in-law do not get on with you, or your husband doesn't behave well and there is instability in the family, your health deteriorates.'

Harmonious social relations also make it easier to have good thoughts, and good thoughts are conducive to health. Bà Chính would explain to me at length about two relatives of hers who had both suffered from poor health due to their very quick tempers. Being constantly angry and dissatisfied, presenting a 'heavy face' to the world, is certainly not good for one's health, Bà would say, clearly hinting at the sad and sullen face of her own daughter-in-law. Or as another woman explained,

> 'Good thoughts express good health. A person who has good thoughts and good behaviour is always a good person who loves life and is optimistic. If people think bad thoughts, they also always feel worried (*bứt rứt*) and unwell (*khó chịu*).'

It is widely recognized that thinking and worrying too much causes illness, and in everyday social life the ability to relax, smile, and take things easy is highly valued. While the requirements of good thoughts and good social behaviour are clearly moral in character, they are also elements in an 'everyday aesthetics' (Desjarlais 1992): harmonious social relations are not only morally proper, they are also aesthetically pleasing. In everyday life, proper and decent social behaviour – knowing one's place vis-à-vis others in social hierarchies, addressing and approaching others in correct manner – is considered beautiful and graceful (*đẹp*), while improper behaviour, answering back or treating others disrespectfully, is 'ugly' (*xâu*). In this sense, health has both ethical and aesthetic aspects; it unites moral concerns with strivings for beauty and grace.

Following Pierre Bourdieu one could say that it is precisely in the everyday 'aesthetic' practices through which morally proper social relations are realized that social cosmologies become 'embodied' and turned into basic and deeply felt personal orientations. Since 'the body believes in what it plays at' (Bourdieu 1990: 73), bodily practices turn social structures and meanings into personal dispositions and orientations. The respect for parents is expressed and affirmed in the way a bowl of rice is handed over to them; male superiority is expressed and affirmed in the central positioning of men in family gatherings, etc. Bodily practices and sensibilities teach us how to feel nausea at some experiences and delight at others; attraction to some things and repulsion at others; balance and relaxation in some situations and imbalance and tension in others. Somatic sensibilities and 'gut' reactions are socially formed and cultivated, born out of specific social experiences and positionings. Particular images of society and social relations are therefore perpetuated by being 'incorporated' into everyday attitudes and practices which – to some extent – make social worlds 'go without saying' (Bourdieu 1977). In this sense, bodies are both sources and reflections of important moral-aesthetic values and orientations, sustaining and enhancing particular ideas about society and social relations. When women feel their bodies to be heavy and exhausted, they often simultaneously feel that something is wrong and disorderly in their family lives, that everyday social relations are 'ugly' and out of balance.

Everyday understanding of body, family, and state as corporate collectivities structured by similar principles of hierarchical order and balance have parallels in classical Chinese medical ideas and socio-political moral ideologies. Medical historian Paul Unschuld (1985) writes that the socio-political theories of Confucianism and the classical theories of Chinese medicine are closely intertwined and have historically been mutually supportive. Along with Buddhism and Taoism, both Confucianism and Chinese medicine were introduced during the almost 1,000 years of Chinese rule of Vietnam. Even though it has been debated 'how Confucian' the

Vietnamese became (Whitmore 1987), there is no doubt that today Confucian cosmology is strongly present in North Vietnamese moralities and social relations (Jamieson 1993); Nguyễn Khắc Viên describes Confucianism as 'the intellectual and ideological backbone of Vietnam' (1975: 16).

Both Confucian socio-political theory and medical theories are based upon the correlative cosmology which emphasizes the inter-relations between bodily, social, and cosmic worlds. In Confucianism, the total normative socio-political order (*tao*) comprises individual bodies, the family, the state, and the cosmos, which are all tied together in analogous and mutually dependent relationships (Schwartz 1985). Within this order everything has its place, and each individual is assigned specific social roles with attendant moral obligations. Roles and relationships are governed by 'objective' prescriptions of proper behaviour (*li*) which, as Benjamin Schwartz writes, 'bind human beings and the spirits together in networks of interacting roles within the family, within human society, and with the numinous realm beyond' (1985: 67). Classical medical texts emphasize how inner bodily balances are maintained through awareness and recognition of such objectively prescribed moral rules for proper behaviour. For instance, Chinese philosoper Hsün-Tzu (238 BC) writes:

> If a person utilizes his body and his nature, his insight, under-standing, and mature consideration in the manner prescribed by custom, order and success will ensue; otherwise, the result is un-predictability and upheaval, idleness and unruliness. If the con-sumption of food and drink, clothing, lodging at home, as well as movement and rest are carried out in the manner prescribed by custom, one will achieve harmony and order; otherwise one is sub-ject to attack and betrayal, and illnesses will occur. If a person arranges his appearance and demeanor, his coming and going, as well as his manner of movement in accordance with custom, he will achieve elegance; otherwise barbaric crudity, depravity, vul-garity, and savagery ensue. This means that man cannot live with-out ceremony, the concerns of daily life cannot be successfully concluded without ritual; without rites, the state cannot exist in peace. (Unschuld 1985: 64)

In other words, the everyday links between health, morality and aesthetics have parallels in traditional Confucian moral-medical theories where good health is a function of proper social relationships while improper social relations cause ill health. In this sense, the body becomes a field where politics and aesthetics meet and intertwine: individual physiologies reflect and refract social relations, and the health of bodies is closely tied in with the harmony and stability of social relations. Against this background, let us now look more closely at the notions of blood and nerves which were central to women's experiences with the IUD.

Core categories in women's health: blood and nerves

As we saw in the previous chapter, two core categories which connect many of women's bodily experiences, both in relation to the IUD and in general, are *blood* and *nerves*. All IUD symptoms relate to one or both of these categories: menstrual disturbances, abdominal pain, and gynaecological infections relate mainly to blood; headaches and backaches relate mainly to nerves; and weakness relates to both blood and nerves. Each of these categories can be seen as a *core symbol* in the semantic networks sketched above; condensing a range of symptoms, feelings, and social situations, and linking social and somatic experiences. Both blood and nerves are crucial for health and survival, and particularly important in relation to women's health and lives. As we shall see, blood and nerves are also aspects of human physiology which are heavy with social and symbolic meanings; condensing a multitude of interrelated meanings and experiences. They are closely related to both 'inner' and 'outer' balances, tying the body together and relating it to its social surroundings.

During fieldwork, my attention was from early on drawn towards the two common ailments: lack of blood (*bệnh thiếu máu*)[11] and nervous disease/nerves (*bệnh thần kinh*), both known as 'women's diseases'.[12] At this stage of fieldwork I often asked open and broad questions, such as 'What are the most common health problems for women here?' To this question, either nerves or lack of blood would often come up, as when Như said:

'Most women here suffer from exhaustion, from lack of "substance" (*chất*). They eat too little, so they suffer from that disease. In the countryside women often suffer from that disease.'
'Which disease – malnutrition?' I asked.

'Nervous exhaustion. You work a lot so the organs in the body are very active, but the food has no substance. I only eat rice with vegetables, so there is not enough substance.'

Also lack of blood is a very frequently mentioned health problem for women and apparently even more common than nerves. Many women suffer from both, and in daily life the two sets of symptom complexes often overlap. At the core of both ailments is a feeling of weakness and exhaustion, of lacking the strength and energy which everyday chores require. Women often also see nerves and lack of blood as causally related: nervous tension leads to a thinning of blood, and lack of blood creates nervous tension.

When talking about their experiences of nerves and lack of blood, women often present different kinds of symptoms and complaints and varying views of the causes of their health problems. In the following account, however, I shall emphasize the shared perceptions of the two diseases which exist among women and only to a limited extent include individual variations in women's perceptions. At the end of the chapter I shall return to the five women we met in the previous chapter in order to illustrate the ways in which the two diseases are experienced by individual women in the context of their everyday lives. Whereas the case histories of the women provided in Chapter 4 focused specifically on family planning and IUD use, the aim in the present chapter is to demonstrate how the physical discomfort caused by the IUD is experienced within a much broader context of stressful social and somatic experiences. But first, let us take a closer look at local understandings of blood and lack of blood.

Blood: a source of vital energy

In everyday notions of the body and health, the body's strength and balances are closely related to the quality and amount of blood (*khí huyết/máu*).[13] Blood is considered as the precondition for all life and activity. It is usually described as a vital substance which nourishes the body, enabling it to live and function. Blood is 'the best thing in one's body' and 'the most necessary'. Having enough blood makes people strong and healthy, while lack of blood causes weakness and ill health. Each person is said to be born with a certain amount of blood which diminishes over time. One woman explained that when a person grows old, she 'dries up' and gets more wrinkled and lacks blood.

Blood loss, however, can be counteracted by the intake of nourishing diets or strengthening medicines. The main influence on the amount and quality of blood is nutrition, since nutritious foods build up the body's 'substance' and blood. But also the quality of social relations influences blood: social harmony and balance make blood stronger and healthier while social tensions and imbalances weaken blood.

As we saw in the previous chapter, blood is also central to women's reproductive health and to reproductive processes. Menstruation, conception, gestation, birth and breastfeeding are all aspects of women's lives that relate directly to blood. According to Richard Coughlin, in traditional Vietnamese thinking menstrual blood, foetal blood and breast milk are the same substance which changes during the reproductive cycle (Coughlin 1965: 250). People in Vải Sơn said that a woman's menstrual blood is transformed into the foetus during pregnancy; during gestation her blood 'concentrates' to feed the foetus; and when the baby is breastfed, the quality and amount of breast milk depends on the quality of the mother's blood. If the mother's blood is weak or bad (*xấu*), the breast milk will be thin and watery (*loãng*).

Due to their reproductive functions, women lose a lot of blood during their lifetimes. Menstruation, abortion, IUD use and birth cause women to lose blood, but deliveries are considered particularly harmful to women's health. When women talk about the different states of health they have experienced in their lives, changes are often marked by the birth of each child: for each childbirth, health deteriorates sharply. These perceptions are supported by national family planning messages which strongly emphasize the harm done to women's health by too many childbirths.

Everyday notions of blood and its functions in the body have a counterpart in traditional Chinese medicine where blood – along with *chi* (matter-energy) – is one of the 'vital forces' of life. In traditional Chinese medical theory, blood nourishes and maintains the body, moving through the blood vessels and the meridians. Blood in Chinese medicine differs from the Western idea of blood by being considered not simply as a moving fluid but as a form of energy (Porkert 1974). Blood is produced from food which is first transformed into a vital essence/substance (*jing*) and then into blood (Kaptchuk 1983). Nutrition is thus fundamental for building up energy and strength in the body. In the paired concept of blood and *chi* (*chi hsueh*), *chi* is mainly *yang* while blood is mainly *yin* and so represents the female aspect of vital energy and 'the ruling aspect of female constitutions' (Furth 1987: 13). Blood and *chi* are mutually dependent, *chi* creates and moves the blood, while blood nourishes the organs that produce *chi* (Kaptchuk 1983). Classical medical texts teach that people are born with a certain amount of vital 'primal *chi*' which is gradually lost through reproductive acts: ejaculation in men and menstruation, childbirth and breastfeeding in women (Furth and Shu-Yueh 1992).

Furth (1987) describes how classical medical texts systematically represent women as the 'sickly sex', weak and vulnerable due to their loss of blood in menstruation, gestation, and childbirth. Since blood is a fundamental source of strength and vitality, women's inevitable loss of it condemns them to weakness and physical fragility. In other words, Chinese gender ideologies viewing women as 'naturally' subordinate to men are supported and rationalized by medical views of women as by definition 'weak' and 'fragile' due to their role in reproduction. Furth also notes that classical medical texts stress the dangerous and potentially socially disruptive nature of female reproductive powers, thus giving women the choice between 'negative sexual power and socially acceptable weakness' (Furth 1987: 9).

In daily social life in Vải Sơn, blood is a very potent metaphor, related both to the personalities of people and to the ties between them. Blood may refer to personality and temperament, as when it is said that someone has 'impatient' or 'hot' blood (cf. Cadière 1957: 106; Tung 1994: 488). But blood also refers to relatedness; both paternal and maternal family and kin are considered as people of the same blood and flesh (*máu thịt/ruột thịt*) as oneself, to whom one is therefore tied by special bonds of intimacy and belonging (cf. Hy Vắn Lương 1989). Infertile couples are often reluctant to adopt children from other families because such children are of a 'different blood', and if children are adopted, they are usually adopted within lineages. Also the proverb 'A person's flesh is deeply impregnated by his blood' (*Máu ai, thắm thịt này*) expresses the close ties between blood relatives (Cadière 1957: 108). One reason why blood relations are special is that they transcend the present; family relations are preceived as a 'stream' (*dòng*) which ties each person to the past and to the future.[14] *Con là máu, cháu là mủ* (Children are one's blood, and grandchildren also) is a common expression which points to the continuation of life through children and grandchildren.

But here and now, the creation of a 'happy family' is an ultimate and core purpose of life to many women. Blood, therefore, is also metaphorically associated with some of the most highly valued capacities in life: the abilities to create, nourish, and maintain close relations to other people, and particularly to one's own offspring. Blood is life, both as 'vital energy' keeping the individual body alive and as the capacity to reproduce and nourish social relations and so contribute to the continuation of personal and social life.

Against this sociocultural background then, what does it mean when women say they suffer from a lack of blood? Lack of blood is a disease that cuts across the two semantic fields outlined in the previous chapter. It is a disease which is has its roots in the field of sexuality and reproduction, where contraceptive use, childbearing, and childraising drain women's bodies of energy and strength. But it is also a disease which is directly related to the many everyday stresses and concerns which affect women's bodies and minds. As mentioned, lack of blood is an experience which nearly all women in Vải Sơn share. When I first said to Lan that I would like to talk to some of the women who suffer from lack of blood, she said: 'Then you can talk to anyone, we all suffer from lack of blood.'

Lack of blood represents both a disturbance of bodily balances and an erosion of bodily strength. As commonly described by women, lacking blood means feeling weak and exhausted, often being dizzy and dazed, and losing appetite and weight. Lack of blood is sometimes also associated with headaches or with an inability to see clearly. A common symptom of lack of blood is menstrual blood that is dark and fetid instead of red and fresh as in healthy women. A yellow rather than rosy complexion is also a symptom of a lack of blood. Women often describe lack of blood as a circle of symptoms and weaknesses: one feels weak, depressed, and tense; one does not want to eat or work, and so one gets even more weak and depressed. Lacking blood means lacking the ability or desire to go on living and working normally; one's arms and legs feel tired (*mệt mỏi*), heavy (*nặng*), or sad/angry (*buồn bực*); one feels sad and depressed inside (*chán nản trong người*); one cannot eat and just feels generally unwell in one's body (*khó chịu*). As one woman said: 'You feel sick and tired. You can't think clearly, you don't want to do anything.' Lack of blood, then, is a state of fatigue and exhaustion which affects mind and body: it is a physical as well as mental feeling of being out of strength, energy, and balance. In the light of the emphasis in traditional Chinese medicine on balance, strength and harmony, the core symptoms of lack of blood – dizziness and fatigue – seem to point to more fundamental imbalances and disturbances of vital bodily functions.

Lack of blood is clearly a 'women's disease'. People usually say that nearly all women lack blood due to menstruation, abortions, IUD use, and deliveries.[15] But it is also closely related to poverty. In Lai's words,

'I once went for a health check, they told me I lack blood, I should go home and eat something nourishing. But what do I have to eat that is nourishing? I have too little food, how should I eat something nourishing? Work I have a lot of, food I don't have, so I lack blood. The other day there was a meeting up there, they said if you lack blood, you should eat fortifying foods. They just said so, so now I know, but how could I eat something fortifying. It is difficult.'

Poverty seems in many ways to affect women more than men. Poor nutrition, lack of sleep and rest, and thoughts and worries are all experiences which – according to women themselves – characterize women's lives more than men's. During family meals, women often eat last and least, taking care of everyone else's needs before their own. It is women who stay up at night, nursing children or taking care of them when they are ill. At the end of a workday in the fields there are never-ending household chores to perform, while men can rest and watch television when they return from work. Women often lie awake at night speculating about how to make ends meet, while men are not concerned with the small and insignificant details of everyday economy. In general, it is women who think and worry –'about the family, about life' – while men are more carefree. Rather than condemning it, however, women often envy men their 'carefreeness'. Feeling worried and tense disturbs the body's balances and weakens the blood; for the blood to be strong and plentiful one should be relaxed and happy, eat well, and sleep well – in short, lead a life which few women in Vải Sơn are able to.

Even though most women clearly see their lack of blood as basically caused by the social and economic situation in which they find themselves, many women resort to medical treatment. The most common way of treating lack of blood is either with various kinds of B vitamins (B1, B6, or B12), which can be inexpensively bought at the commune health station or from private pharmacists, or with traditional herbal medicine (*thuốc bổ*). The B vitamins, and particularly B1, are said to stimulate appetite, while *thuốc bổ* nourishes the blood. Most women say, though, that the best way of treating lack of blood is simply by eating better and resting more. But this is not always easy, and many therefore accept the condition of lacking blood as a fact of life – simply a part of being a woman.

In sum, lack of blood is a disease that cuts across both mind–body and self–social world divides. In the conduct of everyday life, exhausted bodies and depressed minds are inseparable; as lived by women, everyday burdens of work and worries are both physical and mental experiences. When women talk about sad, heavy, and depressed arms and legs, they seem also to be talking about more general states of mental, emotional, and physical exhaustion (see Chapter 7 below for further discussion). Moreover, lack of blood is a disease that connects women's individual bodies to the social bodies of their families and communities. It is closely associated with women's self-sacrifices for their families: women work too hard and eat too little, setting aside their own needs in order to feed and nourish others, depleting the blood of their own bodies in order to keep the social body alive and well functioning. When the social body does not function well, as when family life is full of tension and conflict, this adds further to the weakening of individual bodies. In these respects, lack of blood has several features in common with the other 'women's disease' to be considered here, namely *nerves*.

Nerves: the ability to stay in balance

While blood is vitally important for health and life, the body's strength and stability also depend on the strength of the nerves (*thần kinh*). Nerves are considered as 'the strength of one's body' or 'the strength of one's life'. They are perceived as a network of 'strings' which tie the body together and coordinate its activities. The brain is the centre of the network of nerves, governing and coordinating the body's organs by sending messages to them via the nerves. Through their association with the brain, nerves are directly related to the mental capacities which ideally govern a person's body and life. Having strong nerves means being able to coordinate one's body and behaviour well, controlling and managing physical movements and expressions. It means being in balance and in control of oneself and being able to work, perform, and behave optimally in every respect.[16] Nerves are also related to blood: strong nerves support the free and easy circulation of blood, and if one's blood is good, nerves will function better.

In everyday perceptions, nerves are influenced by a range of different factors, from wind and weather to family tension. 'Harmful' winds or sudden heat or cold may affect the nerves, causing colds (*cảm lạnh*) or 'wind strokes' (*trúng gió*). Other environmental influences such as pesticides or pollution may also affect and weaken nerves. Working too hard strains the nervous system and so may cause weakness of nerves. The influence of stressful and straining thoughts on the nervous system is also very frequently mentioned: if one thinks a lot and does not relax, one's head will be tense (*đầu óc căng thẳng*) and the nerves weaker. This is the reason why sad and stressful thoughts should generally be avoided: they strain the mind and nerves and thus weaken the whole body.

Nerves and the nervous system are both literally and metaphorically associated with specific personal qualities and with social relations and arrangements. Due to their close associations with the mind and brain, strong nerves connote highly valued personal qualities such as determination, will, steadfastness, self-control, intelligence, and initiative – in short, the ability to keep one's balance physically, mentally, and socially. Having strong nerves means being socially competent and capable of living up to one's responsibilities as a family and community member. It means knowing how to perform and how to behave properly towards others. The symptoms associated with weakness of the nerves range from slight headaches to raving madness, thus associating everyday physical frailties with an eventual total loss of self-control. The links between nerves and mental/moral capacities were very clearly expressed in the following excerpt from an interview:

> 'If you think too much, it influences the nerves. Some people have become crazy from that. They don't understand anything, their nerves are weak.'

'In what way are they crazy?'

'They are not normal, they speak in a confused way. They don't know anything anymore. Normal people know how to dress, how to behave towards others, they know who is above and who is below. But crazy people, they don't know who is who. Their nerves can't direct them anymore. Someone at their mother's age they may address as a child.'

Nerves are closely associated with social competency and weakness of the nerves suggests an inability to orient oneself socially – a social and moral disorientation. In this sense, nerves connect individual and social bodies: healthy individual bodies know how to behave and position themselves socially, while ill and imbalanced bodies are socially and morally confused.

While being central to everyday perceptions of the body and health, the concept of nerves does not seem to have an immediate equivalent in traditional Chinese medical thinking. Today, however, the disease category 'neurasthenia' (in Chinese: 'nervous weakness') is one of the most frequently used diagnoses for mental illness in China (Kleinman 1986). The term 'neurasthenia' was brought into the Chinese medical vocabulary at the beginning of the 20th century (Tseng 1973; Kleinman 1986). Based on his own clinical studies in a medical college in China, Kleinman (1986) points to the striking similarities between the disease which in China today is labelled 'neurasthenia' and the disease which in the West is labelled 'depression'. In Kleinman's Chinese patients, common symptoms of neurasthenia were: headaches, lack of energy, weakness, insomnia, dizziness, and a range of other complaints (Kleinman 1986: 152). On the background of his clinical work, Kleinman suggests that 'neurasthenia' in China may represent a 'somatized' version of the Western category of depression. Since somatic dysfunctions are more culturally acceptable in China than mental diseases, both patients and practitioners in China tend to favour somatic interpretations and labellings of symptoms, while discarding their possible social and psychological meanings. Being a somatic rather than mental disease, neurasthenia is more culturally and sociopolitically acceptable than depression, and therefore a diagnosis of 'neurasthenia' is usually preferred to one of 'depression'.

While Kleinman's work is based on clinical research and mainly focuses on medical categories and diagnoses, studies of 'nerves' in other cultures have considered it as a popular illness category employed in families and local communities. A large number of studies have documented various forms of nervous disease in Europe and North and South America (e.g., Low 1981; Davis and Low 1989; Dunk 1989; Lock 1990; Scheper-Hughes 1992a; Migliore 1994; Guernaccia *et al.* 1996). In these studies, nerves are most often seen as a flexible folk idiom of distress, covering a broad range of different symptoms. Nerves are frequently associated with weakness, dizziness, disorientation, diffuse aches and pains, appetite loss, and feelings of sadness and depression. Many studies describe nerves as a predominantly female complaint (e.g., Davis and Low 1989; Dunk 1989; Lock 1990; Rebhun 1993). The experience of nerves is often seen as grounded in social situations of stress and distress, in the family, local community, or at work. While most studies see nerves as originating in different kinds of psychosocial stress and tension, Scheper-Hughes' work in a shanty-town in northeastern Brazil connects nerves with the experience of chronic and acute hunger. In all studies, however, nerves are seen as a culturally acceptable idiom of distress through which social tensions and contradictions are communicated and enacted.

Also in Vải Sơn, nerves are a flexible and fairly diffuse illness category, comprising a variety of different bodily experiences. Headache is a core symptom of nerves, but nerves are also associated with dizziness, disturbed vision, fatigue, trembling in arms and legs, weight loss, diffuse aches and pains anywhere in the body (but most often in arms, shoulders, back, and chest), fainting, falling over, feeling confused (*lẫn lộn*), memory loss, sleeplessness, feelings of 'tightness' in the breast (*tức ức*), depression (*buồn chán/ chán nản*), anger-sadness (*buồn bực/bực mình*) and madness (*điên*). Suffering from nerves may mean suffering from frequent headaches, unexplicable pains in the chest or back, or just from general feelings of weakness, dizziness, and physical exhaustion. All sorts of feelings of physical pain and discomfort may apparently be explained with reference to nerves, as in Lai's case:

'It hurts when I urinate, and there is a pain/pressure in my chest, my back aches and I feel weak ... I guess it is nerves. Because I am very weak, so my body is exhausted. It is because of the nerves that it hurts when I urinate, because the nerves have to think a lot. I have no time to rest, there is too much work, my head is not relaxed but tense (*căng thẳng*). If my financial situation were stable, it would be better.'

Besides physical pain, nerves are also often associated with feelings of sadness and depression, with appetite loss, lethargy and a loss of desire to live. A woman suffering from nerves said,

'I feel fed up with everything (*chán hết mọi việc*), I only want to lie down, I don't want to do anything. I just feel very tired, my arms and legs are tired.'

However, such feelings of sadness and hopelessness are normally only categorized as nerves if they go together with physical symptoms like headaches, dizziness, fatigue, etc. For instance, Nhị told me about her frequent conflicts with her husband and explained,

'Every time it is like this I feel depressed (*chán*). I don't want to work, and I am not interested in eating and suffer more from headaches ... If you think a lot, and feel depressed and have headaches, it is nerves. But normally, if you only feel depressed, it is not nerves.'

Nerves are an ailment which may have either 'external' or 'internal' causes: it may be caused by outside disturbing influences: wind, weather or harmful substances (cf. Craig 1996), or it may be caused by exhaustion of the inner workings of mind or physiology. Such exhaustion may be due to too much hard physical work or to too many stressful thoughts. As Mai said:

'I often have headaches because of thinking a lot. When I don't think there is no problem. [...] When the children are ill, the family finances are unstable, when things don't go as I want them to, my thoughts are strolling like this.'

Like lack of blood, nerves are often seen as a circle of symptoms: overexhaustion of body/mind leads to a weakening of nerves which causes aches, pains, dizziness, fatigue and sadness. Once saddened and weakened, the body has to work even harder in order to manage everyday tasks and responsibilities, thus further exhausting the nerves. Nerves are often seen as directly caused by living in situations of economic need and social stress and tension, where one's mind and body have to work too hard to keep family and finances on course. Mơ said:

'Here, out of ten people ten suffer from that disease... because, for instance like my family, we live under difficult circumstances, so I have to think a lot, I cannot relax. People who relax and who have enough never suffer from that disease. If you are poor and have to think a lot, you get it right away... Your mind (*tinh thần*) is not relaxed, the [family] economy is poor. You think often, so for those reasons you get nerves.'

The straining of thoughts which causes nerves is very often related to family tensions, associated with stressful relations to husbands, children, or parents-in-law. In Quế's words:

'Often it is family affairs which cause people to suffer from nerves. For instance, if there is a lack of harmony (*bất hoà*) between brothers and sisters, fighting and divisions within the house, many people get crazy.'

As mentioned earlier, poverty and family tensions are perceived as being closely related. A stable economy is generally seen as the best way to create a happy family life, while family disharmony often has its roots in a fragile economy. In severe cases, where family relations are very strained, exhaustion of the nerves may lead to madness or 'disease of the thoughts' (*bệnh tư tưởng*).[17]

Like lack of blood, nerves are a disease biased towards women. But where lack of blood is often seen as closely related to women's reproductive physiology, nerves are typically caused by the social and economic circumstances of women's lives. Since women think more about the 'petty details' of everyday life and economy, they are more prone to diseases of the nerves than men. Nhị put it in this way:

'Women suffer from nerves firstly because of the circumstances of the family, you have to work hard and get tired, and secondly because you have to think a lot. Because the family is poor, or because there are contradictions between husband and wife, you think a lot, you strain the nerves, and so suffer from nerves, headaches.'

Women often say that family conflicts tend to take a heavier toll on women's health than on men's, since men are typically more oriented towards the world outside the family, while to women the family and its welfare are major concerns in life. Therefore thoughts and worries about the upbringing of children, about lazy or unfaithful husbands, or quick-tempered mothers-in-law often strain women's bodies and minds, causing weakness and exhaustion:

> 'Eight out of ten people suffer from headaches. Most of them are women who have many children, or whose husbands are not faithful, so there is no happiness. Some have a good income, but they suffer from headaches because their husband has a relationship with another girl outside.'

Even though women clearly recognize that the experience of nerves is rooted in stressful social and economic circumstances, nerves – like lack of blood – are very often medically treated. For headaches, many women routinely take *Seda*, a pain reliever. As general strengtheners, either traditional fortifying medicine (*thuốc bổ*) or vitamin B6 or B12 (as pills or injections) may be used, and acupuncture is a frequently used treatment for backaches. But while medical treatments are recognized as being effective in the short term, all women seem to think that a real improvement in their state of health requires a more fundamental change of the social situation which causes ill health. As Hồng said:

> 'In order to cure nerves, the best thing is to be relaxed ... that there is agreement between husband and wife. Second, that the family has enough to eat and spend so that your thoughts are relaxed. That's the best way to cure nerves.'

When we talked about her frequent headaches, Loan said, 'Medicine does not help. Only a harmonious family life helps.'

Liên confirmed this: 'Medicine cannot cure thoughts.' One woman, telling the story of a young woman suffering from 'disease of the thoughts', said that the girl's parents brought her to a mental hospital, but with no success since 'injections cannot cure this disease, only feelings can cure it'.

While other studies – most notably Scheper-Hughes (1992a, 1992b) – have seen in nerves a medicalization of basic human needs, I do not think that this is the best characterization of the social processes at work when women in Vải Sơn see themselves as suffering from nerves or lack of blood. While Scheper-Hughes describes how shanty-town people are cruelly led to believe that what they need is medicine when what they really need is food and decent living conditions, women in Vải Sơn are acutely aware that medicine does not solve or cure the social problems which are impairing their health. But even if it does not fundamentally solve anything, medicine often takes away the pain and so enables women to keep on doing what they have to do in order to survive and get by every day. Whereas it may be difficult to change the ultimate sources of distress and worry in one's life – poverty and family hierarchies – bodily symptoms can be immediately and directly acted upon.

In short, suffering from nerves means being out of balance physically, mentally, and socially; it means feeling weak and dizzy, sad and depressed, and unable properly to coordinate and control one's own life and activities. Nerves are also often associated with a lack of capacity for correct social behaviour, with an inability to position oneself appropriately in social hierarchies. It is an ailment which is most often caused by too many thoughts/worries or by too much hard work; i.e. by exhausting one's body and mind. The nervous system thus links personal experiences of weakness and dizziness with social values of balance, control, and harmony. 'Nervous disease' indexes both social disharmonies causing personal imbalances and personal imbalances causing social disharmonies. Like lack of blood, nerves breach boundaries between body and mind; thoughts and physiologies are one in the experience of pain, weakness and exhaustion.

Let us now return to the women whose IUD problems were described in the previous chapter: Hảo, Ngọc, Quế, Hạnh, and Tuyết. I shall now broaden my case histories of these women and their lives to describe more of the social situation in which the women live and to include other health experiences than those immediately related to the IUD.

Case illustrations

Hảo: 'If you did not have to worry and think, worry and think ...'

As we sit talking in the darkness of her small house, each holding a cup of bitter green tea, Hảo tells me about the difficulties of her life. Her family's finances are very tight and she has to devote much planning to make ends meet. Her husband is a war invalid, but because he has lost the paper which states that he is an invalid, he does not receive any financial support from the state. He can still work, Hảo says, but he forgets easily and cannot read because his eyes were damaged in the war.

Their children have all been very slow learners, they can hardly read or write even though they have been to school for many years. Hảo worries a lot about their mental health – they do not know how to do anything and they forget everything, she says. They have also always been very sickly and small, much smaller than other children. Hảo worries whether the fact that her husband was in the war and exposed to Agent Orange has somehow damaged the children. Or maybe it is because they were ill so often when they were young, she says – they all had measles; this was before the policy of vaccinations.

The conversation with Hảo is one of the conversations which very soon turns from the IUD to weakness in general. I ask her how she felt after she had her IUD inserted.

'I suffered from stomach aches, sometimes backaches, some-times dizziness. If I rested from work, it helped. But I am weak, so I get dizzy easily.'

I ask what she means by dizzy, and she says:

'Dizzy is to be weak, tired, to feel that you turn around and around. You stand like this and feel as if you are being pushed by the wind. It is because you are weak, you feel like this. It is because of lack of blood.'

In Hảo's own view, her lack of blood is caused partly by the IUD and partly by blood loss from menstruations and deliveries. Suffering from lack of blood makes her feel dizzy and dazed: she often cannot see clearly, and she sometimes loses her balance and falls over. She often suffers from headaches, and she usually feels exhausted. She feels particularly weak during menstruation, she says. Resting usually helps, but normally she has to work no matter how tired she feels.

'I do everything. If I don't work, who does the hard work? If I can't carry a lot, I can carry a little at a time.'

For every year of her life she has become weaker, Hảo says, and she has lost strength with each delivery. Her health deteriorated a lot when the children were young. They were ill so often, so she slept very little and had too little to eat.

'When the children are not well, I feel very depressed and worried and cannot eat,' she says, 'it is the same for everyone who lacks blood. You eat little, sleep little, take care of the children, so your nerves are not relaxed; you worry and think a lot.'

I ask if this is a common condition, and Hảo replies:

'Women often have to think, and therefore suffer from headaches, sleeplessness, it influences the nerves. If you cannot sleep, you get tired and exhausted, arms and legs get tired; the food does not taste good. For instance, if you did not have to worry and think, worry and think, then you could sleep through until morning and would be strong and healthy.'

Hảo sometimes buys fortifying medicine in the market, vitamins B1, B6, or B12. It makes her feel better, but the effect lasts only for a short while.

Due to her physical exhaustion and her constant worries, Hảo also suffers from 'nerves'; she often feels weak and has headaches. Her head is 'strained', confused (*rối loạn*), and she tends to forget things.

'If you worry a lot, it has to influence the nerves, it makes the nerves tense. If you are carefree, your nerves are not affected,' she says.

Even though she feels very weak, her weakness does not worry her; she has accepted it. But her husband is greatly concerned about her and encourages her to buy medicine to make her stronger.

Ngọc: 'Lacking blood makes my body feel sad'

For the last ten years, Ngọc tells us, she has suffered from lack of blood, because she has given birth so often and because she eats an inadequate diet. She often feels dizzy and dazed and has to lean on the wall to prevent herself from falling over. Due to her lack of blood, she also often has headaches and feels completely worn out, and her arms and legs feel tired. The IUD mainly causes backaches, she says, while the headaches are caused by lack of blood and weak nerves.

Lacking blood makes her body feel sad and makes her think and speculate, and all these thoughts make her even weaker. Ngọc is sad that she never had a daughter, because the boys are not very helpful around the house, they are all very lazy. She works hard every day, and she worries a lot about the family finances. Recently, their buffalo died, some chickens were stolen, and three puppies also died. So now Ngọc does not know how to find money to pay for the school for the three youngest boys and for the marriage of the eldest. All this thinking causes headaches and weakness, she says. She has suffered from 'nerves' for many years, but for the last five years it has been more serious than before. She often has headaches and feels dizzy; her mind is unstable. Previously she bought medicine, vitamin B6, in the market, but now she has given it up.

Her husband Giảng encourages her to rest more, and he helps with cooking and other chores on days when she is very weak. Most of the time he is a good and helpful husband, she says, but sometimes he can get very angry and hot-tempered. The difficult thing with him is that she never knows when he will be good and supportive and when he will be violent and 'hot'. Ngọc thinks it is because he was in the war; since then he has had this short and unpredictable temper. When he is 'hot' and shouts at her, she tries not to answer him back – if she does, he will say that she is insolent and be even worse to her. So the best way to protect the harmony of the family is to keep quiet. Ngọc tries not to think about her health, since she has found that thinking and worrying only make diseases worse.

'Only a stable income and a happy family life can really improve one's health', she says.

Quế: 'Men can go anywhere they want'

Quế is yet another woman who has trouble making ends meet. Her family's financial situation is not too good, and she worries a lot about her ability to provide her four children with decent food and clothing. Her husband works in another province and his parents are very old, so Quế has taken over much of what is usually regarded as men's work, including the most physically demanding tasks. In her daily life the IUD does not make her worry very much, she says, she just sometimes feels dizzy and has headaches and backaches, and her menstruations are very painful.

Like almost all other women, Quế suffers from lack of blood: she feels weak, and she often gets dizzy and has black spots before her eyes. In her own view, this is due to the blood she lost during her deliveries, and to her hard physical work and poor nutrition. She works hard to provide for the children, bending over and carrying a lot, so she often suffers from backaches:

'I overwork my body, the nerves in my back cannot take it. I bend a lot, work from six in the morning until lunch, go home and eat a little rice, and work again all afternoon.'

Thinking about her work and the family's economic situation makes her health deteriorate, Quế says, and makes her thin.

Because of her incessant thinking and hard work, Quế also suffers from 'nerves'. Often she cannot see clearly, and she frequently feels weak, sad, and exhausted, and suffers from backaches and headaches. On her bad days she does not want to work anymore or do anything, she just feels tired in arms and legs and generally 'unwell' in her body. As Quế explains, if one works hard, also the nervous system has to work hard and the nerves therefore get exhausted. To strengthen her eyes she takes fish oil tablets, and she also often takes B6 tablets and *Seda*, which ease the pains in head and back, or strengthening injections of vitamin B12.

'Headaches and backaches are typical women's diseases', Quế says. In general, women's health is weaker than men's, because women are physically weaker and have to think more than men.

'Women often have to think more, think more deeply, about the children, about life.'

One thing which also makes Quế think and speculate a lot is the fact that her husband lives and works far away. It is not good for a family to have 'husband in one place, wife in another', and she is worried about whether he has other women when he is away.

'If your husband is faithful, you do not have to think and so you do not become ill.' She often wishes she were a man:

'Men can go any where they want. But a married woman has to lock up her heart, she can't go anywhere, she can't join society outside.'

Hạnh: 'Now I have money and rights'

As we sit in the shade on the porch outside her house, Hạnh tells me that before she had the IUD she was fat and healthy, but now – after giving birth to four children and after having the IUD – she is always sick. Since she had her last IUD inserted more than two years ago, she has suffered from lack of blood. She often gets dizzy and dazed, the whole world turns around and she cannot see anything. This happens particularly often when she goes out to work on very hot days. She sometimes feels so weak and tired that she cannot work at all.

'If your body is healthy you do not feel like this', Hạnh says. But she is weak and lacks blood, and lacking blood makes her think and feel sad:

'Lack of blood influences your mind, you do not want to work, you do not want to be with others. Your thoughts are not relaxed, because the family's finances are in a shambles, the children are often ill. [...] If your body lacks blood, you often think, feel depressed.'

Hạnh sometimes buys blood-strengthening medicine, vitamin B12, in the market. Since she and her husband moved into their own house recently, she has been able to buy medicine for herself – before, when they lived together with her mother-in-law, she never dared ask for money to buy medicine. Her mother-in-law has a difficult temper, and ever since Hạnh and her husband got married 14 years ago, her mother-in-law has been treating her badly. She likes her own three daughters better than Hạnh and usually orders Hạnh to do all the hardest work. Her husband's three sisters also stick together, and they often say bad things about Hạnh to her husband and mother-in-law.

Hạnh is very happy that she and her husband live by themselves now; now at least she has 'money and rights', she says, while before she had neither. But even though she has more economic freedom now, relations with her in-laws are still very complicated. Their new house lies in the same compound as the house of her mother-in-law, so even though the two houses are physically separate, they remain very close in daily life, and Hạnh still depends on her in-laws for assistance with childcare and other tasks. When her husband comes home, he often stays in his mother's house rather than with her, and in the conflicts between her and her mother-in-law, he often sides with his mother.

Thinking about her family and mother-in-law affects her nerves, Hạnh says – she often suffers from headaches and dizziness and feels tired and sad. The more she thinks, the more headaches she has. She has been suffering severely from thoughts and headaches during the past two years, and now she feels very weakened and exhausted. She buys medicine, vitamin B6, to strengthen her nerves, and her husband also buys her medicine and encourages her to get better.

Tuyết: 'I still have to work hard to build up the economy'

Even though Tuyết and her husband are relatively well off compared to many others, Tuyết still worries a lot about their financial situation. She thinks that it is a great responsibility to have three children to take care of and she worries about whether she will be able to bring them up properly. Tuyết envies her neighbour My who lives with her parents-in-law. If one lives with one's parents-in-law, they bear the main responsibility for the household's economy, but living separately, one has to carry the whole responsibility alone, there is no one else to take care of things. Her husband's parents died before he got married, and her own parents live in another hamlet, so there is no one to assist her with daily chores.

Tuyết has suffered from 'lack of blood' for five years now, since she had her first IUD. She knows it is lack of blood because her skin is not fresh and rosy anymore, but yellow, and she feels completely worn out. She feels dizzy, exhausted, and tired in arms and legs. She lacks blood because of her deliveries, because of the IUD, and because she does not eat well. She says:

'If you eat well, you have a lot of blood. You have to build up your health by eating well.'

Tuyết also feels much weaker than before she had children, and she has lost a lot of weight. Before she had children she weighed more than 50 kilos, now she weighs only 42. In her own view, she lost weight because she has given birth to three children, and because she worries so much. When the eldest child was young, he suffered from whooping cough and polio and one of his legs was paralysed, so she worried a lot about his health. Today she still worries, particularly about the family's finances. Even though she is weak, she still has to work hard to build up the finances to provide for her children and make sure they have food and education. She eats only a little, and tries to save as much money as possible for investments in order to secure the future for her children.

Tuyết's thoughts are never relaxed, she says, she is always thinking and worrying, tense and tired, and therefore she suffers from 'nerves'. Her backaches, headaches, dizziness, fatigue, and pains in the chest are all symptoms of nerves. She is terribly afraid that the headaches might influence her brain, causing damage and reducing her intelligence. This happened to her husband; he used to study, but he thought too much and had headaches which damaged his brain, forcing him to give up studying. Tuyết treats her lack of blood with traditional medicine, and *gà hâm*, a specially prepared chicken. For her headaches, she sometimes takes vitamin B6 and *Seda*. Her husband is very concerned about her health; he encourages her to rest more, eat better, and take medicine. He also encourages her to go for health checks, but she feels shy and does not want to go.

⚘

The above five cases all demonstrate the close links that exist between IUD problems and more general feelings of physical weakness and discomfort. The weakness which the IUD causes is embedded within much more general feelings of weakness and exhaustion which are rooted in poverty, hard work, and worries about family and children. The five cases also illustrate the close relationship that exists between 'lack of blood' and 'nerves'. Often the two ailments merge into one feeling of weakness and exhaustion which is grounded in the social, emotional, and economic contingencies of everyday lives. Finally, the cases illustrate how thoughts, worries and physical weaknesses merge into one feeling of stress and exhaustion. Experiences of family disharmony are often experienced together with physical weakness; daily feelings of anger, fear, or disappointment become virtually inseparable from physical sensations of lethargy and exhaustion.

Summing up: the socio-somatics of everyday symptoms

As we have seen in this chapter, women's everyday feelings of physical weakness and discomfort are very often experienced in tandem with social stresses and tensions, and particularly with tensions within the family. In the lives of women in Vải Sơn, close associations exist between the health and the happiness of families. Experiences of bodily discomfort therefore gain significance and urgency from the wider social meanings which they engage, linking aching bodies closely to stressful family lives. Real families are often very far from the ideal 'happy families' pictured both in family planning campaigns and in women's dreams. Daily lives are fraught with marital strifes, tensions in relationships with in-laws, economic problems, worries about the health of children, etc. – and such experiences are all perceived by women as closely intertwined with physical experiences of heavy arms and legs, tired bodies, and aching heads. In other words, feelings of weakness often encompass not only physical but also social strains; dizziness may indicate bodily as well as social disorientation and physical pain is often experienced coterminously with painful social relations. Bodies that are out of balance point to social worlds that are likewise out of balance. In a similar way, pain or exhaustion are not just physical experiences but carry social and moral implications as well.

The common 'women's diseases' of blood and nerves provide particularly clear illustrations of the close interlinkages between body and mind and between individual body and social body. Women in Vải Sơn experience 'nerves' and 'lack of blood' as diseases of the body as well as of the mind, uniting physical experiences of pain and discomfort with feelings of sadness and mental exhaustion. From women's own perspective, they are bodily experiences that have an obvious basis in the social situation of the person suffering from them. They are related to the poverty that forces women to work too hard, rest too little, worry too much, and eat inadequately. They are associated with family tensions and with the specific physical and social stresses of womanhood brought about by menstruations, pregnancies, abortions and deliveries. In this sense, women in Vải Sơn are acutely aware that their everyday symptoms represent more than pure physiological malfunctioning or just 'an unfortunate brush with nature' (Scheper-Hughes and Lock 1987: 31). In common reasoning, symptoms are not just biological signs, but also metaphors for stressful and exhausting living conditions. In the words of Michael Taussig:

> The signs and symptoms of disease do something more than signify the functioning of our bodies; they also signify critically sensitive and contradictory components of our culture and social relations. Yet, in our standard medical practices this social 'language' emanating from our bodies is manipulated by concealing it within the realm of biological signs. (Taussig 1980: 3)

Women's diseases of blood and nerves thus illustrate how bodies come to mean and how physical sensations and sensibilities are closely associated with specific social forms and relations.

In short, this chapter has demonstrated how social and physical experiences are intimately linked. We have seen that social balance and harmony are considered vitally important for health, while ill health is closely associated with social tension. But we still do not know much about the character of the social tensions that seem to form an integral part of women's physical experiences. What does social harmony, or disharmony, mean in practice? Which are the social experiences that bring women's bodies out of balance, making them feel heavy, tense, and anxious? While the above analysis of cultural meanings which cross over between body and society highlighted the ways by which dominant cultural meanings tie together individual and social bodies, it did not tell us much about the ways such meanings are realized, contested, and negotiated in local worlds. For such insights, we need to consider the concrete social contexts in which meanings are enacted and embodied. In the following chapter, therefore, we shall consider the local moral worlds of family and community in which both social and somatic experiences are shaped.

Notes

1. As we have seen in the previous chapter, this clearly influences the ways modern contraceptive methods such as the pill or the IUD are perceived.

2. The distinctions between 'hot' and 'cold' foods seem to be identical to Chinese hot/cold distinctions (see Anderson and Anderson 1974). Meat (particularly dog meat), coffee, alcohol, ginger, chili, etc. are normally considered 'hot', while most vegetables are 'cold' and rice is neutral. See also Cadière 1957.

3. By constitution, each person has either 'hot' or 'cold' blood. People who have cold blood feel cold at night and during winter, while people who have hot blood cannot stand the heat of summer. Cold-blooded people should eat more hot foods than others, while hot-blooded people should eat cold foods. It is usually considered better to have cold than hot blood, since hot-blooded people tend to get ill more easily.

4. When I asked Lan why contraceptive pills prevent pregnancy, she seemed surprised at my stupidity, saying, 'Don't you know what hormones are?'

5. As Unschuld (1985, 1987) points out, traditional Chinese medicine is an extremely complex and varied corpus of different knowledges. Western writers, however, have tended to focus solely on the correlative cosmology while neglecting aspects of Chinese medical theory which are closer to standard Western medical knowledge. In other words, what Unschuld points to is a sort of 'Orientalism' in Western readings of Chinese medical theory, a tendency to stress points of difference between China and the West while ignoring points of convergence. When I emphasize notions of balance, harmony, and systematic correspondences in my discussion of local perceptions of the body, my intention is not mainly to contrast these ideas with Western ideas, but to explain the widespread recognition of the social origins of bodily symptoms which I noted among women in Vải Sơn.

6. For more elaborate expositions of traditional Chinese medical theory, see Needham (1969), Porkert (1974).

7. Also the everyday emphasis on strengthening foods has a parallel in traditional medical ideas; in *thuốc Bắc* strengthening tonics (*thuốc bổ*) are an important part of medical care.

8. Analogical relations between individual bodies, families, and the state are also at the core of national family planning messages, which closely associate the health of bodies, the happiness and wealth of families, and the stability of the nation.

9. The term *nhà* (house) covers most of these social units: *nhà* may be a loving way of referring to one's spouse, i.e. to a person/body; it may mean house, home, or family; *nhà quê* usually refers to one's home village; and *nhà nước* is the most commonly used term for state.

10. Yet, as we shall see in the following chapter, while the idea that a head of household is necessary is generally taken for granted, it is less obvious *who* the head of the household should be or is.

11. The local concept of 'lack of blood' seems closely related to the biomedical category of 'anaemia' even though the two may not be quite identical.

12. In a case study of a Vietnamese woman living in England who suffers from 'wind illness' or somatic depression, Maurice Eisenbruch notes that according to Vietnamese indigenous healers, two factors are directly connected with women's supposed physical vulnerability: first, their weaker 'life essence' due to blood loss from menstruations and deliveries, and second, the fact that women 'tend to brood and to have jittery nerves' (Eisenbruch 1983: 325). In her study of notions of reproductive physiology in Iran, Mary-Jo DelVecchio Good (1980) similarly finds that women are more prone to diseases related to weakness of blood and nerves than men.

13. The term *máu* is Vietnamese, while *khí huyết* is Sino-Vietnamese (Cadière 1958: 107).

14. Since kinship structures are patrilineal, women's position in this 'stream' of life is ambiguous (cf. Wolf 1972; Croll 1994). On the one hand, it is through women's bodies that life continues, while on the other, women (*phụ nữ*) remain *phụ* (secondary) to their husband's lineages.

15. Some women also mentioned that lack of blood may be caused by worms (*giun*) which disturb digestion (*rối loạn tiêu hoá*).

16. Strong nerves are often seen as a precondition for the successful practice of withdrawal as a contraceptive method. As mentioned in Chapter 4, there is quite a lot of prestige associated with the successful use of this method precisely because it demonstrates self-control and intellectual capacities.

17. 'Disease of the thoughts' is often associated with unhappy love affairs, the most common story being the story of the young woman who has been let down in love and who thinks so much that she becomes insane.

CHAPTER 6

Local Moral Worlds

A quiet morning in spring an unusual drama unfolded in Bà Chính's yard. Loud voices suddenly pierced the air, interrupting the stream of ordinary morning sounds of squealing pigs, rattling pots, and shouting children. I went downstairs and out into the yard to encounter a sight I shall never forget. Kiều was standing there with her bike, wearing her wide summer hat and dark sunglasses, apparently ready to leave for work. Opposite her was Bà Chính, with her long black hair – which she normally held tied and rolled in a tight ribbon – hanging loose over her back. In her hand Bà held a long stick with which she lightly slapped Kiều's arm as she spoke, scolding her for being an insolent, lazy, and good-for-nothing daughter-in-law.

The scene bore reminiscences of times long past – had it not been for Kiều's bicycle, sunglasses, and smart summer clothes, this might well have been a clash between mother-in-law and daughter-in-law a few hundred years ago. The walled yard, the stagnant green fish pond behind it, the flies, the banana trees, and two women in violent confrontation. For a few minutes time froze and present and past merged. Then events moved on: Bà Chính removed one of her plastic slippers, lifted it to Kiều's face, and slapped her chin with it. Kiều stood paralysed before she turned around, exclaimed, 'I cannot live like this anymore', got on her bike and went off to work.

'You see,' Bà Chính said, turning to me, 'this is what I told you. People don't know how to behave anymore, they don't know what is up and what is down, they have no morality. How can I live with a spoilt daughter-in-law like this? She even tells me I cook too salty food. Would *you* ever dare tell *your* mother-in-law her food was too salty?'

Without waiting for an answer, she turned to the banana-man who – along with a crowd of neighbours – had witnessed the scene, to continue their discussion of today's price of green bananas.

Shocked, I went to talk the events over with Bình and her husband Quảng, the next door neighbours. It turned out that the conflict was not mainly over too salty food, but over the upbringing of Kiều's eldest son who was growing up to be wilder and more unruly than most boys of his age. But contrary to what I had naively expected, both Bình and Quảng strongly condemned Kiều, rather than showing sympathy with her. Even though Bà Chính is known to be a hot-tempered and difficult woman, they both agreed that Kiều's behaviour was absolutely unacceptable. Under no circumstances was it proper or acceptable for a daugher-in-law openly to contradict and criticize her mother-in-law, as Kiều had done this morning. Quảng was outraged.

'Next time this happens we will call the police and we will have her fired from her job. Behaving like this, how can she be a teacher? A teacher should be a model for her pupils, she should know her place, teach them right and wrong. Behaving like this, how can she do that? This is unacceptable.'

As I realized later, all neighbours agreed with this condemnation of Kiều, finding that she had violated basic codes of conduct and morality. Another neighbour later explained to me:

'No matter what her mother-in-law tells her, being a daughter-in-law she should still speak nicely and behave properly.'

ജ്ര

Daily life in Vải Sơn is fraught with family conflicts such as this. Some are played out in the open, when fights and quarrels get too loud to conceal, but many take place in more hidden, subtle – yet still often violent ways. The cases of Hảo, Ngọc, Quế, Hạnh, and Tuyết have illustrated how everyday work burdens and social tensions in relation to husbands and mothers-in-law often lie at the heart of women's feelings of mental and physical exhaustion. These experiences are rooted in a social and moral universe where women are expected to carry the burdens of housework and childcare, where wives are often expected to 'follow' and comply with their husbands, and where younger women are expected to respect and obey their parents-in-law.

Women's experiences of weakness, dizziness, and headaches seem to reach far beyond the immediate situations of not having enough money to pay for the children's schoolbooks, being angry with a husband over his wasting of money, quarrelling with a mother-in-law over when to work and when to rest, or lying awake at night speculating about the family's finances. These everyday problems are all rooted in structural tensions and in competing moral definitions of what it means to be a mother, a wife, or a daughter-in-law. In order to be able to draw up a more general picture of the social dynamics underlying the tensions and contradictions in women's lives, I shall now make an analytical comparison of the experiences of individual women like Hảo, Ngọc, Quế, Hạnh, and Tuyết, while also exploring the competing moral ideologies which inform daily social interaction in Vải Sơn. In daily lives, widely differing and contradictory moral notions exist, creating a broad array of differing modes of perceiving and evaluating social relations. As we shall see, this moral complexity is rooted in Vietnam's turbulent history and in the syncretic character of today's Vietnamese culture.

The literature on women in Vietnam often discusses whether and to what extent gender equality has been achieved in socialist Vietnam (e.g., Hy Văn Lương 1989; Werner 1997). These are not simply academic questions, but also topics of reflection and lively discussion among women themselves. In this chapter we shall look more closely at the local moral worlds in which women's social and bodily experiences are shaped and at the tensions and contradictions with which these worlds are fraught. I have borrowed the term 'local moral worlds' from the work of Arthur Kleinman (1986, 1992), who employs the concept to refer to the local worlds in which experiences of illness are constructed. Local moral worlds are the local worlds of shared experience which mediate the influences of macrosocial and political forces, shaping their specific local effects. Local moral worlds form local contexts of power in which social risks and resources are distributed, placing some people in positions of greater social and physical stress and danger than others.

To begin with, we shall consider the daily living conditions which women themselves experience as stressful. Women's everyday stresses and worries seem to be related to two central facets of their lives: first, the experience of *overwork*, i.e. very hard work every day and responsibility both for working the fields and for all domestic work including the management of the household economy, and second, the experience of *submission*, i.e. having to 'please' (*chiều*) one's husband and his family. What this amounts to is a double burden of shouldering the responsibility for the welfare of one's family and the main portion of the burden of work and worries, yet still often feeling fettered and dependent.

Everyday experiences of social stress and tension

A recurrent theme in women's discussions about their health is their hard work and the inequitable divisions of labour between the sexes. Both men and women would usually say that men only worry about 'big and important' things, such as large investments or the marriage of a son or daughter, while all the 'small and insignificant' tasks in everyday life are considered as women's responsibilities. As Hôm said,

'Men, they only care about outward representational things, for instance, building a house or buying something big for the family, but the small insignificant activities in the family, that's for women. Money so the children can go to school, or money to make clothes for the children, those things, they are women's jobs. Selling things for the family or raising pigs or chickens to make things for the children or to buy rice for the children, women have to worry about all that.'

Talking about women's health, a woman in one of the focus group discussions said,

'You go to work, come home tired in the evening, the children are a nuisance, the pig screams, you have to cook food for it. You go to sleep, already exhausted, so tired, the child has to be breastfed all night, the husband demands. So it is true that ...'

At this point the other women joined in, laughing, repeatedly chanting the old folk verse which summarizes the daily experiences of many rural women, 'The pig screams – the children cry – the husband demands lustfully; the pig screams – the children cry – the husband demands lustfully' (*Lợn kêu, con khóc, chồng đòi tòm tem*). The daily work burdens and unequal gender division of worries about children and household economy take a heavy toll on women's health. Hảo phrased it like this:

'Women's health can never be like men's. Here we still say a weak ox is stronger than a cow. No matter how healthy a woman is, she will never be like a man. First, because for every childbirth she loses a lot of blood, and second, if a family is poor the woman often worries, often thinks. Moreover, if your children do not have enough, if they have less than others, you also worry. Or if a child is sick, the woman also has to worry more than the man, she has to stay awake at night, run for medicines for the child. Men only worry about big things. Women often have a harder life than men.'

Due to their responsibility for the welfare of the family, women also carry the major burden of worries of everyday life. As mentioned in Chapter 5, women would very often emphasize men's carefree attitude as an important reason for their stronger health. Hồng put it in this way:

'Men forget right away, but women think a lot. Men often don't notice, they think family issues are trivial matters, so they don't think about them.'

Another woman said:

'Men only feel sad for a moment, then they meet their friends, go for a drink, so they forget and are happy again at once. Even though it is very sad in the family, men go outside and forget about it. They play, have fun, drink beer and alcohol. Women can't do that, women have to work, take care of the children. There is no time to go out to drink at all.'

Men often seem to be proud of their carefree attitude, saying like Mỹ's husband: 'Men are carefree. Women always think, that's the way women's feelings are.' Another man said:

'Men only worry about important matters. In the rural family there are many small jobs in the family which women worry more about and think more about. We men, at night we go out gambling, we drink a few bottles, and then we sleep until morning. The women have to worry about the kitchen work, about tomorrow, they have to prepare food for the pig and the chicken, so women have to deliberate a lot about the work.'

Stephen O'Harrow (1995) writes that in Vietnam the height of *machismo* seems to be 'a gentlemanly idleness' at women's expense. An old folksong (cited from O'Harrow 1995: 165) goes like this: 'Drinking and gambling till you're on over your head / But even if you are out of money, your kid's mother is still out there selling her wares.' In his study of Red River delta families, Phạm Văn Bích sums up gender divisions of everyday work:

Women's work in the countryside ranges from the weeding, trans-planting, firewood gathering, water carrying, sewing, cleaning, washing, domestic animal raising to the shopping, cooking, and even serving other family members: usually in the family meal it is the wife who serves others. Women's work never carries with it the prestige of men's work. Men may take the most important family de-cisions. In a lot of families, the wife is alone responsible for every manual work; her husband does nothing. (Phạm Văn Bích 1997: 136–37)

The hardships and work burdens women experience in their married lives are common topics of folksongs and sayings as the following (quoted from Trịnh Minh-hà 1992: 58, 80) demonstrate:

Loving her husband half of the night,
She spends the other half before dawn carrying her
*   merchandise to market.*

With husband, she can't go anywhere,
With children, she can't even have peace for one hour.

With children, she has to endure hardship for the children,
With husband, she has to bear the burden of responsibilities in
*   his family.*

Also the worries associated with having to please (*chiều*) one's husband often exhaust women physically. The idiom of 'pleasing' one's husband is used in many different contexts, referring to both sexual and social relations, and is closely related to women's feelings of having to depend (*phụ thuộc*) on their husband and in-laws. In sexual relations, having to please one's husband may mean having to have sex even if one does not want to. Women often seem to put up with rather than participate in sex, and many women say that they are much too exhausted from hard physical work to be able to enjoy their sexual lives. Quế put it this way:

'Women cannot bear having a lot of sex. It makes you feel tired and worn out like a boiled vegetable.'

Yet women often feel they have to 'please' their husbands and live up to their sexual demands. To the laughter of the other women, one woman in a focus group discussion said: 'One has to please him, he puts it in, who would pull it out?' Or as Như said,

'If you do not want to but have to please your husband, you get angry, but he insists, he forces you, and afterwards you only feel anger, you do not feel any pleasure at all.'

Talking about the use of withdrawal as a contraceptive method, a woman in a focus group discussion said:

'The wife has to please the husband, she is forced to please her husband, so she is forced. She cannot push him out, it is a very unsafe method. They put it in, you get pregnant, you have to care for the child. It is very difficult for women. Giving birth, hardship every month. Being forced. At night, the children wet their beds. It is very difficult.'

Having to please their husbands may also make it difficult for women to practise safe periods or withdrawal, which could otherwise have been alternatives to the IUD. Moreover, if a man does not want to use condoms, there is not much his wife can do about it. Pleasing one's husband may also mean getting pregnant and having another child against one's will, as happened in Quế's case. Getting involuntarily pregnant seems to be the paradigmatic expression of having to please one's husband, combining the sexual and the social meanings of the term. Women often joke about this, saying 'Pleasing one's husband means getting pregnant' (*Chiều chồng là chửa*).

But the idiom of pleasing one's husband is not only related to sexual relations. In daily social life, pleasing one's husband may also mean fanning him while he eats during the hot summer months, fetching water for him to wash himself when he comes home from work, even though one has also just come home tired oneself; or accepting his choices and decisions in various spheres of life. In household decision-making, husband and wife often share minor decisions on expenditures or the wife makes them alone in her husband's absence or due to his lack of interest. But more important decisions – about larger investments, the marriage of a child, funeral arrangements for parents, etc. – are usually made by men.[1] Hương said,

'In reality the husband still has more power (*quyền*)[2] than the wife. For instance, if husband and wife are planning to do something, even though they discuss it with each other first, the husband still makes the final decision. For instance, if they are planning to build a house at the end of the year, and the wife says that if they build it at the end of the year there is not yet enough money and they should wait until next year. If the husband says no, we can always borrow money, we have to build the house right away, then in the end the wife has to accept her husband's idea even if she still wants to wait until next year. If the husband decides so, they have to do it.'

Also Mỹ often emphasized that 'husbands always have more power than wives', saying that women's feelings of powerlessness tend to affect both their bodies and minds:

'The wife has no power. For instance, if your husband decides something, you are forced to listen to him. [...] In most cases, the wife has to depend on the husband. In such situations [of disagreement], you feel depressed, you don't want to eat, because you feel depressed inside, you think all the time. It is very difficult, very depressing.'

Nhị is one of the unlucky women who have found themselves married to men who are lazy workers and drink or gamble the family's money away:

'Whenever there are conflicts in the family, the husband has the power, no matter what the wife says, he still only scolds her, beats her. If she earns money, he goes and gambles it away. Being a wife, she cannot scold him, cannot beat him. She can only get angry, very angry. It is very depressing. You don't want to work anymore, so the family's finances deteriorate. The more the family finances deteriorates, the worse the relations between husband and wife will be, and this often leads to beatings and fights.'

Pleasing one's husband may also mean accepting his bad moods and violent tempers without complaint. Many women live with aggressive husbands and I was surprised to note the apparent prevalence of domestic violence in everyday life. Women living with violent or very 'hot' husbands would usually explain to me that the best strategy when a husband is rude or violent is silent endurance: if one answers back, things will only get worse. Bình – who often suffers from her husband's beatings – described the violence she endures:

'He insults me, many times a day, but I still have to endure. Women live under slavery. [...] I please him, but he still beats me. Sometimes he beats me every day, sometimes a few times a month. Whenever I come home tired and refuse him, he beats me again, he gets "hot" again. I just have to endure, wherever he tells me to go I have to go. When he beats me I just keep quiet, or leave the house.'

The often harsh living conditions of young rural women have also been described by the Vietnamese exile writer Dương Thu Hương. In *Paradise of the Blind* (1994) she writes,

> Many landscapes have left their mark on me, but one in particular haunted me [...]: a certain vision of duckweed floating on the surface of a pond. An ordinary pond, like the kind at home. A pond lost in some godforsaken village, in a place where the honking of cars and the whistling of trains is something mysterious, exotic. A place where young women bend like slaves at their husband's feet. A place where a man whips his wife with a flail if she dares lend a few baskets of grain or a few bricks to relatives in need. A strip of land somewhere in my country, in the 1980s. (Dương Thu Hương 1994: 130)

Of course, not all husbands are the same. Some are good, gentle, hard-working, and understanding while others are lazy, violent, and rude. Regardless of whether they are married to a good or a difficult husband, however, all married women in Vải Sơn share the experience of being dependent on their husbands and their parents-in-law. This dependency is expressed in an old folk verse I often heard Bình quote when she was pondering why her fate had been to end up with this husband who maltreated her: 'A woman is like a rain drop, no one knows whether it will fall into a well or on a rice field' (*Đàn bà như hạt mưa sa, hạt rơi xuống giếng, hạt ra ngoài đồng*). Women's feelings of anxiety and powerlessness are expressed in many folksongs and sayings. The following folksongs are quoted from Nha-Trang (1973: 201) and Lê Thị Nhâm Tuyêt (in Marr 1981: 248):

> *I am like a piece of peach-coloured silk,*
> *Fluttering in the market, knowing not to whom it will belong.*

> *I am like a well by the road*
> *A clever man will use it to wash his face,*
> *A rude one to wash his feet.*

But regardless of how their husbands behave, all women agree that being married is always better than not having a husband at all. In Mai's words:

'If you don't have a husband, other people do not respect you. They will gossip about you and say that you don't have a husband as other people do. Even if a woman is very talented, if she does not have a husband she will be ignored and disrespected by others.'

The importance – and hardships – of marriage are also expressed in folksongs and sayings such as the following (quoted from Trịnh Minh-hà 1992: 67):

Unstable like a hat without a chin-strap,
Like a boat without a rudder, as she is without husband.

She who is married wears a yoke on her neck,
But she who has no husband is like a bed whose nails have
  come loose.

But women's feelings of dependency and submission extend beyond marital relations as such. In a patrilocal society like this, marrying a man means joining his family. Women living with their husbands' parents therefore often feel very dependent and tied in their relationship to their in-laws. In particular the relationship between daughter- and mother-in-law is a frequent source of tension. Many of the women I knew in Vải Sơn experienced constant conflicts with their mothers-in-law over when to work and when to rest, which tasks to do first and which to do later, what to buy in the market and what not to buy, etc. Hương said:

'Living with your parents[-in-law], they have the power. You have to ask for permission, you do not feel relaxed and free.'

Hương found getting married and moving into the house of her parents-in-law very difficult:

'At home I only had to work a little, but when I came to my husband's house I had to do all kinds of work. At home I could work when I wanted to and rest when I wanted to. In my husband's house I had to work in the fields every day, cutting sugarcane, transplanting rice, harvesting and when I came home I had to cook, sweep and work in the house.'

As we have seen, Hạnh also often found it difficult to live with her in-laws:

'Sometimes they scold you even though you don't deserve it. They do all they can to find something to criticize, even if there is hardly anything to comment on. They will excuse their own daughters, but the daughter-in-law they examine minutely looking for something to criticize.'

Parents-in-law usually expect their daughter-in-law to be respectful and compliant, attentive to their needs and wishes and respectful of their wisdom. This, obviously, creates a great deal of tension in situations where the daughter-in-law feels she is being ordered about by a domineering mother-in-law whose views of the world belong to the past. As Mỹ sharply said,

'Here the daughter-in-law often hates her husband's parents because they have the power. Because they say, we have lost money to buy [a daughter-in-law]. They have bought the daughter-in-law so they have the power.'

But of course, mothers-in-law differ, too. Some are good, understanding, and supportive, and may even take the daughter-in-law's side in marital conflicts. This is the exception rather than the rule, however, since, as women often said about their husbands, 'He is their own child, so they always support him' (cf. Phạm Văn Bích 1997: 97). In marital conflicts, therefore, women often find themselves confronted not only with their husband but with his whole family (*nhà chồng*). In cases where the husband and his family agree that the couple should have another child, social pressure is often put on the woman which is very difficult to withstand.[3] Conflicts between mother-in-law and daughter-in-law are very common themes of Vietnamese folksongs and verses. Stephen O'Harrow writes:

Indeed probably nowhere in the world's folk literature is there a richer mine of sayings than the one found in Viet Nam about mothers-in-law, and specifically regarding the hatred that arises between the husband's mother and the young wife. (O'Harrow 1995: 167)

The following two folksongs are quoted from Nha-Trang (1973: 187, 233):

Where are you going all bundled up neatly, young girl?

I am a young bride having just begun the life of a daughter-in-law.
My mother-in-law is very cruel;
I can no longer stay, I must go home to my parents.

And:

> *Father-in-law is a phoenix feather,*
>
> *Mother-in-law is a painted statue,*
>
> *Daughter-in-law is a basket wherein insults are thrown.*

As in Hạnh's case, tensions are sometimes also strong between a woman and her sisters-in-law. O'Harrow (1995: 167) cites a common saying,

> *Bitter and piquant but still blood kin,*
>
> *Sweet and smooth, and yet strangers;*
>
> *When the husband's younger sister lives with the sister-in-law, You'd better watch out*
> *Or come one day, they'll kill each other.*

When a woman lives with a difficult husband, her greatest comfort is the awareness that not having a husband would be even worse; and to a woman who lives with a harsh mother-in-law, the most important comfort is the awareness that 'mother[-in-law] is old, mother[-in-law] will die' (*mẹ già thì mẹ chết*). When women in Vải Sơn talked about having to comply with husbands or parents-in-law, they often did so with an expression of stoic resignation: these conditions of life are difficult but unchangeable, being dependent and feeling exhausted are simply part of what it means to be a woman. Being a woman means having to endure, just as being a woman means suffering from headaches, dizziness, and weakness. But why is it that women feel they 'always have to depend' on men and their families while also bearing the largest burden of family responsibilities? Let us briefly consider the Confucian ideologies which seem to nourish and support everyday moral standards.

Dominant moral ideologies: the Confucian heritage

In Confucian moral cosmology, social roles and relations are spelled out in the 'five relationships' (*ngũ luân*):

- ruler–subject,
- father–son,
- husband–wife,
- elder brother–younger brother,
- friend–friend.

Along with each of these social relations go specific prescriptions for behaviour detailing how parents and children, husbands and wives, rulers and subjects should behave towards each other.[4] Social order and harmony is maintained when all members of a society take up their proper positions within these five sets of relationships and behave in accordance with the conduct they prescribe. Within the Confucian social matrix, then, the position of an individual is always relationally defined: a person may take up one position towards her mother, another towards her younger sister, another again towards her father's elder sister, etc.[5] In this sense, selfhood is not a core but rather a bundle of social relations which change and shift depending on the constellation of persons involved in particular social interactions.

Most important of the five relationships are the three analogic ruler–subject, parent–child, and husband–wife relations, which are sometimes referred to as the 'three bonds' (Marr 1981). Of particular relevance to the present study are the parent–child and husband–wife relations. According to Confucian doctrine, children should always treat their parents with gratitude, obedience and respect, while parents should be compassionate and understanding towards their children. Children find themselves in immense debt to their parents and owe them endless gratitude (*ơn*) for their lives and whole existence. In everyday life, this debt to parents is expressed in a range of proverbs such as 'When drinking water, remember its source' (*Uống nước nhớ nguồn*) or 'When eating fruit, remember who planted the tree' (*Ăn quả nhớ kẻ trồng cây*). The gratitude which children owe their parents extends into ancestor worship after their death: when parents die, their children are responsible for worshipping and caring for their souls (cf. Chapter three).

The notion of 'filial piety' (*hiếu*) refers to the duty of children to honour and obey their parents, and to be 'without filiality' (*bất hiếu*) is one of the worst social sins imaginable. Respect for one's elders is a core social value; by respecting one's elders and showing awareness of the gratitude one owes them, one also demonstrates a more general recognition of the gratitude owed to those who have 'created the conditions' for one's life and accomplishments. The core of everyday morality lies in the often quoted phrase 'knowing who is above and who is below' (*biết trên biết dưới*), which refers mainly to hierarchies of age. Ideally, younger people should obey and respect their elders, while older people should treat their youngers with compassion and understanding. Or, as people often say, one should 'respect those above and yield to those below' (*trên kình dưới nhường*). The moral obligation of younger people to show respect to those older than themselves was one of Bà Chính's favourite topics of conversation. As she said,

'I call them small shrimp, those people who don't know how to live properly (*ăn ở không đúng mức*).
'What is it to live properly?'
'To live properly is to respect people above, people older than oneself. To people below one has to yield, that is, respecting those above and yielding to those below, then there is harmony.'

In arguments with her son and daughter-in-law, Bà Chính often referred to the respect and gratitude children owe their parents, emphasizing her own self-sacrifices for the sake of her son. She explained,

'If children are spoilt and talk back it shows a lack of gratitude (*ơn*). Who gave them food and education? How did they learn to read and write? Their parents had to save and economize to be able to provide them with food and education, so their gratitude should be as high as the sky. That is why people say: "Your gratitude to your father should be as high as the Thái Sơn mountain. Your love for your mother should be like the water that springs from the source." A heart full of worship for mother and respect for father. Fulfilling this is the "way of children" (*đạo con*). Not fulfilling your duties towards your parents means being a heartless person (*con người bất nhân*) [...] That is why I say to my son, "Who took care of you from you were just a drop of blood? If I had not cared for you, if I had remarried, your life would have been miserable."'

But the generational axis is only one of the social axes upon which everyday moralities are structured. The other fundamental social axis is the axis of gender. In Confucian cosmology, gender difference is naturalized and inscribed into cosmic order through the associations of female/male with *yin/yang*, dark/light, earth/heaven, moon/sun, passivity/activity, etc. Confucian classics such as the *Book of Changes* and the *Book of Rites* emphasize women's subordination to men, stating for instance that 'Great righteousness is shown when man and woman occupy their correct places: the relative positions of Heaven and Earth'; or 'To be a woman meant to submit' (Croll 1995: 13–14).[6] In Vietnam as in China, women's social positions are traditionally defined by the 'three subordinations' (*tam tòng*), which also women in Vải Sơn would sometimes mention to explain their socially inferior position. The three subordinations are comprised in the sentence, 'As a daughter she obeys her father, as a wife she obeys her husband, as a widow she obeys her son' *(Tại gia tòng phụ, xuất giá tòng phu, phu tử tòng tử)*. Or as Bình's husband said: 'The boat follows the steering-wheel, the girl follows her husband' (*Thuyền theo lái, gái theo chồng*).

The proper behaviour of women in different phases of their lives is prescribed in numerous moral sayings.[7] The moral guidelines for female behaviour are generalized as the four virtues (*tứ đức*) of labour (*công*), physical appearance (*dung*), appropriate speech (*ngôn*), and proper behaviour (*hạnh*) (Marr 1981: 192). Or, as a classical moral axiom puts it: 'Every young woman must fully practise and scrupulously conform to four virtues: be skilful in her work, modest in her behaviour, soft-spoken in her language, faultless in her principles' (Trịnh Minh-hà 1992: 83). Another morality verse translated by Trịnh Minh-hà (1992: 82) goes: 'The seven deadly sins of a girl: one, sitting everywhere; two, leaning on pillars; three, eating sweet potatoes; four, eating treats; five, fleeing work; six, lying down too often; seven, wolfing her nephew's sweets.'

A prime moral female virtue is chastity (*trinh*): women are expected to stay virgins before marriage and remain absolutely faithful to their husband even after his death. In pre-colonial Vietnam, the moral prescriptions for female behaviour were expressed in morality texts of which one of the more famous is Nguyễn Trãi's *Family Training Ode* from the 15th century. Nguyễn Trãi describes in detail the proper moral behaviour of women, particularly towards parents-in-law, husbands, and children. Two examples, quoted from Nha-Trang (1973: 23, 36):

Owing a debt to your parents for their supporting you with
    great hardship,
You ought constantly to serve them with devotion and respect.

In gratitude to your parents your prime consideration is filial
    piety.

Serve them the best you can.

Do not wait for others to do for your parents the service that you could do yourself,

Lest you be the subject of ridicule in your community and of laughter in the times to come.

Or to cite another example:

Even though you sleep intimately on the same bed and use the same cover with him,
You must treat your husband as if he were your king or your father.

In short, within a Confucian moral framework it is only natural that women have to submit to their husbands and in-laws. Being a woman means being responsible for children and housework, and being faithful, hardworking, gentle, and compliant.

In some ways, such moral guidelines now clearly belong to a time past. Women in Vải Sơn often emphasize that there is much more equality today than in the feudal era, where bride price was paid and women were 'bought' as daughters-in-law to work as 'slaves' while still only being marginal members of the household. The daughter-in-law had to eat alone in the kitchen while other family members had their meals together in the house. Mỹ explained,

'People in the old days said, one has spent money to buy a daughter-in-law, so one drives it through all the way. Scary, isn't it?'

The expression 'driving it through all the way' (*đâm cho thủng*) has several meanings; besides its sexual connotations it also refers to the husband's family putting the daughter-in-law to work and getting all it can out of her labour power, and to her husband's making her pregnant. In short, getting something for one's money. Mơ, who is today a mother-in-law herself, says:

'Now, when the daughter-in-law lives with her parents-in-law, they have understood the new times so they are [socially] aware. It is easier to be a daughter-in-law today, not like before. In reality, now the daughter-in-law also has equality, or she has rights to discuss freely, freedom to choose. Of course there are still people with difficult tempers, but most are informed by now.'

Also Bà Chính noted – with regret – the changes that have taken place in intergenerational relations over the past years:

'My life used to be miserable, living with my mother-in-law, she was over 80 before she died. I never dared to be impertinent, and now I have to live with this mad daughter-in-law. In the old days she would have been beaten for behaving like this. She would have had to ask decently for permission to go anywhere, even just to go outside the house she would have had to ask for permission. But today heaven and earth have changed places, people have no conscience anymore and I have to bear the consequences of that.'

Comparing women's lives today with 'the feudal era', Lý says:

'Before women also had to worry like now, but there was less equality than today. Before women also had to do the hard work, but when there was a banquet or something, women had to sit in the kitchen, they could not come up and sit with the men. Today there is more equality.'

In socialist Vietnam, the emancipation of women has been considered a key element in the creation of a new society. Not least during the wars, women's equal capacity to participate in social and political life was strongly emphasized, and women were encouraged to take an active part in formal employment and politics. Along with the efforts to attain greater equality between women and men, however, state discourses have also perpetuated traditional gender ideologies (cf. White 1987; Barry 1996). In the anti-colonial movement, women's liberation was an element in the struggle for national liberation as much as an end in itself (Hue-Tam Ho Tai 1992; Barry 1996). Since the 1945 revolution, women's traditional virtues as family caretakers have been considered crucially important for maintaining the social and political stability of the nation.

The new Law of Marriage and the Family which was passed in 1960 strongly emphasized women's role as mothers (cf. Vũ Mạnh Lợi 1991), and in a 1974 major policy address on women, Lê Duẩn, the first secretary of the Communist Party, stressed the unique domestic and child-rearing role of women within socialist society (Hy Văn Lương 1989: 752). A slogan that was often used in the 1960s and 1970s to characterize the ideal socialist woman – 'good at national tasks, good at household tasks' (*giỏi việc nước*

đảm việc nhà) – established close and analogic links between
women's responsibilities for family and nation. The 'Five Good'
and the 'Three Responsibilities' campaigns in the 1960s and 1970s
stressed women's traditional responsibilities for the welfare of
their children and families, with the addition of responsibilities for
production and warfare (cf. Werner 1997).[8]

The slogans used in socialist Vietnam to emphasize women's
positive characteristics are strikingly similar to the traditional
Confucian female virtues of chastity, hard work, and proper
behaviour. A 1977 Women's Union leaflet on the mobilization of
women says:

> The Party still appreciates the beautiful and good characteristics of
> women: women are hard working, industrious, creative, cour-
> ageous, loyal, and altruistic. The Party considers women to be an
> important revolutionary resource. (Hội Liên Hiệp Phụ Nữ 1977: 5)

However, whereas the Confucian virtues primarily concerned
women in their family roles as daughters, mothers and wives, the
socialist virtues position woman in a double role as responsible for
both family and nation. Since official discourse establishes direct
links between family welfare and national welfare (cf. Chapter 3),
women's role as family caretakers also has important political
implications, as Lê Thị Nhâm Tuyết writes:

> Family education is no longer a separate undertaking but has
> actually become a component part of the whole process of building
> new kinds of people in the countryside (1991: 216).

In socialist Vietnam, woman thus becomes a 'triangulating
category' that mediates between family and state (cf. Barlow
1994a), and traditional feminine virtues are celebrated and ascribed
new political significance. As one of the women in Trịnh Minh-hà's
film 'Surname Việt Given Name Nam' sharply says,

> Socialist Vietnam venerates the mothers and the wives. The
> woman does not exist, she is only a labourer. The liberation of
> women is understood here as a double exploitation. [...] [As for
> the Women's Union], the Mother-in-Laws' Union, they have
> made of us heroic workers, virtuous women. We are good
> mothers, good wives, heroic fighters ... Ghost women, with no
> humanity! [...] The woman is alone, she lives alone, she raises her
> children alone. She gives birth alone. It's a sea of solitude! The
> revolution has allowed the woman to have access to the working

world. She works to deprive herself better, to eat less. She has to get used to poverty. (Trịnh Minh-hà 1992: 60–62)

But it is not only in official discourse that women's traditional roles and virtues are maintained. As we shall now see, Confucian ideals also persist in the local moral worlds of family and community.

Local moral worlds: the persistence of Confucian ideals

Both gender stereotypes considering men as superior to women and traditional moral ideals of women's modesty, chastity and hard work are alive and well in Vải Sơn today. Men are often said to be of superior intelligence, as expressed in sayings like 'No matter how superficial a man is, his intelligence is a deep well; no matter how profound a woman is, her intelligence is shallow like a beteltray' (*Đàn ông nông nổi giếng khơi, đàn bà sâu sắc như cơi đựng trầu*); or 'No matter how wise a woman is, she is still a woman; no matter how foolish a man is, he is still a man' (*Khôn ngoan cũng thể đàn bà, dẫu rằng vụng dại vẫn là đàn ông*) (cf. Phạm Văn Bích 1997: 236). When talking about women and men, or girls and boys, people often emphasize the 'gentle and mild' character of women in contrast to men's more 'hot and uncontrollable' tempers. Men are tigers, while women are willows. Nhị put it thus:

'Men are not very patient. If their wife scolds them too much, they go out with other women. That's their character. I don't know if it's inherited or what, but no men have patience.'

These stereotypes seem to be both descriptive and prescriptive: this is the way women and men are, and it is the way they should be. Gentle men are called 'hermaphrodites' (*ái nam ái nữ*) and women like Quế who loudly and openly speak their minds are said to be 'like men'. Phạm Văn Bích (1997: 233) notes:

We need to keep in mind that in a society where sharply distinguished gender roles prevail, strong aggressive women are often viewed as highly undesirable. 'Those women do not want husbands, they want to be husbands' – that is the way they are seen and evaluated.

In everyday moral evaluations, women who are mild, gentle, quiet and reserved are often held up as moral examples and considered as people who 'know how to behave'. Liên said to me one day, when I had had a dispute with a leading member of the commune People's Committee:

'Few women are hot-tempered, very few, most are gentle, patient, tough. So you should learn something. Don't be hot again, you are much too hot-tempered, that's what everyone says.'

And her uncle, Hùng, joined in:

'If women are hot-tempered, they can't preserve the happiness of their families. That's why people say, "If the husband is hot, the wife should step back" (*Chồng nóng thì vợ phải lùi*). If both husband and wife are hot, it will cause much pain.'

The ability to control one's temper is valued in both women and men. A favourite saying goes: 'Enduring one thing will give you nine good things' (*Một điều nhịn thì chin điều lành*). Still, it is clearly more acceptable for men than for women to be 'hot' and for boys than for girls to be 'wild'.[9] Women who speak up or talk back to their husbands or parents-in-law are said to be 'terrible/ frightful' (*ghê gớm*), and women who openly defy their husbands or parents-in-law are 'excessive' (*quá đáng*) and 'lack morality' (*không có đạo đức*). People generally agree with Liên's uncle that when men are hot, women should keep cool. An often used saying goes: 'When the husband is angry, the wife should refrain from talking back to him; Rice will never be burned if one lowers the heat when it boils.' (*Chồng giận thì vợ bớt lời; Cơm sôi nhỏ lửa một đời không khê*).

The above moral standards are dominant in the sense that they are widely agreed upon, among women as well as men. In fact, my impression was that women are often the strictest judges of each other's behaviour. Among women, gossiping about other women is often lively and not always particularly friendly. When Kiều openly defied her mother-in-law, she was strongly condemned as 'impertinent' *(láo)* and 'insolent' (*hỗn*), 'rotten' (*hư*), and 'without filiality' *(bất hiếu)* by everyone in her village. One of the neighbours noted:

'The wife should behave as a wife, the mother-in-law as a mother-in-law. It is no good if the wife thinks she can act as a mother-in-law.'

Another woman, who quarrelled loudly with her husband at night, was gossiped about as someone who did not know how to keep her family happy. Mai remarked that if a woman complains about her husband's laziness and her own large work burden, she is likely to be ridiculed by others:

'Some women, even though they are not happy, they still silently work, they work ceaselessly. But there are also some people who say to their husbands, "I work hard like this but you don't help at all." But if you talk to your husband using excessive (*quá đáng*) language, other people will laugh. They will say that this is women's work and they will call you a woman who competes with her husband (*ganh chồng*). [...] A woman who speaks up like that is said to be petty (*lèm nhèm*).'

In contrast, a woman who was being beaten by her husband but did not complain about it was admired and praised by her neighbours and said to be an exceptionally 'good woman'. In general 'good women' are women who accept the hardships of their lives with endurance and resilience and without complaint. As we shall see in Chapter 7, the ability to 'endure hardship' (*chịu khó*) is a central element in the stereotype of Vietnamese women; women, apparently, have a special talent for endurance.

Another important feature of local moral evaluations is that women are usually held responsible for maintaining the harmony and happiness of their families. Regardless of the character or cause of domestic conflicts, the wife is generally held responsible (cf. Vũ Mạnh Lợi 1991: 161). As Mỹ remarked:

'The husband may go with other women, go gambling, or beat his wife and children. He scolds his wife and children, he eats but he doesn't know how to work, but the wife has to endure. If she speaks up, other people will laugh at her, but they don't laugh at her husband, they laugh at her.'

If a couple is divorced, the blame is often attached to the woman. Phạm Văn Bích (1997: 198) quotes a folksong: 'Nobody has the heart to cut the ears of a nice cat; a woman dropped out by her husband has no words of her pride'. This implies that if the wife had been good, she would not have been expelled from the family. While a divorced man 'has the same value as before' and can easily remarry, no man will marry a divorced woman.[10] Mỹ concluded:

If husband and wife have separated, people will think that the wife is no good. Nobody will marry her. It is different with the husband, he can marry another woman. [...] People put the blame on the woman, they say she is so useless that her husband has left her. People don't know how to criticize men at all. So, it is very difficult and unfair in this respect.

Mai had this to say:

'Even if a woman is very badly treated by her husband, even if he is very unfaithful to her, if she asks for a divorce people will say she is no good. She will be condemned even if he didn't treat her well. People will say, "Who does she think she is, leaving her husband like that?" They will scold her like that ... "What kinds of talent and greatness does she think she possesses?" they will say. It is difficult, isn't it? Therefore, whatever the cost, one has to endure.'

In relation to sexuality, the moral evaluations of women and men also differ markedly. Women who are unfaithful to their husbands are strongly condemned as 'lustful' (*đa dâm*), 'wanton' (*đĩ tính*), 'flirtatious' (*lăng nhăng*), 'lascivious' (*đĩ*), 'rotten' (*hư*), 'ill behaved' (*lăng loàn*), etc. Even though men should ideally be faithful to their wives as well, it is widely recognized that men like 'something different' (*của lạ*) and that men – in contrast to women – cannot control their sexual urges when they are away from their wives (cf. Franklin 1993). While women are said to be able to live without it easily, sex is usually considered to be a necessity for men. An old saying goes: 'A man has five wives and seven concubines; a good woman only has one husband' (*Đàn ông năm thê bảy thiếp; gái chính chuyên chỉ có một chồng*). Mai said:

'A man can marry and have children with two or three women, and no one laughs at him. But if a woman who has husband and children has an affair with someone else, she will be condemned, absolutely condemned. Such things are forbidden for women. Women should be "faithful and skilful" (*trung hậu đảm đang*).'

Even though polygamy is considered feudal, it is still commonly accepted under some circumstances. If a woman fails to produce a son, most people find it quite reasonable if her husband tries his luck with someone else (cf. Phạm Văn Bích 1997). Therefore, when Mai had given birth to her fifth daughter in a row, she said to her husband that he could take a second wife if he wanted to. But, as she proudly said, he refused, which shows what a good husband he is.

If her husband dies, a woman should ideally stay faithful to him and not 'take another step' and remarry. Referring to the folk verse 'There is never enough water to fill the river; there are never enough women to please a young man' (Trịnh Minh-hà 1992: 67) Bình said:

> 'Men say, the more water in the river the better, the more wives for a man the better. No matter how many women a man has, it is still not enough. But a virtuous woman only has one husband, she is not allowed to "take another step" (*đi một bước nữa*).'

If a widow does not yet have a son, it is usually considered acceptable if she 'takes another step' in order to secure her future. If she does have a son, however, people will expect her to 'stay behind to take care of her children', since if she remarries, the children will be given to her husband's family to bring up (cf. Nha-Trang 1973). Bà Chính explained that while she 'stayed behind' to take care of Chính and her husband's old parents when her husband died, another village woman in a similar situation re-married. The consequence of this was that the son of her first marriage became a confused, underweight, maltreated child who is a petty criminal today.

Confucian moral ideals and hierarchies of age and gender are also visibly expressed in everyday bodily manners and attitudes. In family celebrations men always take up the central or 'high' positions on chairs or beds, whereas women tend to sit in the marginal and 'low' positions on the floor and at the edges of the room. During his stay in a northern Vietnamese village, the anthropologist Hy Văn Lương noted,

> I was struck by the visible presence of junior adult males at the main table of the family in front of the ancestral altar, almost universally at the expense of their senior female relatives (mothers, paternal aunts), who either sat at the side of the room or ate separately on the floor in the side room reserved for women. [...] The central room of the house is still primarily the preserve of male family members. (Hy Văn Lương 1989: 752)

Yet, as also noted by Phạm Văn Bích (1997), when reaching the status of mother-in-law and grandmother, women often move from the marginal into the central positions during family gatherings.

Women's marginal position in the household is also evident from their close association with the kitchen. Today, as centuries ago, the kitchen is regarded as a female sphere, and in Red River delta communes like Vải Sơn, the kitchen is always built separately from the main house and is made of poorer materials than the house itself. Phạm Văn Bích observes (1997: 103) that the kitchen is often placed lower than the main house, thus associating women with the dark, the low and the wet. Even in wealthy families like Bà Chính's, where the main house is large and bright, with tiled floors and brick walls, the kitchen will usually be small, dark, and smoke-filled, with a dirt floor and mud walls. Women's positioning in the kitchen therefore seems to symbolize and confirm their position within their husbands' households: marginal and inferior.

Also in community meetings women take up markedly different social positions than men. As described in Chapter 2, the first time I was in a meeting in Vải Sơn I was surprised to note the male dominance: the only woman present was Lan, who was busy serving tea most of the time and very modest and almost servile in her attitudes and manners. But these manners, I soon learnt, earn her considerable respect among both women and men for being a morally upright woman who knows how to behave properly.

These observations would seem to confirm Bourdieu's (1977) ideas of correspondences between social and cognitive structures: by always being assigned marginal positions and by learning to behave modestly and self-effacingly, women also learn that they are inferior to males and elders. As Bourdieu says, 'bodies take metaphors seriously' (1990: 71). Through everyday bodily practices which 'naturalize' women's inferiority to men, social structures and hierarchies come to be taken for granted and reproduced.

In daily life in Vải Sơn, then, women seem to be actively participating in the continuation of the moral mechanisms which work to their own disadvantage. Moral evaluations and condemnations of women are often carried out by other women: even women who themselves feel tyrannized by an unfeeling mother-in-law may sharply condemn the woman who openly refuses to comply with her parents-in-law. Similarly, even women who themselves suffer from living with lazy and unpredictable husbands may condemn the woman who shouts at her husband and 'does not know how to preserve the harmony of her family'. Most women are actively striving to be morally good themselves – who doesn't want to be a good mother, a wife who is respected by everyone for her good manners and high moralities, or a cherished daughter-in-law?

In short, this seems to provide an excellent example of *symbolic violence* (Bourdieu 1977: 191). Symbolic violence is violence that is exercised with the complicity of its victims; it is exercised when people internalize dominant perceptions of the world into their own self-understandings and practices, even though these perceptions contribute to the maintenance of their own socially inferior positions. In Bourdieu's view, since given gender arrangements are usually taken for granted not only by the dominating men but also by the dominated women, gender domination is the 'paradigmatic form of symbolic violence' (1992: 170).

Considered from another perspective, however, this is not symbolic violence. The social world in which people in Vải Sơn live is clearly not taken for granted or uncritically accepted by its members. Rather, daily social practices are strenuously debated, and dominant moral orders are often contested by women. While women do tend to accept their everyday burdens of work and worries, they do not think that there is anything natural about given social arrangements – on the contrary, most of the women I knew were very conscious of the fact that social and family burdens could be differently distributed. While Quế accepts that her husband has other degrees of freedom than she has, she is also sharply critical of women's subordination to men. While Hạnh silently yields to her mother-in-law most days, she clearly does not feel that this is the way family life should be.

As we shall see in Chapter 7, it is usually out of pragmatic concerns rather than moral principles that women accept their submission to husbands or elders. Despite the fact that women often actively embrace and employ dominant moral ideologies, many women in Vải Sơn also simultaneously express and live by very different moral notions. Co-existing with dominant moral ideologies are alternative moral visions that emphasize equality rather than hierarchy and individual freedom rather than social duty. Also in these visions, harmony and social balance are striven for, but harmonious social relations are differently conceptualized than in the Confucian moral world.[11]

The existence of alternative moral visions in everyday life

The above account may have given an impression of women as endlessly submissive, patient and enduring. It does not take a long stay in Vải Sơn or anywhere else in Vietnam, however, to realize that women are not always placid and enduring. Stephen O'Harrow (1995) even finds a widespread discontent among Vietnamese men precisely because women do not live up to Confucian moral ideals and men therefore often do not take up their 'rightful' social places. We shall now have a closer look at this 'other side of the coin', at women's indignation over having to submit to males and elders, at their expectations of equality and personal rights, at feelings of being unjustly dominated, and at refusals to comply with dominant moral standards.

First of all, many women feel it is unfair that they alone have to bear the major burdens of childcare and domestic work, in addition to their exhausting work in the fields. Hảo summed up the difference between women and men in the division of daily work chores in this way:

> 'Men come home from work, and they only rest, eat, drink. They don't have to do anything, they watch television, or talk and go visiting. Women have to sweep the yard, feed the pig and chicken, cook the rice, wash clothes, so we are already tired. [...] We work from early morning, from five o'clock in the morning till ten in the evening, we never rest, when one job is done there is another.'

While many women feel that 'the wife is only secondary', the awareness of being the person who keeps family and everyday life together also seems to be a very important source of self-confidence. Women know that no one can take care of the children or of the household finances as well as they can. One saying goes: 'Living with mother you will eat rice with fish, living with father you will eat only vegetables' (*ở với mẹ thì ăn cơm với cá, ở với cha thì ăn là rau*). In popular culture, the wife is often said to be 'general of the interior' (*nội tướng*), and many sayings and proverbs point to the wife's power in the conduct of everyday affairs. The following sayings are quoted from Tai Van Ta (1997): 'The bell of the husband is second to the gong of the wife' (*Lệnh ông không bằng cồng bà*); 'The wife is first, Heaven second' (*Nhất vợ nhì trời*); and 'The man washes the dishes and sweeps the floor;

when his wife summons he hurriedly answers: "Here I am, Madam"' (*Làm trai rửa bát quét nhà; Vợ gọi thì dạ, bẩm bà tôi đây*).

When asked who the head of the household is, women in Vải Sơn sometimes replied, '*I* am the head of the household. My husband is never here', or '*I* am household head, my husband doesn't know how to do anything.' One woman said:

'Do you know why it is men who go to other places to work? A man would never know how to do a woman's work at home.'

Mai's comment was:

'Women are often clever and skilful, they can carry everything, they take everything upon themselves. The husband sometimes only exploits.'

Women often feel that their lack of power is especially unfair when considering the fact that in most respects they are at least as capable as their husbands. In Hương's words:

'My brain is as good as my husband's, but I am only allowed to speak, I don't have any power. My husband will listen to me if he agrees with me, if he disagrees he won't listen.'

The feelings of worth and self-confidence which women also possess are expressed in folksongs like the following two (quoted from Nha-Trang 1973: 214):

A great mob of men is worth only three coins,
One can afford to dispose of them in a cage and abandon them
*   to the ants.*

A single woman is worth three hundred coins.
For her to sit, one should spread a flowered mat.

And:

We honourable sisters are like a mass of boulders in Heaven,
How could you youngsters as small as mice think of disturbing
*   us?*

Cursed be you bunch of mice,
When this rock falls down, your bones will be crushed.

Since few women in Vải Sơn see anything natural in gender hierarchies or in women's supposed inferiority to men, women's obligations to please their husbands are far from taken for granted or passively accepted. In daily life women employ a range of different strategies to circumvent the authority of husbands and in-laws. Not surprisingly, women most often insist on their rights to decide for themselves when it comes to the issues that are closest to the body, i.e. fertility and sexuality. The title of this book is paraphrased from an expression commonly used by women in Vải Sơn: 'The one who has the body has the worries' (*Ai có thân thì phải lo*). Women reason that since it is women who get pregnant and give birth, this is a sphere of life in which women should be in authority. As Hương said:

If you go to the hospital in secret, who will know? If your husband wants more children and you don't, he can't force you. You decide for yourself first. The husband's opinion is only a small part. For women, if you want a child, you have a child. You don't have to say anything to your husband until your stomach is big, and then what can he do? In this respect, women can decide everything for themselves, it is all up to you.

As some women have found out, the 'duty' to please one's husband sexually can be evaded by hiding under the bed and the 'duty' to bear him the additional child he wants can be evaded by having an IUD secretly inserted.[12] Even though most of the women I knew would make decisions related to childbearing and contraceptive use in consultation with their husbands, a few said that these issues were absolutely up to themselves to decide upon. For instance, Nhị said:

'I didn't want any more children, so I decided to have an IUD. I would go whether my husband agreed or not, I didn't ask for his opinion. Because you have to think of your life and your children first. The husband is one thing, the wife is another, but first of all it is difficult for oneself. Having many children is difficult for oneself, later it is difficult for the children so I decided not to have many children.'

Similarly, Hảo said:

'Women are often afraid of giving birth, it is more difficult for women than for men to have many children. Of course it is more difficult for women than for men, so this is something women decide about. Maybe the man wants another child but he can't decide. That's the only thing, in other respects women can't decide.'

Another kind of concern for one's own body was expressed by Như when she told me how she had taught her husband not to beat her anymore:

> I educated him so that he does not beat me anymore. The authorities could not educate him, the Women's Union could not educate him, so I said I have to solve this. If you beat me I beat you back, I said to him. I told him I took care of his children, I even took care of him, so if he kept beating me I would leave him. After some time I had to beat him, he ran away and from that day he was afraid. [...] Nobody could educate him, so I had to oppose him, I had to solve it myself, I had to defend my own body.

Như's success in 'educating' her husband – something many other women do not succeed in – has to do with two important factors: first, she is physically stronger than her husband, and second, she had the support of his family.

In short, even though women may feel they have to comply with and please their husbands, they also feel that their bodies are their own and that (at least in some situations) it is their right to insist on their own wishes and do what they can to realize them. While Nhị would often silently put up with her husband in everyday minor disagreements and quarrels, she insisted on her right to decide for herself when it came to childbearing and fertility control. Quế did give birth to the child her husband's family wanted, but she also felt that it was unfair that she had to do so. Whereas Hảo accepted bearing all worries about the children and their health by herself, she also commented sharply on this unequal division of everyday burdens.

The idea and expectation of equality (*bình đẳng*) seems to tie together many of women's feelings of everyday injustice and harm, and equality was a recurrent theme in women's talk about their lives. The concept of equality was most often used to describe a contrast to current conditions of life, as when Bình talked about what a marriage should ideally be like:

> 'Husband and wife have married each other, they should be absolutely loving and compassionate towards each other, understand each other, that is equality. If the wife wants to do something, and she is weak, her husband should come and help her. That is what everyone calls equality. If the wife works hard

and no one bothers to help her, she will soon be a dead corpse. It is very difficult for Vietnamese women.'

When I asked Bình what she meant by 'equality', she said, 'Equality is when women are like men, men are like women, that is equality.' As commonly perceived by women, the ideal marriage is a union of two people who treat each other with compassion and respect and discuss (*bàn bạc*) things with each other. Mai put it like this:

'In my opinion, if you want to buy something, for instance an electric fan, then husband and wife should discuss, no one should decide alone. If husband and wife agree, they can buy it, if they do not agree, they can't. They have to act in unity (*thống nhất*).'

An often quoted saying expresses the importance of marital harmony and agreement: 'If wife and husband agree, together they can empty an ocean' (*Thuận vợ, thuận chồng bể đông tát cạn*). Women often stress complementarity as the ideal in husband–wife relations: the wife does the housework, the husband does the work outside the house, but the important point is that they share work tasks and responsibilities equally. As Hôm said,

'If both husband and wife worry about the finances it is easier. If the wife worries but the husband does not worry, it is miserable for the woman.'

A similar gender complementarity exists in the traditional division of labour in rural Vietnam where 'the husband plows, the wife transplants, the buffalo harrows' (*chồng cày, vợ cấy, con trâu đi bừa*). Notions of marital complementarity and equality are also expressed in folksongs like the following (quoted from Nha-Trang 1973: 170):

In the way of husband and wife,
Depending on each other is essential to guard against the
    adversities of life

Dreams of equality and mutuality, however, often collide with everyday realities, where neither husband–wife nor daughter-in-law–mother-in-law relations are equal. Mỹ told me:

'When you get married you are very dependent. For instance, if the husband's parents sit by the table drinking tea, you may not be allowed to sit with them. If you sit down to have tea with them, they will scold you, because you have to sit on the bed, separately. [...] It is very difficult for women in Vietnam, very difficult. Life is never relaxed, there is no equality. It is very feudal.'

Many women talk in a discourse of rights (*quyền*) and emphasize women's lack of rights within their families. For instance, Mai said:

'In the countryside women do not have the same rights as men.'
'What do you mean?'
'To take the most simple example: in the countryside the husband can say *tao* ["I"; used by a superior when talking to an inferior} to his wife, but the wife can never use *tao* when talking to her husband. Second, when attending a banquet the men sit above while the women sit on the ground. Third, in the family the husband does the important work, but the women have to do the insignificant things, tending animals, cooking. Men do not have to do trivial work. [...] In some cases there is equality, husband and wife working together, but in many cases there is not.'

Mỹ commented on the discrepancies between women's rights 'in society' and within their families:

'The wife only has rights in the outside world. In the family, if someone comes to borrow something, she has the right to lend it to them, but that is the only right she has. In the family, the husband has the rights, in society both husband and wife have rights. So the wife's rights are only outside in society, in the family she does not have any rights.'

While women in Vải Sơn often mentioned the contrast between women's formal rights in society and their lack of the same within their families, one of the women in Trịnh Minh-hà's film also pointed to women's lack of rights in public and political life:

'Our bosses are often men, women assist them ... This is what equality amounts to! We fight very tightly for our rights, but the men always succeed to win over. [...] In meetings, women never take the floor to claim or demand, they speak but only in a feminine spirit... [I mean] a spirit eager to please. To please their boss. They can't say simply "we think" or "we want"... It's very difficult to speak freely when one does not have the power.' (Trịnh Minh-hà 1992: 73)

Besides equality, also freedom (*tự do*) and independence (*độc lập*) are important values in everyday life, and are often contrasted to constraint and dependence. Bình would sometimes compare her own life to mine, saying how lucky I was to be 'like a bird that can fly'. Women most often use concepts of freedom and independence when they describe visions of a life where one does not have to depend upon one's husband and his family but is able to decide for oneself how to live. Mơ, who is now 48 years old, has had a difficult life as second wife to her husband. After being very badly treated by her husband and his elder wife and after giving birth to a child weighing only 1,800 grams, Mơ decided to return to her parents' house to give birth to her second child. The way she described this clearly demonstrates both the values of freedom of independence which are important to her and the ways in which social stresses affect her body and her thoughts:

'My thoughts were relaxed, I was not under anyone's power anymore, what I earned was my own, I did not have to think anymore, I could do what I wanted to, I became much more healthy, and this child weighed 4 kilos when I gave birth to him, I gave birth to him in my parents' home. I did not have to depend on anyone anymore. I worked when I wanted to work, ate when I was hungry, rested when I was tired. My thoughts were relaxed, so I gave birth to a 4-kilo baby.'

Whereas some women feel happy and content living with their husbands' parents, many other women prefer living separately (*ở riêng*), i.e. as a nuclear family, since living separately gives one a degree of freedom and independence which women who live with their husband's parents rarely achieve. Hương ruminated:

'In the house of your parents-in-law you are very dependent. You are awakened early in the morning to go to work. You cannot relax when you sleep; you cannot relax when you eat. If the children are naughty, you are not forgiven. Living separately, feelings between husband and wife are also more relaxed. There is more freedom, much more freedom. [...] Living separately, you can eat what you want to. If you have the money you can buy what you want to, whereas over there, if your parents-in-law buy something you just have to accept it.... Once you lives separately, what you want to eat or spend, what you want to do is in your own hands, you are not dependent.

In short, whereas social duties, obedience, hierarchy and respect form the core of Confucian moral ideologies which to some extent are shared by women in Vải Sơn, most of the women I knew would also simultaneously stress moral ideals of equality and independence and emphasize their rights to decide for themselves. In Confucian ideology selfhood is relative and relational, while women in Vải Sơn also clearly see themselves as fairly autonomous and independent beings.

So how are we to account for these moral complexities? Where do the 'alternative moralities' with their strong dreams about equality and independence come from? Possibly, ideas of equality are a universal feature of human society, as James Scott (1977) has suggested. But ideas of equality and independence are also rooted in Vietnamese history, and particularly in its last 50 years. In the following section I shall briefly mention some of the points in Vietnamese history where alternatives to Confucian moral ideologies have been articulated, in order to throw some more light on the sources of the moral ambiguities which women in Vải Sơn experience.

Sources of alternative moral visions

Several researchers have noted the co-existence of 'patrilineal' and 'bilateral' kinship structures in Vietnam (e.g., Whitmore 1984; Hy Văn Lương 1989; O'Harrow 1995). Along with double kinship structures there also seems to be a double social ethics, encompassing ideas of gender equality or complementarity as well as ideas of gender hierarchy (Nha-Trang 1973; O'Harrow 1995). It is often assumed that the existence of such 'double' structures of kinship and morality is due to a merging of earlier 'indigenous' Southeast Asian and later 'imported' Chinese models of kinship, and that pre-Chinese Vietnamese culture was much less gender-hierarchized than Confucian culture (e.g., Taylor 1983; Whitmore 1984).

The existence of numerous female gods and national heroines such as Hai Bà Trưng and Triệu Thị Trinh is often taken as an indicator of the earlier stronger position of women in society (e.g., Mai Thị Thu and Lê Thị Nhâm Tuyết 1978). Triệu Thị Trinh – a young peasant woman who led 30 battles against the Chinese and who was said to be 9 feet tall, with 3-metre-long breasts which she threw over her shoulders as she rode on an elephant – is attributed with the following declaration (Trịnh Minh-hà 1992: 63):

'I only want to ride the wind and walk the waves, slay the big whales of the Eastern sea, clean up frontiers, and save the people from drowning. Why should I imitate others, bow my head, stoop over and be slave to a man?'

Another remarkable character in Vietnamese history is the 18th-century female poet Hồ Xuân Hương, who is still immensely popular today. Hồ Xuân Hương's poetry is unusual for its sharp criticism of the dominant male order and its very open allusions to sex and eroticism; it defies all Confucian notions of proper womanly manners and behaviour and challenges social and sexual norms. Alexander Woodside (1971: 49) writes that the existence of such an 'improbable figure' as Hồ Xuân Hương indicates that along with the Confucian traits in Vietnamese culture, other and less orthodox outlooks existed. As also pointed out by Nha-Trang (1973), Confucian social ethics and actual norms and practices apparently did not always converge in 18th- and 19th-century Vietnam. One of Hồ Xuân Hương's most famous poems laments the fate of the woman who is married as a 'second wife' (quoted in Nha-Trang 1973: 230):

One wife is covered with a quilted blanket,

One wife is left alone in the cold,

Cursed be the life of sharing one husband!

Very infrequently you may possess your husband,

Not even twice a month.

You work hard for some glutinous rice

Only to receive it cold and tasteless;

You are resigned to renting yourself for services,

Only to obtain no wage.

Had I known how miserable this lot is

I would rather have been content with

Remaining unmarried.

Another famous poem by Hồ Xuân Hương is the following (quoted in Nha-Trang 1973: 226):

Being pregnant without having been married is remarkable,

(While) there is nothing unusual about being pregnant by a husband.

Also songs, sayings, and proverbs from the period prior to the arrival of the French often protest against the demands imposed on women by Confucian morality and formulate alternative views of gender relations. The two following folksongs (quoted in Nha-Trang 1973: 228, 233) exemplify this 'critical discourse':

Chastity is truly worth a thousand gold coins:

Counting from my ex-husband to you,

I have had five men.

As for lovers that I have had in secret,

Hundreds of them have gathered on my belly

as they would have in the market.

And:

Because of my affection for my husband I ought

To cry over the death of my mother-in-law;

I and the old woman were definitely not relatives.

Vocabularies for the articulation of notions of equality and individual freedom were systematically introduced in Vietnam with the arrival of the French in the late 19th-century. The French brought with them concepts such as freedom, equality, equal rights (*bình quyền*), and democracy (*dân chủ*). With the new and powerful ideas of a Vietnamese nation which grew out of colonialism (Marr 1981; Tønnesson 1991), new ideas of the relationship between individual and society also emerged. With the establishment of a modern nation, notions of the individual as a person in his/her own right, independent of family and kin relations, came into being. In the modern nation, the individual is no longer totally immersed in kin relations, but has a legal and official status as a singular and autonomous being.[13]

At the centre of the lively cultural and political debates in colonial Vietnam was the opposition between the 'old' and the 'new' world order (Jamieson 1993). The 'old' order with its social hierarchies, its submission of the individual to the social, and its strict social and sexual morality was criticized in public debates and counterposed to the 'new' concepts of individual freedom and equality. In the 1920s and 1930s gender inequality and women's rights were the topics of lively debate, and as David Marr writes,

'Women became conscious of themselves as a social group with particular interests, grievances, and demands' (Marr 1981: 191). In literature, the products of the 'self-reliance literary group' (Tự Lực Văn Đoàn) clearly expressed a search for new moral frameworks.[14] The new literature of the 1930s was very different from both Confucian and socialist moral didacticism; placing individual experience and personal emotional turmoil at the centre of literary expression (cf. Lockhardt 1992). Tự Lực Văn Đoàn writers were fascinated by the new ideas of personal freedom and individual rights, and their writings celebrated free love and personal happiness while criticizing the strict family structures which constrain individual freedom and creativity. They would often depict modern, Westernized young women demanding equality in relation to both men and mothers-in-law. For instance, Loan, the main character in the novel *Đoàn Tuyệt* by Nhất Linh, refuses the traditional role of a daughter-in-law, having only to obey, work and give birth. She complains that her husband's family does not respect her right to be a person (*quyền làm người*) and insist that everyone in the family is a person with equal rights, no one a lesser person than the others (Filimonova 1992).

Also state and party discourses have been important vehicles for the critique of 'feudal' family structures and gender relations, depicting the patriarchal family as a remnant of pre-revolutionary society (cf. Barry 1996). Since before the 1945 revolution, women's liberation has been an important theme on the socialist agenda, and the 1946 Constitution made gender equality an institutional right. The 1960 Marriage and Family Law abolished concubinage, polygamy and forced marriages and emphasized women's equal rights with men. In the socialist era, women's liberation and national liberation have been perceived as closely related issues – as Hồ Chí Minh said, 'If women are not liberated, society is not free.'[15] Terms such as liberation (*giải phóng*), equal rights, equality and self-determination (*tự chủ*) have been used both in relation to women and to national liberation and independence (Marr 1981), and talk about women's situation has often been used as a metaphorical language for speaking of the national situation (cf. Barry 1996). As we have seen, state discourses have in some respects contributed to the perpetuation of traditional gender stereotypes; but state messages on women's liberation and equality also seem to have provided women with a vocabulary for the expression of sentiments which might other-wise have been more difficult to articulate. For instance Moʼ said:

'In the time of the French, parents still had a feudal attitude. In the family the daughter-in-law only had to work and give birth, she had no rights to discuss. She only knew how to walk round and round in the kitchen, she did not know anything. [...] But the Party's policies have taught people that women also have rights to equality like men and that in the family women also have rights to discuss. [...] Since the time of the French, society and culture have developed day by day.'

It seems as if state slogans on freedom, independence, and equality have contributed to the creation of a new awareness and an expectation that women should have social rights equal to those of men or elders. It is probably not least against the background of such expectations that one of the women in Trịnh Minh-hà's film says,

'You have to be careful when you look at our society. There is the form and there is the content. Truth is not always found in what is visible ... Our reality is inhabited by silent tears and sobs ... Women's liberation? You are still joking, aren't you?' (Trịnh Minh-hà 1992: 73)

In addition to the expectations created or nourished by socialist rhetoric, today's increasing contact with the world outside Vietnam through media, tourism, and foreign investments also bring alternat-ive notions of morality and family relations (cf. Pelzer 1993). The Mexican television soap *Maria*, depicting 'loose' sexual moralities, was avidly watched while I was in Vải Sơn, and in general foreign products and television programmes are extremely popular. Women would often explicitly compare their own lives to what they assumed were the social realities of the West, as when Lý said,

'In Denmark, if you don't want this person you can marry another, that's normal. In Vietnam you can't: if you have married someone you have to endure whether you are happy or not.'

Summing up: the articulation of moral notions in daily life

As we have seen from the analysis of local moral worlds, two different sets of everyday moral ideologies can be analytically distinguished: a dominant moral ideology based on Confucian doctrine, and an alternative moral ideology emphasizing individual rights, self-determination, and equality. Coexisting with the idea that women are 'lower' – secondary to men – is another set of moral notions that emphasizes the equal personal rights and freedoms of all human beings. In daily lives these two sets of ideas often merge: in both their practices and verbal expressions, all the women I knew in Vải Sơn would sometimes emphasize the moral ideals of female endurance and self-sacrifice and at other times emphasize their rights to self-determination and equality.

The important difference between the alternative moral notions and Confucian ideologies is their mode of articulation in everyday life. Whereas Confucian moral notions are vociferously expressed and very frequently employed in daily moral evaluations of the attitudes and behaviour of others (cf. Madsen 1984), alternative moral visions are much less openly articulated. I heard women express ideas about freedom and self-determination most often either during one-to-one conversations or when small groups of like-minded women were together, sharing with each other the hardships of their lives. But in the conduct of normal everyday life, few women talk openly about the stresses and worries of their lives or are overly critical of dominant moral ideologies. As I shall discuss in the following chapter, most women strive to keep family conflicts within the family, and many women would rather comply with their husbands or mothers-in-law than create scenes and quarrels. They silently keep their feelings of anger and indignation to themselves. Women sometimes explicitly voiced their feelings of being unable to talk. This is what Hạnh said:

> 'As a daughter-in-law you have to accept, because you do not dare speak. If you speak, people will say that you are answering your parents-in-law back. They have more power, they can speak. Answering back means you do not listen to your parents-in-law. But if you do listen they will make you work hard, and over-working yourself also makes you angry. That's the way it is.'

And Liên said:

> 'If I speak up, I am afraid that people will laugh so I don't dare say anything. If I speak, I am afraid my household will break up, so I don't dare speak. I am afraid of getting a bad reputation. I am afraid people will know that something is the matter between my

parents-in-law and me. If I speak I am afraid it will become a big affair, so I am forced to keep silent. I only know in my heart.'

In short, Confucian moralities are dominant in Vải Sơn in the sense that they are socially legitimate and generally accepted within the local moral worlds of family and community, while the alternative moral notions are much less accepted socially. As we have seen, women who 'talk back' to their parents-in-law are strongly condemned for being impertinent and lacking filial respect, and women who demand their rights vis-à-vis their husbands tend to be ridiculed for 'envying' their husbands and for not knowing how to preserve the harmony and happiness of their families. Much less openly articulated than the dominant moral ideology, the alternative version of everyday morality can be compared to what James Scott has termed 'hidden transcripts': the 'discourse – gestures, speech, practices – which is excluded from the public transcript by the ideological limits within which domination is cast' (Scott 1990: 28). Hidden transcripts contain those perceptions of reality which go against the dominant world-view and as such represent resistance to dominant social orders. Yet, as we have seen, women often simultaneously embrace and resist dominant moral notions, living with a double and equally valid set of moral ideals.

Women's experiences of overwork and submission seem to be rendered more stressful by the fact that many women are conscious of the contingency of dominant moralities and articulate about their visions of a different and more equal social order. Experiences of physical weakness and imbalance often seem to be related to social situations where women feel worn out, angry, and upset, but still have to 'grit their teeth' and endure. The physical and emotional experiences associated with women's diseases of blood and nerves – feelings of sadness (*buồn*), heaviness (*nặng*), weakness (*yếu*), fatigue (*mệt mỏi*), 'tightness/choking' (*ức, tức*), anger/tension (*tức bực, tức*), loss of appetite and loss of desire to live and work – often seem to be related to situations where different moral notions are in conflict and where women feel that they have to comply with social hierarchies despite their dreams and ideals of personal rights and equality. Hạnh very clearly expressed the associations between social and bodily feelings of distress when she said:

'If you are very angry and cannot speak to anyone, you feel too tight, choked inside, uncomfortable, and automatically you get tired, tense, and then you become ill and weak, tired of life.'

Mỹ consented:

'I have to endure like this, so I feel depressed and tired inside, my stomach feels really hungry, but I still cannot swallow anything. [...] I haven't done anything wrong, but my husband still scolds me, so I feel self-pity but I have to endure. I do not dare open my mouth and cannot speak to anyone, so I feel self-pity. In other countries husband and wife are equal, it is not like in Vietnam. In Vietnam one has to endure like this, so life is very miserable for women in Vietnam.'

In brief, then, pain and discomfort can be seen as the lived bodily experience of larger socio-cultural and historical tensions. Women's everyday experiences of social inequality often collide with their dreams and expectations of equality, and it seems to be not least the bodily refractions of such collisions that are at issue when women feel weak, exhausted and dizzy.

The question that remains is: Why does it make sense for women to 'bear the hardship' and silently endure rather than openly defy the social and moral orders which they know are not preordained and which bring them both social and physical pain?

Notes

1. Several other studies of family life in Vietnam have noted that women tend to be responsible for day-to-day economic affairs, while more important decisions are often taken by men (e.g., Đặng Nguyễn Anh 1989; Vũ Mạnh Lợi 1991; Khuất Thu Hồng 1991; Phạm Văn Bích 1997).

2. In Vietnamese, the term means both power and rights. I shall translate it as either/or, depending on the context.

3. In the survey we did in Vải Sơn, 23 per cent (46) of women said they had not wanted the last child they had, and of these more than one-fourth (12 women) said they had been pressured by their husbands or other family members to have another child.

4. See Jamieson (1993) for a more detailed account of such Confucian moral prescriptions in the context of Vietnam.

5. In everyday life, this is reflected in the use of pronouns and person-referring forms which shift depending on the speaker's social position vis-à-vis the persons he/she addresses or refers to (cf. Hy Văn Lương 1990).

6. In Vietnamese, the most common word for woman is *phụ nữ*; the term *phụ* meaning secondary, minor, subordinate.

7. As pointed out by Barlow (1994a, 1994b), in classical Confucianism the category 'woman' is not simply a binary and oppositional category to that of 'man'. Since identities are defined also by age and generation, there are many different kinds of (kins)women rather than one singular category of essential womanhood. In Imperial China, Barlow argues, gender was not primarily defined by the body and physiology but by different social positions in networks of kin (see also Ebrey 1990).

8. As presented in the Women's Museum in Hanoi, the 'Five Good' campaign (*phụ nữ 5 tốt*) in 1961–65 aimed at 'good solidarity and production; good recognition of the policies of the Government; good knowledge of politics, culture, technology; good management of family and children; good participation in economic management'. The 'Three Responsibilities' campaign (1965–75) encouraged 'responsibility for production and work; responsibility for the family; responsibility for national defence' (cf. Mai Thị Tu and Lê Thị Nhâm Tuyết 1978).

9. A sociological study conducted by Vũ Mạnh Lợi in the Red River delta in 1985 notes that parents tend to pay attention mainly to the 'outward orientations' of sons, i.e., to their opportunities for social promotion, whereas for daughters, the 'inside-family orientations' are emphasized, i.e. preparations for the role of a 'good housewife and gentle family female member'. While sons are expected to be 'good in education', daughters are expected to be 'good in behaviour' (Vũ Mạnh Lợi 1991: 153).

10. The difficulties women encounter if they wish to remarry are probably exacerbated by the current demographic imbalance between women and men in Vietnam where there is a shortage of men of marriageable ages (Allen 1990, Goodkind 1994b).

11. There is a parallel in these observations to the work of James Scott (1976, 1977) on peasant politics and rebellion in Southeast Asian history. Juxtaposing the dominant culture of the elite with the 'alternative moral universe' of peasants, Scott notes that dominant moral orders are rarely uncritically accepted by the dominated; 'peasants are hardly in the thrall of a naturally ordained social order' (1976: 239). However, whereas Scott tends to see the moral universes of peasants and elites as fairly distinct, separable, and internally homogeneous, the argument I want to pursue is that 'dominant' and 'alternative' moral notions co-exist and merge in daily lives and experiences.

12. In some respects, however, it is difficult to circumvent male authority. It is not easy, for instance, to put a condom on a man who does not want it, and it may be difficult to keep one's IUD a secret. One woman said: 'One cannot have an IUD in secret forever. Eventually he will find out, or he may marry another woman if he really wants the child.'

13. For a more detailed description of this process, see Marr (1981: 93–99).

14. For a detailed discussion of the Tư Lực Văn Đoàn and the moral-political debates in the 1920s and 1930s, see Jamieson (1993).

15. Also in nationalist writings womanhood and nation are closely linked. The revolutionary nationalist Phan Bội Châu urged young women who were asked 'Do you have a husband yet?' to reply, 'Yes, his surname is Viet and his given name Nam' (Marr 1981: 210).

CHAPTER 7

The Expression of Distress

It is late afternoon and Bình and I are sitting on the edge of one of the simple wooden beds in her house, having spent a long afternoon together tending sugarcane and weeding between cabbages. The whole family, Bình, Quảng and their two sons, live in just one dark and sparsely furnished room with dirt floor.

This afternoon the boys are out playing and Quảng is in Hanoi. Bình and I are both tired, our arms are swollen and itching from touching the sugarcane leaves and our eyes feel strained from too much sun. As she talks, Bình shuffles her feet in her cheap, worn-out plastic slippers. On our way back from the fields I had asked her what the saying '*cá chuối đắm đuối vì con*' (the *chuối* fish sacrifices itself for its children) meant. Even though I had often heard women quoting this saying to describe their own lives, I still had not fully understood it, and failed to see the link between the lives of fish and women. While we were walking, Bình evaded my question, but she now returns to it.

'You see,' she says, 'the *chuối* fish is a special kind of fish which plays dead and gives itself up to the fisherman in order to save its children. Women do the same, they sacrifice themselves for their children.'

After these words she starts to cry, changing from the smiling and cheerful Bình I have known for months into a different woman. With my question about the *chuối* fish, I have obviously touched on a sensitive issue. I put my hand on Bình's arm and ask her why she is crying. She then tells me a long story about her life; how she grew up in a family with many children, always beaten by a violent elder brother; how her parents arranged her marriage with Quảng, how she soon realized that he was even more violent than her brother had been. Once he beat her so badly that she had to be hospitalized for weeks. Now she lives in constant fear of his temper which tends to erupt as soon as he gets something to drink.

'Wouldn't it be better to get a divorce?' I ask naively.

'No, no, no,' Bình says, 'this is what I tried to explain to you: I can't get a divorce because I feel pity for the children. I could leave him, but then the children wouldn't have a mother. That's why people say, the *chuối* fish gives itself up for its children. I can't first give birth to children and then leave them, I feel pity for them.'

'What about his family,' I ask, 'couldn't you get help from them?'

'They can't do anything,' Bình says. 'In the beginning they tried to talk to him and to explain things to him, but now they have given up. There is nothing to be done. But I have learnt to manage. Most days I try to stay happy and treat him mildly and gently, and if he gets violent I leave the house until he has cooled down. You know, it is always better to smile and present a happy face.'

৵৻৻

While the previous chapters have illustrated how the feelings of weakness, exhaustion and various kinds of aches and pains which women associate with the IUD are closely related to everyday experiences of social distress, the question to be considered in this chapter is how women express and communicate their feelings of distress. How are negative feelings – of anger, bitterness, resentment, disappointment – handled in daily life? We shall have a closer look at the status and meanings of emotion in daily life in Vải Sơn, with particular attention to social implications of the expression of negative feelings. In other words, whereas the previous chapters considered physical symptoms mainly as experience, the focus of the present chapter is on symptoms as communication and performance. When talking about their bodies and health, people do not just describe symptoms and states of the body – they also do something with the things they say. In this sense, physical symptoms represent not only 'passive' suffering, but also 'active' performance and communicative practice (cf. Good 1977; Lock 1993b), and 'local moral worlds' are not only sites for the construction of illness experience, but also fora for the expression of distress (cf. Kleinman 1992). To start with, we shall briefly consider some of the studies of emotion and somatization in China which are relevant for a discussion of the Vietnamese situation.

Emotion and somatization in Chinese cultures

Several recent works in anthropology have pointed out that human feelings are not just biological or natural facts (e.g., Rosaldo 1984;

Kleinman and Good 1985; Lutz 1988; Lutz and Abu-Lughod 1990). Human emotions are fundamentally social, they are deeply integrated with everyday structures of value, meaning, and social interaction. A person's feelings come into being through social situations which carry specific meanings for that person, and they are expressed in ways that are culturally organized and recognized. Yet while recognizing the fact that emotions are socio-cultural constructs, it is important to keep in mind that as lived and felt, emotions are also urgent existential and bodily experiences and crucial to people's whole experience of themselves as persons in a social world. Charles Taylor (1985: 48) writes that emotions are 'affective modes of awareness of situation'; it is through our emotional attachment to specific values and goals that experiences become meaningful and that human lives gain direction and force. People orient themselves and act in social worlds that matter to them through being 'moved' in some ways. Since emotions are both deeply personal and existential and closely related to social situations and expectations, they can be seen as 'intersections' between selves and social worlds. In the words of Lyon and Barbalet (1994: 48), emotion is 'the experience of embodied sociality'.

A range of anthropological works have been concerned with emotional expression among the Chinese (e.g., Hsu 1971; Kleinman 1982; 1986; Potter 1988; Sun 1991). These studies converge on a number of points: they claim that the Chinese avoid talking about personal feelings; are much less introspective and self-scrutinizing than Westerners; pay more attention to social relations than to inner feelings; and use somatic rather than psychological idioms for the expression of distress. Of particular relevance to the present study is Arthur Kleinman's (1986) work on somatization and mental disease in China. Kleinman argues that negative feelings are socially unacceptable among the Chinese and that a very limited vocabulary exists in which to express disturbed feelings and distressful experiences. These norms, he suggests, 'overdetermine a somatic idiom for the expression of personal and social distress among Chinese' (Kleinman 1986: 55).

Several studies have summed up the difference between Chinese and Westerners in the *sociocentric/egocentric* dichotomy: while Chinese people are said to think of themselves primarily in terms of their relations to others, Westerners are assumed to perceive themselves in terms of autonomy and independence.[1] There is an interesting disagreement, however, between Arthur Kleinman (1980, 1986) and Sulamith Heinz Potter (1988) concerning the social significance of human feelings in Chinese cultures. While Kleinman claims that emotions are socially dangerous and therefore often repressed by the Chinese, Potter asserts that emotions are socially irrelevant in China. According to Kleinman, the Chinese learn from very early childhood that feelings should not be openly expressed, since emotional expression may create social imbalance. It is better silently to endure negative feelings than to express emotions which may bring social relations out of balance. In Potter's view, however, feelings are far from socially dangerous in China; they are simply socially insignificant. In the West, she says, social relationships are maintained by individual feeling and personal enactment, while in China, social structure is perceived as having an existence independent of individuals. Nothing is gained or lost socially by expressing one's feelings. Emotions are mere idiosyncrasies and are never the legitimizing rationale for any socially significant action. Social order requires affirmation only in behaviour and not in feelings; what counts socially is what people do and how they behave towards each other rather than how they feel inside.

Against the background of these studies and their differing views of emotion in Chinese social life, let us now return to women in Vải Sơn. In what follows we shall take a closer look at local understandings of selves, emotions and social relations. Are negative feelings socially dangerous or are they socially irrelevant?

The importance of emotion in everyday life

During my first months in Vải Sơn I found the absence of any emotion discourse striking. People very rarely talked about their personal feelings – they would tell long and detailed stories about what happened during a particular social event, who said and did what, but rarely a word about how they themselves felt about it. I had great trouble formulating the questions I wanted to ask, such as 'How did you feel about that?', since this was not a normal phrase in people's conversations. There hardly even seemed to be a generalized word for 'feelings'. Terms for specific feelings – anger, happiness, sadness, etc., do exist, but the closest one can come to a generalized term for 'feeling' is probably *tình cảm*. But the term *tình cảm* has slightly different connotations than 'feelings'; it usually refers either to feelings between people or to the capacity to feel for others rather than to an individual's inner emotional life.[2]

But two things soon dawned on me. One was that my distinction between feelings and thoughts was not always shared by people in Vải Sơn. In everyday life, 'feelings' and 'thoughts' are often not considered as distinct phenomena but as basically the same. When people talk to each other about a sad or disturbing event, they will usually ask 'Do you think (*nghĩ*) a lot?', rather than 'How do you feel?' When women talk about 'having to think all the time' and about thoughts exhausting their bodies, this also seems to be a way of communicating emotional distress. For instance, Như described the hardships of her marriage in the following way:

> 'I work very hard, from early morning, during lunch hours, I harvest a little paddy, my husband sells it and goes gambling, but I can't say anything [...] He sells everything, there is nothing to eat in the house. It is very difficult so I always think inside (*trong người mình lúc nào cũng bị suy nghĩ*).'

In other words, disturbed feelings often seem to be communicated in idioms of stressful thoughts. The term *tư tưởng*, which the dictionary translates as thoughts, also comprises feelings: when a woman says that her 'thoughts are not relaxed' (*tư tưởng không thoải mái*) or that she always has to 'think inside' (*nghĩ trong người*), she also says that she feels emotionally out of balance.

The other thing that dawned on me was the peculiarity of my own expectation that people should scrutinize and verbalize their inner selves and feelings. Feelings can very well be communicated and experiences can be shared without much verbal self-scrutiny or introspection. When one woman tells another about her seriously ill child, she does not need to describe in detail her inner feelings for the other woman to be able to understand and empathize with her. When Bình told me about her husband's quick temper I could comprehend her very well even though she did not explicitly label her feelings about the situation. When a woman says that yesterday her father-in-law was 'hot' again, other women know precisely what she means. In other words, among people in Vải Sơn, empathy and understanding are often relied upon in the communication of emotion rather than self-scrutinizing verbal idioms.[3]

In everyday life in Vải Sơn, the ability to share the feelings of others is a highly valued human quality. To most people, sharing the joys and sorrows of each other's lives seems to be what social life is all about. While I was in Vải Sơn, several of the older people I knew became ill and seemed to be approaching death. When this happened, as in the case of Bà Hôm, the house would be crowded with people who came to support the dying person and her family. For days, people would come and go, asking about the old person's health, drinking tea, holding hands, and sharing the difficulties of death with the family. Similarly, when someone died, the house of the deceased would be crowded with people from near and far who came to 'share the sorrow' (*chia buồn*) with the family. Illness is another occasion for compassion and sharing of feelings: when Lan's daughter was ill with German measles, the neighbours brought her so much fruit that she could hardly eat it. If someone is sad and depressed, as happened to a woman in Liên's hamlet who lost her husband at an early age, her neighbours will come to cheer her up and encourage her to return to life among others. People often emphasize the importance of sharing with others the problems and worries of one's life. One woman said:

'If one is angry about something it is better to talk to someone, confide all one's misery in someone, then it gets lighter.'

Lan declared:

'If you lie at home thinking it only makes you more sad. You have to go out and be with other people, and the sadness will decrease, you forget about it. If you are alone you think too much. If you can talk to others you think less.'

In cases of serious economic crisis there is nearly always help and consolation to be found among family and neighbours: Khanh's house burned down to the ground, but people in the hamlet assisted her family with money and loans to build a new one.

Also happy situations are shared, as when a child is born and people come to congratulate, bringing presents of meat and sugar; or when a young couple gets married and family, friends, and neighbours come to celebrate and congratulate. All of these are situations of *tình cảm*, a sharing of feelings and experiences. When people in Vải Sơn compared the Vietnamese to other people, they would often emphasize *tình cảm* as the essence of what it means to be

Vietnamese: the distinct and special feature of social life in Vietnam is the importance and centrality of *tình cảm*. Maybe Vietnam is poor, people would say, but at least it is rich in *tình cảm*. Also capacities for compassion/pity/love (*thương*) and sympathy/understanding (*thông cảm*) are often emphasized in daily life, where feeling compassion for or sympathizing with someone is always a good and acceptable reason for acting in certain ways. For instance, Bình often emphasized that she stayed in her marriage out of compassion/pity for her children: if she left, she would have to leave her children behind with her husband's family. Như said that she stayed with her husband because she felt pity for him since his health was very weak.

In other words, Potter's observations of the social irrelevance of emotion do not seem to fit with my experiences in Vải Sơn.[4] Even though personal feelings are rarely verbalized, there is a lively exchange of feelings in everyday life, and the ability to understand and share the feelings and experiences of others is highly valued. There may be some truth in Potter's statements about the lack of importance of emotion in social life, though, in the sense that people would rarely use their *own* feelings as the rationale for a given social action. This would clearly be considered selfish and morally inappropriate. But since the most valid and legitimate reason to act in certain ways is acting out of concern or feeling for *others*, it does not seem correct to claim that human feelings are socially irrelevant.

Kleinman and Kleinman (1991) also note that the idea of emotions being mere idiosyncrasies in China seems to render Chinese people less than human. If the Chinese do not act in certain ways because things and other people matter to them, why would they act or live at all? But how about Kleinman's remarks about the social illegitimacy of negative feelings then? Can anger, sadness, and frustration be legitimately expressed or should such feelings be controlled and kept inside? In this context it is important to bear in mind the close relations that exist between emotion and morality. Negative feelings – of pain, stress, discomfort – are moral sentiments in the sense that they often serve as indirect comments on the situation in which one lives. In Kleinman's words:

To feel is to value or disvalue, to connect with or stand apart, to act in resistance to or to be paralyzed by our embodied social circumstances and our socially projected bodily experiences (1986: 177).

Expressing distress is a way of taking up a moral position in one's social world and commenting on the social relations and arrangements within which one lives. The expression of negative feelings also often affects one's social surroundings, making other people feel embarrassed, angry, or sad. Since emotional expression also affects others, people in Vải Sơn draw close links between the ability to show concern for others and capacities for emotional self-control.

Hearts and minds: the virtues of endurance

While the sharing of emotion is strongly emphasized in daily life, it is equally important to express feelings which may bring disturbance to other people's lives with some care, and in ways that show a concern for others and a sense of situation. Ideally, one should be aware of the effects of negative sentiments on others and able to control one's feelings in situations where they may harm or hurt others. Therefore, when Lan's husband finally came home after a year in the South she did not tell him about her worries about her health. Instead, she concluded: 'He has enough to worry about already'. Similarly, Hạnh did her best every day not to reveal her anger towards her mother-in-law in order to protect her family from instability and emotional turbulence. Everyone knows that both negative and positive feelings are contagious, they spread and affect other people. Outbursts of anger or resentment are therefore negative social acts in that they may easily hurt others and undermine feelings of harmony and solidarity. People in Vải Sơn therefore generally think that the expression of negative and resentful sentiments should ideally be avoided if one wants to maintain good social relations and a peaceful, happy, and harmonious family and community.

This is not to say that less perfect and self-controlled behaviour is always and necessarily condemned or looked down upon. It is widely recognized that getting angry and losing one's temper is only human, and everyday lives are full of open conflicts, quarrels and biting comments. It is generally acknowledged and accepted that people whose tempers are 'hot' or 'difficult' cannot control themselves, but 'must' erupt and give their opinions straight out. In such cases, the crucial moral issue is not so much the outbreak of hot temper in itself as whether the 'hot' persons later manage to 'think again' and admit their possible mistakes. But even though quarrels and hot tempers are everyday and normal phenomena, mild and gentle social behaviour is clearly more positively valued than 'rude' and violent actions and expressions. It is socially more valued to have a 'happy/joyful temper' (*vui tính*) than a difficult or hot temper (*khó tính/nóng tính*).

The expectations that people have of their own and each other's capacities for emotional self-control are closely related to the ideas that 'hearts' are inseparable from 'minds', i.e. that feelings and intellectual capacities are not distinct but closely intertwined. We have already seen that in everyday life in Våi Sơn, thoughts and feelings are regarded as two sides of the same phenomenon rather than as distinct and separable. Also Léopold Cadière (1957) has described the 'inability' of the Vietnamese to distinguish clearly between cognition and emotion. Cadière notes the 'imprecision' and 'confusion' characterizing the Vietnamese language, which seems to confound the intellectual and the emotional, lacking the ability to separate will from passion, intention from emotion, etc. When asked where thoughts/feelings are located, most people in Våi Sơn would say that they are located in the brain (cf. Eisenbruch 1983). Usually, if a woman was talking about her feelings of sadness and depression and I asked her 'where' she felt sad, she would point to her head. The metaphors used in daily life, however, often place thoughts and feelings in the stomach, as when people say 'one thinks in one's stomach' (*nghĩ trong bụng*) or talk about feeling 'jealous in one's stomach' (*ghen trong bụng*) (cf. Cadière 1957). Everyday notions of the inseparability of cognition and emotion seem to have a counterpart in classical Confucian teachings, where the concept of *xin* (heart-mind) is a core term (Tu 1985: 24). *Xin* is both a cognitive and an affective faculty, it is consciousness as well as conscience. It is the sensibilities of the *xin* which enable people to take others into account, to understand and feel with other people, and to form their own conduct so that it resonates with the lives and feelings of others (see also Elvin 1985, 1989).

While there is very little explicit talk about emotions in everyday life in Våi Sơn, there is a strikingly well-developed and highly elaborate moral discourse on mental and intellectual capacities (cf. Cadière 1957). This everyday emphasis on intellectual capacities seems partly to reflect the Vietnamese emphasis on scholarship and learning – as Alexander Woodside notes: 'Vietnam is and always has been one of the most intensely literary civilizations on the face of the planet' (Woodside 1976: 2). But it probably also needs to be seen in the light of the close intertwinings of the emotional and the mental – or of hearts and minds – in everyday understandings.

In daily life in Vải Sơn, talking about brains seems to be another way of talking about hearts, and intellectual capacities are also social/emotional capacities. Hearts and minds often merge in the concern for others: 'having a heart' (*có tâm*) or 'having a conscience' (*có lương tâm*) means being able to feel with other people, knowing how to show concern and compassion for others. But since a precondition for treating other people well is that one is conscious and aware of the social situation and of the needs and concerns of others, the concept of 'having a heart' is closely related to the notion of consciousness/awareness (*ý thức*). To be conscious means knowing how to take others into account and how to respond properly to others in a given situation, while lacking consciousness means behaving selfishly, without thought for others. For instance, one shows consciousness by helping someone who needs it without first being asked; or by leaving the room if one senses that the two people in it would like to be alone. In other words, even though 'consciousness' clearly refers to mental capacities, these capacities are usually also social and applied, referring to a concrete awareness of situation rather than to abstract insights which can be dissociated from the social world.

In this sense, mental and emotional capacities merge, and feelings are not something 'natural' and 'uncontrollable' which can be counterposed to rational thought. Rather, thought-feelings are one inner field of force which it is up to each person to govern and form appropriately. Everyone has both good and bad forces in them, and it is up to each individual to cultivate the good and check the bad in him/herself. In daily life, much emphasis is placed on the ability to discipline oneself (*kiên trì*), to 'train' and educate oneself (*rèn luyện mình*), and to learn from one's previous experience (*rút kinh nghiệm*) in order to become a better and more

socially conscious person.[5] Tough/enduring/disciplined people
(*người gan*) are generally admired for their self-control and good
manners and for the social awareness with which these personal
qualities are associated. In this respect, Lan is a role model who
always controls her outward expressions and behaves in proper
and appropriate ways. Ideally, one should always be aware of the
effects of one's behaviour on others and think before one speaks
or acts. As Lý said,

> 'About people who don't think, but speak in a disorderly
> manner – babble – people will say that they are not mature, too
> excited, just like children who don't understand anything. [...]
> You have to think before you speak.'

As already mentioned, another personal quality that is highly
valued in daily life is the ability to 'endure hardship' (*chịu khó*) or
to 'put up with' (*chịu đựng*) the trials and tribulations of life. By
silently enduring hardship one avoids disturbing other people's
peace of mind or making others feel sad. Enduring hardship is an
act of selflessness and compassion and as such a demonstration of
some of the most highly valued social virtues. In addition to
shouldering social burdens, by gritting one's teeth and enduring
hardship, one also shows 'toughness', steadfastness, and determination, which are all highly valued human qualities.

The concept of *ethos* has been used by Gregory Bateson to
describe core emotional emphases in a culture. He defines ethos as
'the expression of a culturally standardized system of organization
of the instincts and emotions of the individuals' (Bateson 1958:
118). Schieffelin (1985: 108) notes that ethos is thus both a characterization of a culture's style of expressing emotions and a
standard according to which people's behaviour is evaluated. It
seems to make a lot of sense to talk about an *ethos of endurance* in
Vietnamese social and cultural life.

In the light of this ethos it is not surprising that the 'alternative
moralities' described in the previous chapter are often not openly
articulated by women. Within the ethos of endurance, to bear
hardship quietly and to sacrifice oneself for the welfare of others
are highly valued social acts. By contrast, to insist on one's rights
to freedom and self-determination comes out as very selfish and
socially illegitimate behaviour. Therefore, even though women
may often feel that their 'rights to be a person' are not respected,

loudly insisting on such rights would only demonstrate self-absorption and a serious lack of community feeling and concern for other people. In contrast, by quietly enduring hardship, women place themselves within the category of morally virtuous and respectable people.

We have to bear in mind that even though the above moral expectations are generally valid and all members of society are somehow expected to live up to them, they also exist in a hierarchical moral world where social risks and resources are unequally distributed and where gender expectations differ markedly. While the risks of social and physical stresses seem to be higher for women than for men, women are also usually expected to be yielding, mild, and gentle, and keep cool when men are hot. Even though everyone is expected to be attentive to the needs and wishes of others, the moral expectations of self-sacrifice and endurance seem to be directed more towards women than towards men. Women themselves often see direct links between their 'low' social position and their need to endure and sacrifice themselves for others. As Hương said: 'Women have to endure everything. Women are always lower than men, so they still have to endure and comply.' Or as Mai said:

'Women know how to put up [with situations], to endure. Men often flare up so it is mostly women who endure. The majority endure because they don't have any power. Men don't know how to do anything but they still show off about being the husband. They have the power to be husbands.'

Obviously, though, women do not always endure and comply. As mentioned, fights and quarrels are everyday occurrences, 'as normal as eating rice', as one woman said. Women often 'erupt' in loud and angry voices, talking back to mothers-in-law or trying to 'educate' their husbands. But in daily life most women clearly also strive very hard to endure and to 'hold back' (*nhịn*) their feelings of anger, bitterness, or resentment and to stay calm and happy, at least on the surface. In other words, endurance does not come naturally, but requires a lot of effort in everyday life. Hạnh commented:

'Sometimes I say to myself I should endure, yield, let my parents-in-law say what they want. But spontaneously when they say something, spontaneously I erupt and talk back.'

Hương explained how she usually tries all she can to 'hold back' and not talk back to her husband when he comes home and is in a bad mood, scolding her because the children are too noisy and the food is not ready. Talking about her relations to her family-in-law, Liên said:

> 'Even if it is very difficult, you still don't complain. Often you are so angry that your blood boils, but still you don't say anything.'

In short, despite anger and self-pity, many women still strive to keep turbulent feelings inside and stay as calm and collected as they can, preferring to grit their teeth (*cắn răng*) and silently endure rather than openly expressing anger or discontent. If asked directly about what makes it meaningful for them to conceal their feelings of anger or sadness in spite of the difficulties they experience in doing so, women would usually reply that 'tears do not solve anything' or 'crying does not make it better at all'. Reacting with open anger or sadness usually does not solve any problems or take one much further in life. The best thing one can do, most women would agree, is to forget about troubling incidents and get on with life. Lan put it in this way:

> 'If you think too much and feel sad, you have to try to forget about it. You have to force yourself: in general women have to try to force themselves to forget, not to think too much. You have to forget so that you can get on with living.'

When women comply and endure, however, a range of other concerns seem to be at issue as well.

The creation of selves in local moral worlds

By expressing emotions one both negotiates relations to others and creates oneself as a certain kind of person. In the words of Edward Schieffelin (1985: 106), 'Particular feelings, or at least their expression, are normatively part of the constitution of, and the participation of, the self in a social situation.' By acting and behaving in certain ways, through particular expressions of face and body, one turns oneself into a certain kind of person – a sullen and obstinate daughter-in-law, a strong and hard-working wife, a loving mother, etc. Since being a certain person means being someone who acts on the basis of certain moral values and convictions, identity-making is closely tied in with morality. Charles Taylor writes:

> To know who I am is a species of knowing where I stand. My identity is defined by the commitments and identifications which provide the frame or horizon within which I am capable of taking a stand. (Taylor 1987: 27)

By demonstrating specific moral commitments, one also creates oneself as a certain kind of person.

As we have seen, the social relations where women often experience distress – in relations to husbands and mothers-in-law – are also relations that are highly circumscribed by explicit moral ideologies. Whether Confucian moral ideals are adhered to or not, they do tend to set the agenda for everyday moral reasonings and evaluations. In daily social life, being a morally good person means knowing one's place socially and knowing how to treat other people in appropriate ways. A good person is one who is modest and selfless, sensitive to the needs and concerns of other people, and aware of her/his place vis-à-vis others. By behaving in morally proper ways one maintains personal as well as family honour (*danh dự*) and keeps up a good reputation (*tiếng*). In contrast, behaving in morally inappropriate ways exposes one to the gossip, ridicule, and contempt of the local community. Being the object of such gossip often makes people feel embarrassed and ashamed (*xấu hổ*). Feelings of shame are most often produced in situations where moral shortcomings of oneself or one's family are openly exposed to the outside world. Since feelings of shame and embarrassment are obviously very unpleasant, most people do their best to avoid placing themselves in situations where others may 'assess' (*đánh giá*) and talk negatively about them. So what does this mean, then, for women's handling of difficult and stressful family relations? Let us first consider women's relations to their mothers-in-law.

When I had problems tackling Bà Chính's decisions about what was good or not good for me, what I should do and not do, whom I should be with and not be with, I often went to Lan, Liên or other women for advice. Their advice was nearly always the same: in situations of conflict or disagreement with a parent or parent-in-law, one should always speak and behave respectfully towards the older person. Then later, when tempers have cooled, one can try to explain one's ideas and opinions. Saying one's opinion openly and directly at the time of conflict would show insolence (*hỗn*) and a lack of filiality (*bât hiêu*). One woman explained:

'As a daughter-in-law you often have to comply and endure (*nhún nhịn*). Even if you know you are right, you still have to keep quiet and endure. Talking back means lacking filiality. If you talk back, people will say you are ungrateful (*bạc*).'

Being patient and polite, however, is often easier said than done. Living with a mother-in-law who is overly critical, who incessantly looks for faults and shortcomings, may of course easily make tempers flare up rather than encourage obedience and politeness in the daughter-in-law. Still, to protect her reputation and to be a morally decent person in the eyes of others, it is always better for the woman to keep quiet and silently endure. Lý explained:

'You have to listen to those above you, those older than yourself. Even if they are wrong you still have to keep quiet, then later you can speak ... About obedient daughters-in-law people will say they are good at enduring, which means that whatever their parents-in-law say they don't talk back. That's what their character is like. But those who can't endure, they feel offended and therefore they talk back. Answering back means getting a reputation of being a "rotten" (*hư*) daughter-in-law.'

Quế remarked:

'Many old people have very difficult tempers. Maybe they scold and abuse, but the daughter-in-law still has to care for them and she can't talk back to them. If she answers back she lacks filiality (*hiếu*).'

In this sense, Potter (1988) may be right: what a person 'really' thinks and feels in some situations is less important; it is her/his manner and behaviour towards others that count socially. In order to maintain a reputation as a decent and respectable person and protect one's honour in the eyes of others, one should know how to treat parents-in-law with respect and how to keep hurt and angry feelings of injustice to oneself. Openly defying or disrespecting parents or parents-in-law usually exposes one to the malicious gossip and contempt of other community members and so incurs embarrassment and shame. To avoid becoming the object of gossip and ridicule, one should therefore always act as if parents/

parents-in-law were in authority, treating them with respect, being attentive to their needs, and retaining politeness in manners and speech. Whether one is obedient and compliant in reality or not is less important; what matters most is maintaining an outward appearance of correct and smooth family relations. Lý remarked:

> 'You have to show responsibility towards your parents or you will be condemned by others. People are greatly afraid of being condemned. If you are discussed in public and considered a bad person it makes you feel deeply ashamed (*xấu hổ*), so nobody dares risk that.'

But how about marital problems and frustrations then? Do the same moral requirements exist *vis-à-vis* wives as for daughters-in-law; are wives also expected to endure almost no matter what their husbands say and do? Not quite. Whereas the respect for elders is socially almost sacrosanct, and whereas older people are clearly 'above' and younger 'below' in social hierarchies, the dominant moral ideals of husband–wife relations are more egalitarian. Even though people often say that 'the wife has to follow the husband', wives are definitely not expected to show the same unconditional recognition of the moral authority of their husbands as they are of their parents-in-law. This is demonstrated when people gossip about the marriages of others: both husband and wife often come under fire. Numerous sayings emphasize the importance of marital agreement and cooperation, without particularly stressing the duty of either party to comply with the other. 'The drum plays in one tone, the horn in another' (*Trống đánh xuôi mà kèn thổi ngược*), or 'Grandfather does not agree, grandmother does' (*Ông chẳng bà chuộc*) are sayings children use to tease other children whose parents fight a lot or are divorced.

Still, it often seems to be women who suffer most from marital conflicts: they feel ashamed and embarrassed about their failure to create a happy family life. The ability to form a happy, peaceful, and harmonious married life was extremely important to most of the women I knew in Vải Sơn, and seemed to be at the core of their feelings of self-respect and worth. Therefore, the costs to women of family quarrels are often high in terms of embarrassment, shame, and fear of social ridicule and exclusion. Hương noted:

'If we argue and don't listen to each other, people will say: "The husband doesn't listen to the wife, the wife doesn't listen to the husband." It makes you feel really ashamed.'

As mentioned, women also worry much more about family conflicts and quarrels than their more carefree husbands. In women's accounts it is nearly always wives and hardly ever husbands who lie awake at night tormented by thoughts about the lack of family harmony. Nhị put it in this way:

'Husbands are more carefree, wives think more. About the misery of one's life, that one is not as good as others. The children are one thing, disagreements between husband and wife are another, the third is that my husband doesn't respect me, he disrespects me, shouts at me for nothing. We don't fit very well, so it is very difficult.'

In short, then, it often makes a lot of moral sense to women to endure hardship without complaint. By silently enduring, a woman may create an image of herself as a good and responsible wife and a dutiful daughter-in-law who is doing her best to create a happy life for herself and her family, thinking of others rather than herself and recognizing community norms and values.

However, a woman's character is defined not only by her individual qualities and characteristics, but also by the moral character of her family. The moral qualities of both living and dead family members may affect the ways in which an individual is assessed and judged by other community members. It is commonly held that the sins and virtues of parents may be transferred to their children and grandchildren: if parents behave in socially indecent ways and violate moral codes, their children may have to suffer punishment for their sins (*gánh tội*).[6] This is expressed in the common saying: 'If the father eats salty food, the son will be thirsty' (*Cha ăn mặn con khát nước*). The birth of a deformed child in Vải Sơn was explained by people as being due to the moral misbehaviour of the child's grandfather; similarly, the sudden death of a young man was explained with reference to his father's maltreatment of another young man several years before. In daily life, numerous sayings express the negative effects which the behaviour of parents may have on their children: 'If the tree is green, the leaves will be green; do try to live properly in order to give virtue to your children' (*ở đời này cây xanh thì là mói xanh, ai ơi cứ ở cho lành để đức cho con*), or 'Happiness and virtue follow the model' (*Phúc đức tại mẫu*). Besides their implications for the transferral of sins and virtues from generation to generation, the close socio-moral relations between family members also affect daily social life and the reputations of individuals and families. People who behave in morally inappropriate ways, without due recognition of who is above and who is below in the social hierarchy, are said to be 'children of a family without education' (*con nhà mất dạy*). As one woman said, 'Not respecting one's parents, it means the family education (*gia giáo*) of that house is not good, the family has a bad morality.'

A person's behaviour therefore affects not only her/himself but the entire family. When Hương explained to me why she had followed the wishes of her parents and had not married the man she in fact loved, she emphasized the consequences for her family's reputation of her going against her parents' wishes:

'Not listening to what your parents say means disrespecting them. It means not following your family, that you do not follow what your parents say. So people will talk about this bad behaviour and your parents will have to get a bad reputation.'

Similarly, if a family has a negative reputation this invariably influences the ways its individual members are looked upon and socially evaluated. As mentioned in Chapter 2, I had a hard time finding out why Bà Chính placed Hương in the category of 'bad persons'; but one of the reasons I eventually discovered was that her husband's family was considered locally as 'not good' due to their behaviour during the resistance to the French fifty years before. People say: 'The buffalo leaves his skin, people leave their reputation' (*Con trâu để da, con người để tiếng*). In marriage negotiations people still consider the family history (*lý lịch gia đình*) of the prospective bride and groom, scrutinizing their families for moral flaws. This is expressed in sayings like, 'When marrying a woman consider her family, when marrying a man consider his breed' (*Lấy vợ xem tông, lấy chồng xem giống*) (cf. Bélanger and Khuất Thu Hồng 1995).

It is not surprising then that it is vitally important to most people to protect the honour or 'value' (*giá trị*) of their families and avoid giving 'outsiders' (*người ngoài*) a negative impression of them and of internal family relations. An old saying says that it is always better to 'let family issues be discussed behind a closed door'. Women in Vải Sơn often strive to keep family discords a secret, keeping conflicts and disharmonies within the family, and women who know how to protect the honour of their family are usually considered to be 'good women'. As a model for female behaviour, Liên's uncle Hùng pointed to a woman who did not show any signs of emotional disturbance when a neighbour entered their house in the middle of a violent quarrel between husband and wife:

'Even though she felt endlessly indignant (*ức*) inside, out of respect for her husband she pretended nothing was wrong. Maybe as soon as the neighbour leaves they will resume fighting. That shows how good Vietnamese women are. They know how to defend the happiness of their families.'

By expressing feelings of anger, sadness and despair – in the form of fights and quarrels or in tears and complaints – one reveals the faults and flaws of one's family to the outside world. Thus openly laying bare the weaknesses of one's family is called to 'show one's naked back' (*vạch áo cho người xem lưng*). Even if one is tormented by fears that one's husband is unfaithful, to express these thoughts openly would bring shame to both him and oneself (*xấu cháng hổ ai*).

In small and tightly-knit communities, such as the villages in Vải Sơn, to have a bad reputation or to be exposed to the ridicule and contempt of others can be very painful indeed. However, a concern about reputation and moral ideals does not seem to be the principal reason for women's endurance. Hương said that she didn't care much about her reputation:

'If others talk, let them talk. They themselves are the only ones to listen to it. I don't care.'

What seems to matter more to women than moral principles, honour, shame and reputation are the immediate everyday consequences of expressions of distress – the ways such expressions affect the children, the economy and family life. In other words, we may have to consider emotional expression not only as an element in self-creation, but also as performance or strategy: as a way of doing things and affecting one's social surroundings.

The pragmatics of emotional expression: protecting the happiness of the family

One day I was talking to Hương about the reasons why she and other women would often 'hold back' and keep quiet in situations where they felt offended. 'Let me write it down for you', she said, and put down in my notebook:

1) It is not good for the children if parents fight and quarrel.

2) Love/feelings (*tình cảm*) between wife and husband are ruined by too much quarrelling.

3) It is more difficult to work and build up family finances if husband and wife are in disagreement.

4) The neighbours will speak badly about you if you always fight with your husband.

When I asked her which one of these reasons is most important, she pointed, as I knew she would, to the first. Concerns about reputation have already been dealt with, so let us consider the other three, which also happen to be three of the most important issues in women's lives: children, love and the family's economic situation.

As in Bình's case, women often stay in violent and unhappy marriages out of pity for their children, knowing that if the marriage breaks up, the children will suffer. The children will be teased because their parents do not know how to get along, and in all likelihood they will have to stay with their father's family and so lose their mother. As one woman said:

> 'Many people continue to live together for the children's sake. If the husband is a lazy worker, does absolutely nothing, drinks alcohol, the woman has to try to persuade him to improve. Some people cannot endure and they divorce, but there are also some people who endure and who live for their children, trying to protect them from hardship.'

In order to explain to me why she stayed in her marriage despite her husband's quick temper and frequent beatings, Bình taught me an old folk verse: 'A child sits looking at jumping rain drops, saying: "If mother gets married again, with whom should I live?"' (*Trời mưa bong bóng phặp phồng, mẹ đi lấy chồng con ở với ai?*). Even if an unhappy marriage does not break up, the children will still suffer from their parents' fighting and quarrelling; they will get scared and feel sad. People often say that 'Children also know how to think', and if their parents frequently fight and dis-agree, the children will suffer. To protect their children from worries and rumours, most women therefore do their best to build a happy, stable, and peaceful family, and silently endure rather than openly react to strained family relations.

Women's awareness of the fact that parents serve as 'mirrors' for their children is another important motive for their strivings to avoid open quarrels and conflicts within the family.[7] This was an issue which Mai often brought up. She said that children see what their parents do and later they will copy what they see:

'Parents are mirrors for their children, the children repeat what they say. It is the same with the behaviour in the family. If you respect your parents, give them food before everyone else, then later your children will do the same for you.'

This is also expressed in the saying, 'If those above don't know their place, those below will be disobedient' (*Ở trên mà chẳng chính ngôi, để cho ở dưới chúng tôi hỗn hào*). If you behave rudely towards your elders, the children will copy this and treat you in the same way once you become old and helpless. Stephen O'Harrow (1995) points out that mothers often – more or less consciously – build up 'gratitude' (*ơn*) in their children by letting them know how hard they are working for them and how much they are sacrificing for their sake. In this sense, silently enduring a difficult marriage can be a strategic way of securing one's future, creating a stable environment for one's children so that they will grow up to be grateful and dutiful to their parents. Finally, silent endurance may also be a way for women to win the sympathy of their children and gain their support in family conflicts. As Lý said,

'Mother and child are often very close, the mother lulls her child to sleep, comforts it, takes care of it. [...] So children often have to follow their mother. If parents quarrel, the children will comfort their mother and so the husband feels lonely and has to think again.'

But too much fighting and quarrelling not only scares the children and teaches them the wrong way to behave, it also affects *marital love and sympathy*. If a woman insists on her own point of view, the price is often endless fights which undermine family order and happiness and spoil her dreams of marital harmony and mutual understanding. Nhị said:

'If the wife does not follow the husband, the house is not happy, you see, because everything has to be agreed to by the husband. You can still insist on doing as you wish, but it will not be happy, not peaceful.'

Or as Mai said:

'Answering each other back creates disorder in the family (*gia dình lủng củng*), it spoils the nice cosy atmosphere, ruins feelings, and leads to quarrels.'

Many women therefore prefer to 'follow' their husbands and comply with their wishes rather than creating scenes and quarrels. Ngọc's considerations of whether or not to borrow money against her husband's wishes provide an example of this:

'Our financial situation is very unstable and I wanted to go and borrow some money. I discussed it with my husband but he was against the idea so I had to accept [his decision]. I didn't dare borrow the money. If I had, when I came home we would have quarrelled and there would be disorder in the family, no happiness. There is no point in insisting on going to borrow the money. Otherwise, when I came home and my husband found out about it, he would reproach me, we would quarrel.'

Besides the immediate loss of love and feelings, women also often fear losing their husband to another woman if they are too tough on him. Women's jealousy is a very frequent topic of everyday conversations and jokes and I was often asked if I knew of any women in the world as jealous as Vietnamese women. Many women in Vải Sơn seem to comply with the wishes of their husbands out of a fear that creating too much trouble and marital disharmony may make them turn to other, more placid women. In this sense, refraining from complaining may be a way of holding on to one's husband. While some women fear that their husband's infidelity will ruin marital love and intimacy, others simply say as one woman in a focus group discussion:

'I am not afraid of losing feelings. I am only afraid of economic loss.'

Many women also seem to have realized that in order to 'get things done', it is always better to treat one's husband sweetly and address him mildly and joyfully rather than to engage in open conflict. A hot temper usually only incites fights and quarrels, while being gentle and mild may make one's husband 'think again', realize his faults, and regret his behaviour. One woman said:

'To be able to get things done (*được việc*) I try to be gentle, I accept, in order to make him agree. If he is very "hot" and I am like him it is impossible to get anything done. I try to make him think again. If I am "hot" as well, we will not be able to succeed in anything (*hoàn thành*) so I have to be modest and step back.'

Talking about the different sexual needs of husbands and wives, Quế said:

'If the husband demands sex and the wife does not want it, it often leads to quarrels. If the husband demands more, one has to solve it by explaining, encouraging, and speaking sweetly to him in order to make him agree.'

When Nhị's husband was unfaithful to her, she succeeded in 'educating' him by quietly and patiently explaining right and wrong to him instead of making a scene:

'When we were young there was a time when my husband was chasing after other girls. But I encouraged (*động viên*) him to give up those relationships. At the time when I had just given birth he also had relations with other women, but I explained right and wrong to him and he listened and stopped having such relations.'

One day Quế and Mai were comparing their tempers and Quế envied Mai her gentleness and patience. Mai has always been the mediator, they said, she has been mediating in fights and quarrels ever since they were children. Today she is clearly more clever in handling her husband than is Quế: while Quế easily loses her temper, Mai keeps calm and collected and thus usually succeeds in persuading and 'educating' her husband. She said:

'The more clever one is, the more harmony there will be' (*Cáng khôn khéo cáng hoà thuận*).

Mai explained that she would speak 'cleverly' to her husband in order to persuade him to stay at home and help her instead of going out 'playing':

'If he is on his way out to "play", and you shout at him in an angry voice: "Will you come here and do this or that?", then he definitely goes straight out. No, I say to him in a gentle, joyful voice, "Couldn't you give me a hand with this a second?", and then he helps. In order to be happy one has to be clever. If one is not clever there will be disharmony and fights between husband and wife.'

Similarly, Mai managed to make her husband assist her by joking about his scant knowledge of pig breeding:

'I did not say anything directly to him at all, I just joked with the neighbour: "He doesn't know whether the pig eats with its head or its tail." I joked like that, and from that day, when I came home from washing clothes in the morning, he had already fed the pig. He has progressed.'

Women's realization of the advantages of keeping calm rather than bursting out in anger or impatience and their awareness of the need to be gentle and clever (*khôn khéo*) when handling their husbands are also expressed in folk songs like the following (quoted from Nha-Trang 1973: 183):

When her husband was angry, the woman immediately made peace;
Smiling gently, she said, 'What has offended you?'
My beloved husband, please do not be angry with me,
If you want, I will find a concubine for you

Or as one of the verses in Nguyễn Trãi's Family Training Ode (cf. Chapter 6) goes (Nha-Trang 1973: 38):

If you are unfortunately married to a man who has a lust for wine and women,
Or if your husband turns out to be a gambler,
Implore him discreetly in soft language and gentle voice;
Only with patience can you hope to change him.
If your husband is inconsiderate, bear your pains in silence,
It only hurts you to openly express your disagreement.

Women also often emphasize that too much fighting in a family makes it difficult to build up the family finances. In order to improve the family's finances everyone needs to cooperate, and it is detrimental to these efforts if husband and wife are pulling in different directions. Mo' stressed the importance of cooperation:

'To get things done husband and wife have to agree, then both will be happy and the economy will develop. But if "the drum blows in one tone, the horn in another", that is, one person wants something but the other wants something else, then the family's happiness will not be secured, the economic situation will decay, it will not develop.'

Women also often emphasized that when the finances are secure, the risk of disagreement between husband and wife reduced and women have more freedom to make their own economic arrangements. Hương said:

'It all has to do with the finances. If there is enough to eat and you can buy what you need, there is nothing to quarrel about. If there is not enough to eat and you cannot buy anything there will be discord and quarrels. If the family is poor, happiness cannot be achieved. One person will scold the other, there will be quarrels. If the financial situation is good, you don't have to think about anything, you can be smiling and joyful, people outside will praise you. [...] If the household economy is good, happiness will be complete.'

In short, silent endurance is often an element in women's efforts to create and protect the 'happy family'. Women readily and voluntarily sacrifice themselves, as they say, in order to protect family happiness and harmony (*em cửa em nhà*) and avoid family disorder and confusion (*gia đình lủng củng*). The dreams women may have of freedom, equality, and independence are therefore often overridden by their wish for a happy and harmonious family life. As Lai remarked:

'I have to bear insults (*nhẫn nhục*) in order to preserve the happiness of my family, out of love for my children. It is all for the children, you know.'

I asked whether her husband also had to defend the happiness of the family, to which she replied:

'He does. But he does not have the same degree of responsibility as I do.'

In other words, when women submit to and comply with the wishes of their husbands or parents-in-law, they do not do so because they agree with the principles of women's social inferiority vis-à-vis men or elders, but rather out of pragmatic concerns with the daily welfare and happiness of their families. Keeping the family happy and stable simply matters most and makes all kinds of daily sacrifices worthwhile. Mỹ sums it up like this:

'When you come home, you should try to be joyful, both husband and wife should try, so that there can be happiness. If not there will be fights, and perhaps the husband will leave his wife. How could a wife leave her husband? She has to stay with her children. So both have to do their best, but women often have to try harder.'

Everyday expressions of distress

If in many everyday situations women strive to 'hold back' their feelings and endure hardships in order not to provoke conflict, then how is distress communicated to others? I shall now outline four of the most obvious ways in which women communicate and share the feelings of anger, sadness, or indignation which they may feel towards husbands, mothers-in-law, or other people. Women may express distress through

1) confiding in other women
2) 'foot-dragging'
3) abstaining from food
4) somatic expressions.[8]

One of the most important and common ways for women to express distress is simply by talking about and *sharing stressful experiences* with other women. Even though women can be very tough on each other in their gossip and moral evaluations, it is also among like-minded women that they are most likely to find understanding and support. Women of similar age often experience similar kinds of distress, and other women know exactly what it feels like if a husband flirts around with other women, if a mother-in-law is intolerable, if the children are disobedient, or if a hospitalization knocks the bottom out of the family budget. When women are together, voices often suddenly drop and suspicions about a husband or frustrations over the

difficult temper of a mother-in-law are shared. Sharing the hardships of one's life with other women seems to be an age-old mode
of expressing distress, as the following folksong indicates (Nha-
Trang 1973: 212):

> *My husband is good for nothing;*
> *He wastes his money freely in card games.*
> *It is a shame for me and embarrassing for him if I speak out,*
> *He will get angry and destroy the house.*
> *However, I would like to confide in you, sisters.*
> *Though I had only several baskets of rice and some bales of*
>   *cotton left,*
> *I was forced to sell them in order to pay my husband's debts.*
> *I have resigned myself to endure whatever circumstances for*
>   *the happiness of my family.*
> *My tongue has always savoured the bitter taste of the*
>   *soapberry,*
> *Look at my situation with a husband inferior to many others.*
> *Though you may laugh at me, I cannot help revealing the fact:*
> *Coming from a literate family, I have unfortunately married a*
>   *dull-witted man.*
> *Just as a golden dragon feels it disagreeable to bathe in a*
>   *pond of muddy water,*
> *A wise one like me is annoyed living with a stupid one like*
>   *him.*

There is one problem about confiding in friends and peers, however: one has to be sure that one can trust them. One woman said:

> 'No one can keep things inside forever, you have to confide in
> other people. But you have to find people who will understand
> you; you can't speak to anyone about it. If you do, they won't
> understand and they will say you are a daughter-in-law who talks
> badly about her parents-in-law.'

And Hồng remarked:

> 'If you feel sad you only talk to close friends about it ... because
> if you speak to people outside it is complicated, you get a bad

reputation and the neighbours begin to stare. You only dare to complain to those you are closest to.'

Confiding in others also always carries the risk of being mis-understood, ridiculed, and condemned. This is where the immense importance of understanding each other (*hiểu nhau*) comes in. In everyday life there is a lot of talk about whether people understand each other or not, and misunderstandings and misjudgements are often seen as being due to a break-down in communication. The very common experience of self-pity (*tủi thân*), which also Stephen O'Harrow (1992) noted, often seems to spring pre-cisely from the experience of being misunderstood and misjudged, of being wrongly condemned and ascribed motivations and in-tentions which one does not really have. In a small and close-knit society, the experience of being unfairly condemned and ridiculed can be very unpleasant indeed. This is what makes people feel 'proud' (*tự ái*), distancing themselves from a community which then distances itself from them.

Women in distress may also sometimes turn to their natal family. Hương talked about conflicts in relations to parents-in-law in this way:

'If your husband understands he can suggest to his parents that next time, they shouldn't behave like that ... but some husbands don't understand, they defend their parents so you have to endure and go home and confide in your own parents or brothers and sisters.'

As we saw earlier, when her marriage became too stressful, Mơ returned to her parents' house to give birth to her second child. When Hương came home after several weeks of hospitalization, her mother moved in with her family for some days to take care of and comfort her. Sisters and sisters-in-law (*chị em hai bên*) are often the ones with whom both work tasks and worries of everyday lives are shared: thoughts and feelings are exchanged over the fetching of water, washing of clothes, or shopping in the market. In other words, most women have a strong social support network of other women – sisters, mothers, friends – in whom they can confide thoughts, worries and anxieties. Even though women can sometimes be the hardest judges of each other's behaviour, they can also be most understanding, compassionate and supportive, providing mutual comfort, advice and encouragement. The kind of

behaviour which seems to turn other women into strict judges
rather than supportive sisters is behaviour that expresses arrogance
and a lack of recognition of the standards and norms of one's
community. Living with an attitude of 'above me is only the sky'
(*trên Trời dưới mình*) and not recognizing one's dependency on
other people seems to invite condemnation and social exclusion,
while being able to 'think again' and recognize one's mistakes are
highly valued social skills.

Notably, however, the advice women give one another is often
very conservative. Usually, women encourage each other to keep
enduring, stay where they are and try to accept and live with the
hardships of their lives. Underlying this conservative advice seems
to be a realization that the alternative to endurance and compliance
is rarely very attractive: open revolt usually only gives a woman a
bad name and causes other community members to shun her.
Ultimately, her husband or parents-in-law might throw her out of
their house, forcing her to return to her natal family – if they will
accept her. Therefore, when one woman told another how sad and
angry she felt about her husband's infidelity, her friend said, 'You
have put up so far, so you can put up a little longer, do try to
endure.' Mai remarked:

> 'Women encourage each other to try to stay in their marriage,
> saying "The *chuôi* fish sacrifices itself for its children." They say: in
> the end it is better to close your eyes and endure, don't leave each
> other, go home and stay with your husband to the end of your days.
> No one says: if he behaves so badly then you should go and ask
> for a divorce, no one would dare encourage her to do so.'

Another way of expressing dissatisfaction and distress is by
foot-dragging: doing what one's mother-in-law wants or what
one's husband expects, but doing it only slowly and sullenly.
Ideally, women should work hard but happily, exhausting themselves with a smile. Therefore, there is quiet provocation in a
daughter-in-law's silent acceptance of tasks which she then per-
forms slowly and with a sullen face, sending angry and hateful
glances at her mother-in-law, or in the way a wife puts the rice-pot
on the ground in front of her husband with a hard and angry
"clonk". There are clear limits to the social effectiveness of foot-
dragging, however. Few women ever seem to take it very far, since
– as with open conflict – the children would be the ones to suffer

most from their mothers' refusals to perform household duties properly. Excessive foot-dragging would turn into a self-destructive weapon and would undermine the very meaning of it all: the creation of a happy family.

Losing appetite and *abstaining from food* is another common way of expressing distress. The refusal of a wife or a daughter-in-law to eat together with the rest of the family should be considered in the light of the very important social meanings that are attached to food and the sharing of meals in daily life. Social exchanges of food create and confirm social bonds: giving food to others before one starts to eat expresses appreciation and respect; gratitude for help and support is often shown through an invitation to share a meal; and a mother's love and care for her child seem to be condensed in the phrase: 'Eat, child' (*ăn đi con*). The sharing of meals is a core expression of family solidarity (cf. Phạm Văn Bích 1997), and all the families I knew in Vải Sơn would eat three regular meals of rice a day with all family members sitting together around the tray.

It is a common experience, however, that feeling sad or thinking too much disturbs and reduces appetite, so that one 'cannot swallow a bit'. This experience is also described in an old folk song which goes, 'I'm hungry and I eat a starfruit or a fig, then I take one look at your mother and I can't swallow a thing' (O'Harrow 1995: 167). Women sometimes deliberately refuse to share meals with their family, thus openly negating family solidarity. In one family, the daughter-in-law would eat alone in the kitchen during periods of family conflict and tension, mumbling that she was 'unable to eat' in the presence of her mother-in-law. Ironically, by taking up the position in the kitchen, she confirmed her own marginal and inferior position in her husband's household while also protesting against it (see Chapter 6).

The parallels between abstaining from meals (*nhịn bữa*) and abstaining from expressing one's feelings (*nhịn*) are striking. Both imply a withdrawal from community or family life and both may express a quiet protest to constraining family relations. But a woman's refusal to eat may also call the attention of others to her experience of distress. This is very obvious in the everyday talk about weight loss; women who did not seem visibly thinner to me would often complain of having lost weight lately. Complaints about weight loss often seem to be invitations to talk about other issues of concern and about the thoughts and worries which may have caused the woman to lose weight. This leads us to *somatic expressions* as a fourth mode of expressing distress.

I use the term somatic expressions in order to avoid the concept of 'somatization', which has most often been used to describe 'displaced' experience or affect, i.e. bodily expressions of feelings and experiences which are 'in reality' social or psychological (e.g., Kleinman 1986). Instead of seeing somatization as displaced experience, it seems more appropriate to consider bodily experiences and expressions as ways of feeling and acting which are both social, somatic, and affective. Robert Desjarlais (1992: 150) has suggested that we replace the term 'somatization' with 'somatic sensibilities', since 'somatization' has such strong overtones of displaced social/emotional experience. He defines 'sensibility' as 'a lasting mood or disposition patterned within the workings of a body' (1992: 150). A sensibility denotes a 'particular way of being' and so shapes the ways a person engages with her world: it is through somatic sensibilities that we experience our worlds and that social experiences come to have specific meanings for us. But while Desjarlais' concept of 'somatic sensibilities' captures well the fact that pain embodies rather than represents social distress, it ignores another important aspect of the notion of somatization, namely that pain may also be performative.

Several anthropological studies have suggested that somatic idioms of distress are socially and politically 'safer' than overt expression of discontent and emotional disturbance (e.g., Nichter 1981; Kleinman 1986; Scheper-Hughes 1992b). Since the expression of pain or discomfort may importantly influence and change one's social surroundings, sickness may also be seen as cultural performance (Frankenberg 1986) or as a form of bodily action (Rebhun 1993; Scheper-Hughes 1994). We may therefore need to supplement the concept of 'somatic sensibilities' with those of 'somatic expressions' or 'somatic practices'. Nancy Scheper-Hughes writes that it is important to focus on

> the body's wisdom, its intentionality and purposefulness in its production of unruly and 'chaotic' symptoms that continuously breech the boundaries between mind and body, nature and culture, individual and social bodies (Scheper-Hughes 1994: 232).

We have already seen that in the lives of women in Vải Sơn, experiences of social and emotional distress are often inextricably bound up with the experience of physical discomfort. But while women often strive to control their expressions of social and emotional distress in order to protect the welfare and well-being of their families, experiences of physical weakness are usually openly shared and discussed. As mentioned in Chapter 5, there is a lot of talk in everyday life about various kinds of physical ailments and weaknesses and a lively exchange of advice on how to handle them. When women are together, talk about health problems often glide over into talk about life problems in general: a conversation which starts from headaches or weak nerves will often progress to talk about workloads and worries. Similar divergences also took place in my own conversations with women: often they had health issues as the point of departure but moved from there into other daily problems and concerns. Also contact with health professionals seems to be a common way of sharing distressful social experience. Even though I did not systematically observe clinical encounters or women's communication with pharmacists, I did notice that health station staff were often very caring in their ways of treating patients and that pharmacists would often enquire into the lives and well-being of their customers. In other words, seeking professional help may also be a way of seeking care and advice – not only on aching bodies but on distressful lives.

Notably, distressful bodily and emotional experiences are often expressed in similar terms. For instance, the terms *bực* or *bực tức* convey feelings of bodily irritation, restlessness, and tension, while also referring to anger, irritation, or displeasure with other people. The terms *tức* and *ức* refer to a bodily feeling of being 'stifled', 'tight', or choked, while also indicating anger and annoyance. *Buồn bực* may describe a feeling of bodily tenseness and heaviness, while also describing an emotional state of anger/ sadness/irritation. In other words, emotional and bodily experiences often coincide, and talking about the body may be another way of talking about emotion. Léopold Cadière (1957) writes that Vietnamese culture apparently lacks the 'logic' and 'precision' of Occidental culture which operates with a clear distinction between psyche and soma. According to Cadière, the Vietnamese confuse and confound body and mind, and Vietnamese language does not distinguish clearly between physical states and states of mind and feeling. Similarly, Thomas Ots has noted that among the Chinese, somatic changes are not differentiated from the concomitant emotional changes. The somatic and the psychological are recognized as being two sides of the same entity:

> The difference between the Western and the Chinese view is not that of a dichotomized Western and a supposedly holistic Chinese view of body-mind. The difference lies in the Chinese assessment of an emotional body. (Ots 1990: 26)

Besides being media of communication, experiences of physical pain and discomfort are also often occasions for the display of care, concern, and mutual feelings. When someone is ill, others will try to 'encourage' her and advise her on how to get well again, just as when someone is sad, others will provide comfort and encourage him to return to life. As we saw from the cases of Hảo, Ngọc, Quế, Hạnh, and Tuyết described above, when women feel weak and unwell, their husbands, sisters, or mothers-in-law may also assist more than usual with daily work chores.[9] Most husbands are well aware of how dependent they are on the ability of their wives to work and take care of the family. One man said that without a good wife, no man will be able to succeed in life (*hoàn thành*). Knowing how much they depend on their wives, most husbands are very concerned about the health of their spouses, and as we have seen, this is also a common reason for men's opposition to their wives' getting a sterilization performed or an IUD inserted. In Bình's words:

> 'For instance, I am weak like this, so if my husband sees me do some hard work he feels pity for me and he comes to help me. That is called to cherish each other, to help each other. [...] I am weak so I have to protect my health, not overwork myself. If for instance I am ill then my husband has to assist me in order to avoid a situation where his wife gets much too weak, so he helps.'

In this sense, times of illness may be occasions where damaged social relations are partially repaired and where social disharmonies are replaced by care and concern. Husbands who are usually insensitive may become more caring, and mothers-in-law who generally seem hard and unfeeling may have a chance to show themselves in a new and more compassionate role. In short, it seems to make sense to suggest that women in Vải Sơn often express disturbed and disturbing feelings through their bodies rather than through verbal idioms, i.e. that physical symptoms become not only an embodiment of stressful living conditions, but also a language for the expression of stressful social experience.

Summing up: symptoms as somatic practice

As we have seen, open expressions of distress or anger may have a range of negative consequences for women: it may ruin their reputation; it damages the harmonious atmosphere in the family; it makes it more difficult to bring up the children to be good people; and it rarely makes husbands more considerate or mothers-in-law more understanding. In contrast, somatic complaints often seem to have effects that prove socially beneficial to women. Weakness tends to call forth social assistance, care and concern; when weak women are allowed to rest more than usually and maybe to eat special foods such as *gà hầm* (a specially prepared chicken) or take tonics (*thuốc bổ*) to regain their strength. In contrast to social distress, physical weakness does not directly accuse or criticize other family members but is an outlet of frustration and distress that from a social and moral perspective is relatively safe and acceptable. While headaches/abusive husbands, backaches/dominant mothers-in-law, physical exhaustion/discontent about unequal distributions of work and worries, the IUD/a strict family planning policy may all be co-experienced phenomena, there are certain benefits to women in talking more about the somatic than the social side of such experiences. By communicating distress through somatic idioms, women avoid being categorized as 'rotten' daughters-in-law or as bad wives and mothers. On the contrary, their physical weaknesses only emphasize the fact that they are hard-working, self-sacrificing and think of others before themselves, exhausting themselves for the welfare of their families.

In his work *The Moral Economy of the Peasant*, James Scott (1976) argues that peasants living close to the subsistence margin, always on the brink of economic disaster, tend to live according to a 'safety first' principle and avoid social and economic risk whenever they can. Similarly, in a social situation where energy and resources are scarce, the expression of distress through somatic idioms may be socially safer and less costly for women than open and direct expressions of distress. In many respects, physical suffering may be the best way to alleviate stressful social circumstances or to change the behaviour of other family members. By drawing attention to their physical rather than social suffering, women stay within an accepted model of female behaviour – being weak, patient, enduring – while also actively affecting and changing their social surroundings. When women suffer from headaches, dizziness and weaknesses, their husbands may feel obligated to show concern and to 'think again' about their own behaviour, and mothers-in-law may lessen strict demands on the labour and services of their daughters-in-law.

In the absence of more direct forms of power, being physically weak may therefore be a very effective strategy for women to influence their social surroundings. Many women seem to be aware of this and emphasize how their husbands show a more caring, considerate, and understanding side at times when their wives' health seems poor. In this sense, women's physical suffering is not only passive, but may also be seen as active performance and agency, as the most effective and least costly way of influencing their social environments. During my stay in Våi Sơn, I often found it difficult to match my impressions of the women I met with their own self-representations. The physical and mental strength and resilience I observed in women often seemed to belie their own constant insistence on their physical weakness and frailty. While I definitely do not want to deny or downplay the fact that women do have very good reason to feel weak and exhausted, it seems important to point to the fact that physical weakness may also, simultaneously, be socially and strategically useful to women. What I suggest is not that women are play-acting or inventing symptoms, but rather that they are skilfully monitoring their bodily and emotional expressions in the ways that best suit their purposes. In other words, women are not only passively subjected to the stresses of their lives, they also suffer actively and strategically, managing their lives by the means that are available to them.

Notes

1. The socio-centric/egocentric dichotomy was first introduced by Schweder and Bourne (1984) who, summarizing cross-cultural literature, identified two ideal types of self: the Western concept of person which is autonomous, acontextual, abstract and independent as opposed to a non-Western self that is context-dependent, concrete and socially defined. While this distinction may be heuristically useful, it should definitely not be taken too literally and its explanatory value seems limited. A rigid

dichotomization into egocentrism/socio-centrism obviously essentializes differences between cultures and ignores intra-cultural complexity and heterogeneity (for critiques see for instance Kleinman and Kleinman 1991; Spiro 1993; Holland and Kipnis 1994). As the previous chapter has indicated, the ego-centric/socio-centric division often crumbles when one looks more closely at people's lives and self-perceptions. Women in Vải Sơn clearly understand themselves as people who exist through their relations to parents, husbands, and children; but they also feel they are distinct and individual beings with a body and a life of their own.

2. Kleinman and Kleinman (1991) note that in traditional Chinese medicine, emotion is not a general phenomenological descriptor. Instead, there are seven specific emotions – joy, anger, melancholy, worry, grief, fear and fright.

3. For similar observations concerning Chinese society see Hwang (1987), who notes that there are close connections between emotion and empathy in China: it is expected that people can understand the emotional responses of others to various circumstances in life.

4. As noted by David Marr, this may also be due to cultural differences between Vietnam and China (personal communication, 1996).

5. There are clear parallels between this everyday emphasis on learning and self-education and classical Confucian ideas of self-cultivation (cf. Munro 1969; Tu Wei-Ming 1985).

6. For a discussion of the philosophical basis of everyday beliefs concerning human souls and the transfer of sins/virtue between generations, see Chánh Công Phan (1993). He writes that these ideas are closely related to the practice of ancestor worship in which the social and moral relations between family members are constituted, expressed and confirmed. Chánh Công Phan argues that the 'Đạo of Vietnamese Ancestral Worship' consists in a blending of folk beliefs with the philosophies of Confucianism and Taoism.

7. The idea that parents are 'mirrors' for their children is in line with the emphasis in classical Confucian thinking on moral example and learning through the emulation of models (cf. Munro 1969: 96–99).

8. Probably many other modes of expressing distress exist, but these are the ones that are most obvious in everyday life. Also worth mentioning, however, is the exchange of folk verses, sayings, and poems, and the consulting of fortune tellers or sorcerers.

9. Also the first month after a delivery is a time when women are exempted from normal duties and work burdens. Women often talk about the weeks immediately after giving birth as about a feast or a holiday where the social world is turned upside down. This is a time when everything is done for the new mother; her husband now has to serve her, the care and attention of family and neighbours is concentrated on her, and she just has to take care of her baby and regain her strength.

CHAPTER 8

Conclusion

Anthropologies of Suffering and Resistance

A few days after the family planning campaign has ended, I pass by Thanh's small house again. I wonder how effective Nhưng has been in her attempt to persuade Thanh to have an IUD – did she actually go to the health station that afternoon to have another IUD inserted, and if so, how does she feel now? As I arrive, Thanh is washing a large pile of clothes in a battered tub behind the house, her hair hidden in a faded flowery scarf, her thin body bent. It is a good day for washing; the weather is milder than it has been for weeks, the sunshine is reflected in the puddles in the yard, and birds are twittering. I put my bag on the ground and help Thanh hang out the clothes to dry, thinking how difficult it must be for the children to keep warm in these thin polyester shirts and torn sweaters.

While we hang up the clothes I ask her, 'So, in the end, did you go to the health station the other day?' She looks at me smiling wryly.

'I did. I am very afraid of getting pregnant again and my husband is even more afraid. Our finances cannot cope if we have another child. If I have one more child we will die, so I have to endure and have an IUD. Nhưng is right, isn't she, one has to think of the happiness of one's family first.'

'But you said you were so afraid of the IUD. Are you still afraid now?', I ask.

'I am,' Thanh replies, 'since I had the IUD inserted I have been feeling weak and dizzy, weaker than before. But this is not at all like your country, you know. Life is difficult for Vietnamese women, very difficult. In Vietnam, women have to know how to endure.'

⚭

We are now in a better position than we were at the outset to understand both what compelled Thanh to have an IUD inserted in spite of her fears of it and how her feelings of weakness and dizziness are experienced and produced. In the preceding pages we saw that women's use of the IUD is closely linked to their dreams of the 'happy family', that IUD experiences are deeply interwoven with everyday experiences of physical weakness and exhaustion; and that the effects of IUDs on women's bodies cannot be understood in isolation from the wider social contexts in which their lives unfold. We also saw that women's suf-fering from bodily aches, pains, and weaknesses may express more than a 'passive' exposure to stressful social circumstances. Symptoms may also be considered as somatic practices through which women negotiate everyday social relations and influence their immediate social environments.

Since women's IUD experiences appear to span both suffering and resistance, both 'passive' endurance and 'active' agency, I shall conclude by reflecting on the possibilities and limitations of anthropological interpretations of human suffering and in par-ticular suffering as the embodiment of resistance. This chapter therefore focuses on two important and closely related questions: the analytical problem of how we interpret human suffering, and the moral-political problem of how we engage people who suffer. In the final section of this chapter I shall discuss some of the questions for further research which the present study raises.

Women's agency: the implications of contraceptive 'choice'

All over the world, men and women make decisions about fertility control within the given social constraints of their society and lives. One important issue in this study has been the question of what compels so many women in Vietnam to accept an IUD in a situation where they, like Thanh, are deeply fearful of what this device may do to their bodies and health. The examination of this question has provided insights into the ways in which individual choice and motivation are always socially produced and con-strained. As we have seen, contraceptive choices are structured by social and political conditions and saturated with cultural meanings.

Since the Vietnamese family planning policy has a strong de-mographic orientation, an obvious question to ask first is whether Vietnamese women are forced against their will to adopt a modern contraceptive method like the IUD? Even though the family planning policy clearly aims at a reduction of birth rates and a creation of an economic and normative climate conducive to fertility limitation, this study does not provide evidence of the use of direct force in Vietnamese family planning. Family planning cadres do their best to persuade women to adopt a modern method of contraception, but they also respect women's own wishes and preferences, and the final decision to adopt a contraceptive method lies with the woman herself and her husband. But even if women are not directly forced to accept IUDs or other contraceptive devices, their contraceptive choices are obviously framed and formed by a range of social and political circumstances.

First, the contraceptive choices that women are able to make are constrained by the availability of contraceptive methods, and consequently by the national and international forces that de-termine which contraceptive methods are available in a given social setting. The reliance on the IUD in Vietnam is related partly to a political preference for long-lasting, provider-controlled methods, and partly to the Western world's post-war aid freezes and trade embargoes which led to a reliance on the provision of contraceptive supplies from Eastern bloc countries. In this way, women's most intimate bodily experiences are directly tied to local relations of power and to global relations of trade and aid.

Second, the quality of care in family planning service provision has a strong impact on the kinds of choices women are able to make. From a user perspective, the most serious problems in Vietnamese family planning appear to relate to inadequate quality of care rather than the use of coercive or abusive measures: a very limited range of contraceptive methods is available for women to choose from; information on contraceptive methods and their possible side effects is inadequate; contraceptive counselling is still practically non-existent; and the technical skills of providers are not always optimal. In practice, contraceptive choice therefore often narrows down to simply a yes or no to the IUD.

Third, women's contraceptive choices are shaped by the local moral worlds in which they are made and are strongly conditioned by family and gender relations. In Vietnam as elsewhere, fertility control tends to be considered as an area of female responsibility, while not always being an area of female autonomy. Even though husband and wife very often agree on the need to control fertility, and even though they are equally interested in keeping the size of the family small, they do not always agree upon the method of contraception. Fertility control is generally seen as a burden and a nuisance due to the frequent negative effects on health and well-being. In many marriages, therefore, the woman ends up accepting the IUD, either directly forced by her husband's unwillingness to use a male method of contraception or 'readily sacrificing herself' in order to protect him from the physical or mental discomfort involved in contraceptive use.

Fourth, contraceptive choices always take place within local health cultures where some methods of contraception are perceived as more acceptable than others. Due to its longstanding use in the Vietnamese family planning programme, the IUD is generally considered to be a 'normal' method of contraception and thus safer than methods that have only recently been introduced. Women whose health is fragile and whose physical resources are scarce therefore often tend to feel they are better off using the IUD – which has been used by their mothers, sisters, and neighbours before them – than a new and untried method of contraception.

But contraceptive choices, no matter how constrained, are also expressions of women's active strivings to shape their families and to deal with the contingencies of their lives. In Vietnam today, fertility control represents not only an ambition of the state to curb population growth, but also an attempt by women and men to escape poverty and create brighter futures for themselves and their children. To many rural women, a prime ambition in life is the establishment of a happy, wealthy, stable family, and fertility control is one of the most direct and viable paths to reach this goal. The happy families that women are striving to build are very similar to the families portrayed in the government's family planning messages. At present, then, state discourses and women's deepest feelings and motivations meet and intertwine in the dream of the 'happy family' which forms both the central tenet of current political ideologies and the heart of women's lives. The irony of this is that women's overwork, self-sacrifice and ensuing physical exhaustion are often closely associated precisely with their dreams about the happy family. Striving to keep their families happy and harmonious, many women work harder than they are physically capable of and accept the IUD in spite of the physical suffering that they fear will follow.

Not surprisingly, the IUD is often perceived by women as a burden and a self-sacrifice, as a necessary tribute paid for the stability and economic survival of their families. Since the IUD is a device which most women fear before it is inserted and which many women see as a symbol of female subordination, it is probably not a coincidence that many everyday symptoms and complaints tend to be articulated precisely around the IUD.

In sum, while on the one hand potentially providing women with an important tool for reproductive self-determination, IUD use also supports and confirms a range of dominant gender stereotypes, emphasizing both women's social roles as responsible for family and children, cultural ideals of heroic female self-sacrifice and endurance, and notions of women's physical weakness and fragility.

Women's health: the everyday politics of symptoms and side effects

Considered from an anthropological perspective, contraceptive side effects involve much more than 'raw' physiological reactions to technological interventions on human bodies. This study has demonstrated that the effects of the intrauterine device on women's bodies cannot be understood apart from the wider social contexts and 'textures of meaning' in which women's lives unfold. The side effects of an IUD are usually co-experienced with a host of other health problems, and the IUD is an artifact that con-denses a wide range of stresses, worries, and anxieties in women's lives. In this sense, women's physical symptoms represent much more than mere physiological malfunctions: they are socially structured and generated experiences which are produced by the constraints and demands of daily lives and which gain specific meanings through their association with important and often stressful facets of women's lives. Therefore, if we want to take women's complaints about their health seriously and remain loyal to their own experiences of their lives, contraceptive side effects need to be considered within these broader frameworks of social meaning.

Whereas some studies have drawn direct links between state policies and individual experiences of distress and disease, the present study points to the importance of paying close attention to the social processes unfolding at the 'intermediate' level of daily family and community life where 'macro' social and political forces are transformed into personal experiences of pain and distress. The analysis of women's experiences with the IUD brought us directly into the social and moral spheres of family and community, where women's bodies and minds are strained by various kinds of work burdens and worries. Women often see their physical weakness as closely associated with family problems and tensions, and experiences of physical discomfort seem to gain importance and urgency from the analogic relations that exist between the health of the body and the quality of family relations, thus connecting physical health with family happiness.

An important feature of the moral worlds of family and community is the complexity of the norms and values by which they are structured. Everyday moral ideologies are anything but clear and consistent, and the social and bodily stresses which women experience often seem to be located precisely in the tense spaces created between the contradictory and competing moral ideologies within which daily lives unfold. In order to comprehend the dilemmas and ambivalences which women face today, a historical perspective on today's social worlds is required. Limiting our horizons to today's local moral worlds would seriously constrain our understanding of the processes through which social tensions and moral ambiguities are produced.

In Vietnamese history, a range of very different cultural traditions meet and intertwine, and the competing moral doctrines of today's everyday lives are anchored in wider cultural and historical traditions. Both the moral ideologies and social hierarchies of Confucianism, the early 20th-century emphasis on personal emotional experience, the egalitarian ideology of socialism, and the consumerism and media images of the *đổi mới* era co-exist in today's local moral worlds. Such moral com-plexities often give rise to conflicts between women's dreams of freedom and autonomy and their daily experiences of dependency and submission. Yet even though women may dream of freedom, equality and self-determination, what matters most in their daily lives and shapes their actions and emotional reactions is the practical concern of keeping their families happy and harmonious. In the conduct of daily life, women are guided less by moral principles than by pragmatic considerations – and to women for whom family harmony and happiness are overarching values, to accept and silently endure family hierarchies often makes more sense than to insist on their own dreams of individual rights and self-determination.

It is in this context that physical symptoms may be viewed as 'somatic strategies', as the most effective ways for women to manage their daily lives and affect their social surroundings. Everyday health problems may be ways for women to quietly object to their daily work burdens and to refuse to go on working beyond their own physical capacities. The combined demands of agricultural and domestic work take a very heavy toll on women's bodies and health, and both women themselves and their social surroundings place high expectations and demands on their ability to work and perform. In this context, physical weakness and ill health provide the most – perhaps the only – legitimate grounds on which women may grant themselves a break from back-breaking work without being ridiculed for 'not knowing how to work' or tormented by feelings of guilt and inadequacy.

Everyday weakness and pain may also be ways of gently handling oppressive social relationships, particularly within the family. Both in family conflicts and in the conduct of daily life, women tend to gain more by emphasizing their physical weakness and suffering than by asserting their personal rights or liberty in open confrontation. Openly or angrily insisting on rights and freedoms usually only leads to social conflicts in which women know that they will be the losers – deprived of both the respect of other community members and of the family happiness and stability that they are working so hard to build up. From this perspective, physical symptoms may be considered as socially safe 'weapons of the weak', as means used by women to negotiate more tolerable daily lives for themselves without causing too much social disruption.

This leads us to the question of whether we can understand women's physical suffering as forms of everyday *resistance*? Do women resist dominant moral ideologies and oppressive social relations through their bodies? Or does an understanding of suffering as resistance represent a social-scientific appropriation of women's bodies and lives which turns them into something very different from what they are as experienced? An interpretation of women's physical suffering as forms of everyday resistance would be in line with studies in medical anthropology which have considered human illness and suffering as forms of dissent and resistance – as modes of protesting and resisting hegemonic relations of power (e.g., Comaroff 1985; Ong 1987; Taussig 1980). There are several problems, however, in viewing suffering as embodied resistance. First, this interpretation risks distorting the sufferer's own experience of her suffering. Kleinman and Kleinman have phrased it like this:

> What is lost in biomedical renditions – the complexity, uncertainty and ordinariness of some man's or woman's unified world of experience – is also missing when illness is reinterpreted as social role, social strategy, or social symbol ... anything but human experience. (Kleinman and Kleinman, 1991: 276)

It is important not to overlook the fact that to women themselves, their headaches, backaches and dizziness are, more than anything else, just disturbing feelings of pain and discomfort which make bodies heavier and lives harder.

A second problem in the interpretation of women's suffering as resistance is that we may be brought to overlook the fact that women also often accept and embrace the very social values and ideologies which they 'resist'. While suffering under, and sometimes openly criticizing patriarchal family structures and dominant moral ideologies, most women also simultaneously accept these social forms and values and actively employ them in their moral evaluations of other women. A too narrow focus on 'resistance' may therefore lead us to overlook the social and cultural complexities at work in local moral worlds, turning the subtle and symbolic forms of power which permeate everyday lives into much more crude oppositions between separate and clear-cut ideologies.

Third, the concept of resistance may lead us to misattribute to women forms of political consciousness other than those implied by the practical and pragmatic politics of everyday life. The notion of resistance suggests forms of political consciousness and strategizing action that are very different from the pragmatic everyday tactics which women employ in their lives. Even though women may use their symptoms strategically, what they do is not to rebel or revolt. Rather, they get by, manoeuvring within social fields of constraint and demand as best they can, trying to minimize social and physical pain and risk. If symptoms are weapons, they are weapons used for survival and self-defense rather than for rebellion. In short, the danger in interpreting suffering as resistance is that we 'romanticize' suffering and thus distort the very feelings and experiences which we set out to understand.

However, trying to abstract suffering from its social and cultural contexts would probably represent an even more serious distortion of what is at stake when women feel that their bodies are weak, aching, and exhausted. Anthropological accounts, if content with being 'experience-near', risk losing their ability to reveal the contingencies of social worlds and moral ideologies. This study has clearly indicated that human suffering is deeply political and social. As Davis (1992) has phrased it, 'social organization sometimes hurts'. In order to comprehend human experience, we need to investigate it in the context of the larger social and cultural forms through which it comes into being.

Against this background, and provided that the above caveats are taken into account, I believe that it does make sense to see women's everyday symptoms as forms of resistance – as objections to excessive work burdens and to oppressive social relations and moral ideologies. Recognizing the fact that physical symptoms may embody refusal and resistance to social pressure is particularly important in relation to the question of how anthropology may engage people who suffer. Ignoring the ways in which women's bodies index and express social stresses and conflictual social relations would make it difficult for us to contribute anything to the relief of their pain or to changes in the social and political orders in which it is grounded. As this study has demonstrated, physical pain is often a social product, generated by unequal divisions of social risks and economic resources. Attempts to alleviate human suffering therefore need to take into account the broader social and political contexts in which pain is produced.

In short, women's IUD symptoms and the networks of other symptoms with which they are associated can be considered both as the lived and felt experience of social tension and as ways in which women actively respond to stressful social circumstances. This is not to say that women play-act or invent symptoms in order to manipulate their social surroundings. But in daily lives where physical symptoms and social stresses merge, there may be considerable benefits for women in emphasizing and expressing the somatic rather than the social side of health problems. The problem in this response to social stress, however, is that the social benefits obtained are usually only short-term and individual. Rather than challenging or changing them, women's somatic strategies tend to perpetuate existing social and moral orders. They confirm the dominant cultural stereotype of women as weak, fragile, suffering and physically and socially inferior to men. Thus, while immediately useful to individual women, somatic idioms of distress may be self-defeating in the long run and simply perpetuate the very gender ideologies from which much of women's everyday distress seems to emerge.

'Nature' and 'culture': challenges in contraceptive research

Enormous efforts are being put into the development of safer and more effective models and methods of contraception. At present, this field of research is characterized by a fairly sharp division of labour between basic/biomedical research into the effects of contraceptive methods on human physiology, and applied social science research on users' perspectives and experiences with contraception. The question that I would like to raise here is whether this division of labour between scientific disciplines is useful, and whether more joint and inter-disciplinary work in the field of contraceptive development and research might not be valuable. As we have seen, contraceptive users are boundary-crossing creatures; their bodies are 'cultural' as much as 'natural', thus challenging conventional divisions between the sciences. To conclude, I shall therefore present some reflections on the forms which future research within this field might take in order to deal more constructively with some of its present 'blind spots'. These reflections start from the issues dealt with in the preceding pages, but they also go beyond the present study and speculate further on some of the questions it raises.

This study suggests that contraceptive side effects involve social experience as much as physiological change. In that they are mediated by wider cultural meanings as well as social events and circumstances, the reactions of a woman's body to a contraceptive device seem to involve much more than just 'raw' physiology. This observation fits well with the fact that the same contraceptive device may cause widely differing reactions in women in different social settings – i.e., even though contraceptive methods are universally and cross-culturally applied, women's physical reactions to them are far from uniform (see Chapter 1).

While the focus of attention in the present study has been on the social experience of physical symptoms, there also seems to be a range of good physiological reasons for the problems that Vietnamese women experience with their IUDs. Service delivery conditions are often far from optimal, and IUDs are frequently inserted by providers whose technical and counselling skills are limited. Many women are undernourished and anaemic, and may therefore have difficulty in coping with the increased blood loss caused by the IUD. Reproductive tract infections seem to be common in Vietnam, and the IUD may therefore further increase women's risks of contracting pelvic inflammatory disease. Women themselves often see their hard physical work and demanding everyday lives as hindrances for successful IUD use, and both health care providers and local women in Vietnam have suggested that the currently-used, US-imported IUD may be too large for the uteri of Vietnamese women.

In this context, an important question that may be raised is how the physiological processes involved in IUD use interact with the social conditions of everyday lives and with the processes through which physical pain and discomfort come to gain specific meanings and implications. While the cultural meanings and social implications of strenuous work, poor diet, and social stresses have been important concerns of this study, an understanding of the complex processes through which such social conditions and cultural meanings are woven together with physiological changes would require joint efforts across scientific disciplines.

The more general question at issue here is the relationship between biology and culture. Most contraceptive research tends to consider human biology as something culturally invariant and universal, as an underlying and stable layer which is basically there, beneath all cultural and social mediation. In the same vein, it is assumed that physiological reactions to contraceptive devices

are universal and may be generalized within and across populations (see Chapter 1). Yet if women's physical reactions to
contraceptive technologies are shaped and mediated by their daily
life situations and by the local meanings attached to heavier
bleedings, headaches, dizziness, etc., then perhaps we should
rethink the idea of biology as something stable and universal and
investigate whether there may be systematically different physical
experiences and reactions across and within cultures. Medical
anthropologist Margaret Lock (1993a) has argued that by affecting
the way we put meaning into physiological facts, culture may
affect physiology itself. And Donna Haraway says:

> Neither our personal bodies nor our social bodies may be seen as
> natural, in the sense of existing outside the self-creating process
> called human labour. What we experience and theorize as nature
> and as culture are transformed by our work. (Haraway 1991: 10)

To illustrate her point, Lock uses Engel's discussion of the
human hand as an example: the hand is not just the organ of labour,
it is also a product of labour in the sense that it has gradually
changed over time as a result of what it has been used for.

Rather than being simply responses to external stimuli, then,
physical changes – whether anatomical, chemical or physiological
– are the products of human activity, resulting from our active
engagements with and cognitive appraisals of our environments.
While undeniably 'hard' and physical, human biology is also 'soft'
and social, evolving through intimate interaction and engagement
with culture. In this light, it hardly makes sense to keep seeing
human biology as something universal and acultural. What is
required, therefore, are concepts which, instead of maintaining
dualistic divisions between nature and culture, or biology and
society, enable us to grasp the 'naturalness' of culture and the
'culturalness' of nature and to study the complexities of nature–
culture mediations (see Latour 1993). As a way out of conventional dualistic mazes, Margaret Lock suggests that we employ
the concept of 'local biologies', which allows for an understanding
of physical experience as the outcome of 'an ongoing dialectic
between biology and culture in which both are contingent' (Lock
1993a: xxi). The notion of 'local biology' suggests that biologies
may actually be different in different populations, as a result of the
exchanges and engagements taking place between culture and

physiology. In the context of IUD use in Vietnam, an investigation of 'local biologies' might include (a) a consideration of the ways in which work burdens, diets and social stress affect women's bodies, lives and self-perceptions, and so influence their social and physical responses to contraceptive devices; and (b) an examination of the ways in which health problems are tied to poverty, gender inequality and other forms of structurally determined social constraints.

In general, in order to investigate the ways in which contraceptive technologies may affect the hormone levels, tissues and nerves of human bodies in different ways across cultures, depending on the social activities and local cultural meanings involved, it may be worthwhile to pay closer attention to what Rachel Snow (1994) has termed the 'physiological synergies' between contraceptive technology and women's underlying reproductive health. Of interest here could be the ways in which physiological changes of menstrual bleeding patterns interact with the cultural meanings which are ascribed to menstruation and with the wider social cosmologies in which such meanings are embedded; or the way backaches as physiological phenomena are linked to social experiences of everyday work burdens and cultural meanings of pain and distress. Rachel Snow points out that because of the ways in which research is currently designed, clinical trials represent an important but unused opportunity for integrated research into the links between the biological bases and the social experiences of contraceptive side effects. In order to overcome the limitations of existing data, therefore, future studies of the interactions between reproductive technologies and human bodies would ideally be interdisciplinary and comparative in focus, combining attention to physiological changes with investigations of the making-of-meaning processes to which they are intimately tied. The ideal research strategy for the study of contraceptive technologies would transcend the dichotomy between the social body and the biological body, allowing us to question our usual distinctions between the 'hard facts' of nature and the 'softer' facts of culture.

References

AFPC-UNFPA, 1995. *Results of Survey on Reproductive Tract Infections in Vietnamese Rural Women*. Hanoi: AFPC-UNFPA

Ahern, Emily M., 1975. 'The Power and Pollution of Chinese Women.' In: Margery Wolf and Roxane Witke (eds), *Women in Chinese Society*. Stanford, California: Stanford University Press.

Allen, Susan, 1990. *Women in Vietnam*. Hanoi.

——, Adam Fforde and Gillian Robson, 1995. *Poverty in Vietnam. A Report for SIDA*. Canberra: Aduki Pty Ltd.

Allman, James, Vu Qui Nhan, Nguyen Minh Thang, Pham Bich San and Vu Duy Man, 1991. 'Fertility and Family Planning in Vietnam.' *Studies in Family Planning*, vol. 22, no. 5, pp. 308–17.

Anagnost, Ann, 1991. 'Socialist Ethics and the Legal System.' In: J.N. Wasserstrom and E.J. Perry (eds), *Popular Protest and Political Culture in Modern China. Learning from 1989*. Boulder, Colorado: Westview Press.

——, 1994. 'The Politicized Body.' In: Angela Zito and Tani Barlow (eds), *Body, Subject and Power in China*. Chicago/London: The University of Chicago Press.

——, 1995. 'A Surfeit of Bodies: Population and the Rationality of the State in Post-Mao China.' In: Faye D. Ginsburg and Rayna Rapp (eds), *Conceiving the New World Order. The Global Politics of Reproduction*. Berkeley, Los Angeles/London: University of California Press.

Anderson, E. N. & Marja L. Anderson, 1975. 'Folk dietetics in two Chinese communities, and its implications for the study of Chinese medicine.' In: Arthur Kleinman, Peter Kunstadter, E. Russel Alexander, James L. Gale (eds), *Medicine in Chinese Cultures*. Geographic Health Studies, John E. Fogarty International Center for Advanced Study in the Health Sciences.

Angle, Marcia A., Laura A. Brown, Pierre Buekens, 1993. 'IUD Protocols for International Training,' *Studies in Family Planning*, vol. 24, no. 2, pp. 125–31.

Arditti, Rita, Renate Duelli Klein and Shelley Minden (eds), 1985. *Test-Tube Women. What Future for Motherhood?* London/Boston/Melbourne/Henley: Pandora Press.

Bakken, Børge, 1994. *The Exemplary Society. Human Improvement, Social Control and the Dangers of Modernity in China*. Oslo: Department of Sociology, University of Oslo.

——, 1995. 'Principled and Unprincipled Democracy: The Chinese Approach to Evaluation and Election.' Paper prepared for the international workshop 'Democracy in Asia'. NIAS, Copenhagen.

Balsamo, Anne, 1995. 'Forms of Technological Embodiment: Reading the Body in Contemporary Culture', *Body and Society*, vol. 1, no. 3–4, pp. 215–37.

Banister, Judith, 1993. *Vietnam: Population Dynamics and Prospects*. Berkeley, California: University of California, Institute of East Asian Studies.

Barlow, Tani, 1994a. 'Politics and Protocols of Funü: (Un)Making National Woman.' In: Christina Gilmartin, Gail Hershatter, Lisa Rofel and Tyrene White (eds), *Engendering China. Women, Culture, and the State*. Cambridge, Mass.: Harvard University Press.

——, 1994b. 'Theorizing Woman: Funü, Guojia, Jiating.' In: Angela Zito and Tani Barlow, (eds). *Body, Subject and Power in China*. Chicago/London: The University of Chicago Press.

Barry, Kathleen, 1996. 'Introduction.' In: Kathleen Barry (ed.), *Vietnam's Women in Transition*. London: MacMillan Press/New York: St. Martin's Press.

Bateson, Gregory, 1958. *Naven*. Stanford: Stanford University Press.

Becker, Gary S., 1960. 'An Economic Analysis of Fertility.' In: *Demographic and Economic Change in Developed Countries*, National Bureau of Economic Research. Princeton, N.J.: Princeton University Press, pp. 209–31.

Bélanger, Danièle and Khuât Thu Hông, 1995. 'Marriage and the Family in Urban North Vietnam, 1965–1993.' Paper presented at the Annual PAA Meeting, San Francisco.

Beresford, Melanie, 1994. *Impact of Macroeconomic Reform on Women in Vietnam*. Hanoi: UNIFEM.

Bourdieu, Pierre, 1977. *Outline of a Theory of Practice*. Cambridge: Cambridge University Press.

——, 1984. *Distinction*. London: Routledge.

——, 1990. *The Logic of Practice*. Cambridge: Polity Press.

——, and Loic J. D. Wacquant, 1992. *An Invitation to Reflexive Sociology*. Cambridge: Polity Press.

Burkman, Ronald T., 1996. 'Intrauterine Devices and Pelvic Inflammatory Disease: Evolving Perspectives on the Data,' *Obstetrical and Gynecological Survey*, vol. 51, no. 12, pp. S35–S41.

Cadière, Léopold, 1957. *Croyances et Pratiques Religieuses de Viêtnamiens, I–III*. Paris: École Française d'Extrême-Orient.

Caldwell, John C., 1982. *Theory of Fertility Decline*. London/New York: Academic Press.

Casper, Monica, 1995. 'Fetal Cyborgs and Technomoms on the Reproductive Frontier. Which Way to the Carnival?' In: Chris Hables Gray, Heidi J. Figueroa-Sarriera and Steven Mentor (eds), *The Cyborg Handbook*. London/New York; Routledge.

—— and Barbara A. Koenig, 1996. 'Reconfiguring Nature and Culture: Intersections of Medical Anthropology and Technoscience Studies,' *Medical Anthropology Quarterly*, vol. 10, no. 4, pp. 523–36.

Chan, Anita, Richard Madsen and Jonathan Unger, 1984. *Chen Village: The Recent History of a Peasant Community in Mao's China*. Berkeley: University of California Press.

Chánh Công Phan, 1993. 'The Vietnamese Concept of the Human Souls and the Rituals of Birth and Death.' *Southeast Asian Journal of Social Science*, vol. 21, no. 1, pp. 159–98.

Chi, I-cheng, 1993. 'What We Have Learned from Recent IUD Studies: A researcher's perspective,' *Contraception*, no. 48, pp. 81–108.

Clifford, James and George E. Marcus (eds), 1986. *Writing Culture. The Poetics and Politics of Ethnography*. Berkeley/London: University of California Press.

Comaroff, J., 1985. *Body of Power, Spirit of Resistance: The Culture and History of a South African People*. Chicago: University of Chicago Press.

Condominas, Georges, 1977 [1957]. *We Have Eaten the Forest. The Story of a Montagnard Village in the Central Highlands of Vietnam*. London: Allen Lane.

Corea, Gena, renata Duelli Klein, Jalna Hanmer, Helen B. Holmes, Betty Hoskins, Madhu Kinshwar Janice Raymond, Robyn Rowland, Roberta Styeinbacher (eds), 1985. *Man-Made Women. How New Reproductive Technologies Affect Women*. London: Hutchinson.

Corrêa, Sonia, 1994. *Population and Reproductive Rights: Feminist Perspectives from the South*. London: Zed Books, in ass. with Development Alternatives with Women for a New Era (DAWN).

Coughlin, Richard, 1950. *The Position of Women in Vietnam*. Cultural Report Series, New Haven: Yale University Press.

——, 1965. 'Pregnancy and Birth in Vietnam.' In: Donn V. Hart, Phya Anuman Rajadhon and Richard J. Coughlin (eds), *Southeast Asian Birth Customs. Three Studies in Human Reproduction*. New Haven, Connecticut: Human Relations Area Files Press.

Craig, David, 1996. 'Household Health in Vietnam: a Small Re-form.' *Asian Studies Review*, vol. 20, no. 1, pp. 53–67.

——, 1997. 'Familiar Medicine: Local and Global Health and Development in Vietnam.' PhD thesis, Research School of Pacific and Asian Studies, Australian National University, Canberra.

Croll, Elizabeth, 1994. *From Heaven to Earth. Images and Experiences of Development in China*. London/New York: Routledge.

——, 1995. *Changing Identities of Chinese Women*. London/New Jersey: Hong Kong University Press and Zed Books.

Csordas, Thomas J., 1990. 'Embodiment as a Paradigm for Anthropology,' *Ethos*, no. 18, pp. 5–47.

—— (ed.), 1994. *Embodiment and Experience. The Existential Ground of Culture and Self.* Cambridge: Cambridge University Press.

Đặng Nguyễn Anh, 1989. *Women, Work, and Family Planning in Two Rural Communes in Vietnam.* Women's Union Baseline Survey 1989, Preliminary Report. Hanoi: Institute of Sociology.

Darney P.D., E. Atkinson, S. Tanner, S. MacPherson, S. Hellerstein and A. Alvarado, 1988. 'Acceptance and Perceptions of Norplant among Users in San Francisco, USA,' *Studies in Family Planning*, vol. 21, no. 3, pp. 153–60.

Davis, Dona L. and Setha M. Low, 1989. *Gender, Health, and Illness. The Case of Nerves.* New York/Washington/Philadelphia/London: Hemisphere Publishing Corporation.

Davis, John, 1992. 'The Anthropology of Suffering.' *Journal of Refugee Studies*, vol. 5, pp. 149–61.

Desai, Jaikishan, 1995. *Vietnam through the Lens of Gender. An Empirical Analysis using Household Survey Data.* Hanoi.

Desjarlais, Robert, 1992. *Body and Emotion. The Aesthetics of Illness and Healing in the Nepal Himalayas.* Philadelphia: University of Pennsylvania Press.

Dixon-Mueller, Ruth and Judith Wasserheit, 1991. *The Culture of Silence. Reproductive Tract Infections Among Women in the Third World.* New York: International Women's Health Coalition.

Đỗ Trọng Hiếu, 1993. *Report on IUD Contraceptive Use-Dynamics Study.* Hanoi: Ministry of Health, Vietnam.

——, John Stoeckel and Nguyen Van Tien, 1993. 'Pregnancy Termination and Contraceptive Failure in Vietnam.' *Asia–Pacific Population Journal*, vol. 8, no. 4, pp. 3–18.

——, Hoang Ti Van, Peter J. Donaldson and Quan Le Nga, 1995a. 'The Pattern of IUD Use in Vietnam,' *International Family Planning Perspectives*, vol. 21, no. 1, pp. 6–10.

——, Dao Quang Vinh, Nguyen Kim Tong, Cynthia Waszak, Karen Katz, Robert Hanenberg and David Sokal, 1995b. 'A Retrospective Study of Quinacrine Sterilization in Vietnam.' Report presented at the Quinacrine Sterilization Dissemination Meeting in Hanoi, Vietnam.

Đoàn Văn Hán, 1989. 'The Viewpoint of Traditional Medicine on Childbirth.' *Vietnamese Studies* no. 23 (93), pp. 83–116.

Douglas, Mary, 1966 [1992]. *Purity and Danger.* London/New York: Routledge.

——, 1970. *Natural Symbols.* London: Barrie & Jenkins.

Downey, Gary Lee, Joseph Dumit and Sarah Williams, 1995. 'Cyborg Anthropology.' In: Chris Hables Gray, Heidi J. Figueroa-Sarriera and Steven Mentor (eds), *The Cyborg Handbook.* London/New York: Routledge.

Dunk, Pamela, 1989. 'Greek Women and Broken Nerves in Montreal.' *Medical Anthropology,* vol. 11, no. 1, pp. 29–46.

Dương Thu Hương, 1994. *Paradise of the Blind.* Harmondsworth: Penguin Books.

Easterlin, Richard A. and Eileen M. Crimmins, 1985. *The Fertility Revolution: A Supply–Demand Analysis.* Chicago: University of Chicago Press.

Ebrey, Patricia, 1990. 'Women, Marriage and the Family in Chinese History.' In: Paul S. Ropp (ed.), *Heritage of China: Contemporary Perspectives on Chinese Civilization.* Berkeley/Los Angeles/Oxford: University of California Press.

Eisenbruch, Maurice, 1983. '"Wind Illness" or Somatic Depression? A Case Study in Psychiatric Anthropology.' *British Journal of Psychiatry* vol. 143, pp. 323–26.

Elvin, Mark, 1985. 'Between the Earth and Heaven: Conceptions of the Self in China.' In: Michael Carrithers, Steven Collind and Steven Lukes (eds), *The Category of the Person.* Cambridge: Cambridge University Press.

——, 1989. 'Tales of *Shen* and *Xin*: Body-Person and Heart-Mind in China during the Last 150 Years.' In: M. Feher (ed.), *Fragments for a History of the Human Body.* New York: Zone Books.

Farr, G. and R. Amartya, 1994. 'Contraceptive Efficacy of the Copper T380A and the Multiload Cu250 in Three Developing Countries,' *Advances in Contraception,* no. 10, pp. 137–49.

Fathalla, Mahmoud F., 1994. 'Fertility Control Technology: A Women-Centered Approach to Research.' In: Gita Sen, Adrienne Germain and Lincoln C. Chen (eds), *Population Policies Reconsidered.* Harvard Series on Population and International Health, Cambridge, Mass.: Harvard University Press.

Featherstone, Mike and Roger Burrows, 1995. 'Cultures of Technological Embodiment: An Introduction.' *Body and Society,* vol. 1, no. 3–4, pp. 1–19.

Filimonova, T.N., 1992. 'The Problem of a Family and an Individual in the Novels *Doàn Tuyêt* and *Lạnh Lùng* by Nhât Linh.' Paper presented to the NIAS symposium on 'Problems of literature, culture, society, and history in Viet Nam: the Self-reliant Literary Group and transformations 1930s–1980s.' NIAS, Copenhagen.

Fong, Monica, 1994. *Gender and Poverty in Vietnam.* ESP Discussion Paper Series. Education and Social Policy Department, Human Resources Development and Operations Policy, The World Bank.

Foucault, Michel, 1977. *Discipline and Punish.* New Your: Vintage Books.

——, 1978. *The History of Sexuality, vol. 1.* Harmondsworth: Penguin Books.

Fox, Richard G. (ed.), 1991. *Recapturing Anthropology. Working in the Present.* Santa Fe: School of American Research Press/University of Washington Press.

Frankenberg, Ronald, 1986. 'Sickness as Cultural Performance: Drama, Trajectory, and Pilgrimage Root Metaphors and the Making of Disease Social.' *International Journal of Health Services*, no. 16, pp. 603–26.

Franklin, Sarah, 1993. 'Life Itself.' Paper delivered at the centre for Cultural Values, Lancaster University.

Furth, Charlotte, 1987. 'Concepts of Pregnancy, Childbirth, and Infancy in Ch'ing Dynasty China.' *The Journal of Asian Studies*, vol. 46, no. 1, pp. 7–36.

——, and Ch'en Shu-Yueh, 1992. 'Chinese Medicine and the Anthropology of Menstruation in Contemporary Taiwan.' *Medical Anthropology Quarterly*, vol. 6, no. 1, pp. 27–48.

Gammeltoft, Tine, 1996. 'Women's Bodies, Women's Worries. Health and Family Planning in a Vietnamese Rural Commune.' Unpublished PhD dissertation, Institute of Anthropology, University of Copenhagen.

——, and Rolf Hernø, 1998. 'Human Rights in Vietnam. Exploring Tensions and Ambiguities' (forthcoming).

Ginsburg, Faye and Rayna Rapp, 1995. 'Introduction: Conceiving the New World Order.' In: Faye Ginsburg and Rayna Rapp (eds), *Conceiving the New World Order*. Berkeley/Los Angeles/London: University of California Press.

Good, Byron, J., 1977. 'The Heart of What's The Matter. The Semantics of Illness in Iran.' *Culture, Medicine, and Psychiatry*, vol. 1, pp. 25–58.

——, 1994. *Medicine, Rationality, and Experience*. Cambridge: Cambridge University Press.

Good, Mary-Jo Delvecchio, 1980. 'Of Blood and Babies: The Relationship of Popular Islamic Physiology to Fertility.' *Social Science and Medicine*, vol. 14B, pp. 147–56.

——, Byron J. Good and Arthur Kleinman (eds), 1992. *Pain as Human Experience: An Anthropological Perspective*. Berkeley: University of California Press.

Goodkind, Daniel, 1994a. 'Abortion in Vietnam: Measurements, Puzzles, and Concerns.' *Studies in Family Planning* vol. 25, no. 6, pp. 342–52.

——, 1994b. *The Vietnamese Double Marriage Squeeze*. Working Papers in Demography no. 47. Research School of Social Sciences, Canberra: The Australian National University.

——, 1995. 'Vietnam's One- or Two-Child Policy in Action.' *Population and Development Review*, vol. 21, no. 1, pp. 85–111.

Gordon, Deborah, 1988. 'Tenacious Assumptions in Western Medicine.' In: M. Lock and D. R. Gordon (eds), *Biomedicine Examined*. Dordrecht: Kluwer Academic Publishers.

Greenhalgh, Susan, 1993. 'The Peasantization of the One-Child Policy in Shaanxi.' In: Deborah Davis and Stevan Harrell (eds), *Chinese Families in the Post-Mao Era*. Berkeley: University of California Press.

——, 1994. 'Controlling Births and Bodies in Village China.' *American Ethnologist*, vol. 21, no. 1, pp. 3–30.

——, 1995. 'Anthropology Theorizes Reproduction: Integrating Practice, Political Economic, and Feminist Perspectives.' In: Susan Greenhalgh (ed.), *Situating Fertility. Anthropology and Demographic Inquiry.* Cambridge: Cambridge University Press.

GSO, 1995. *Vietnam Intercensual Demographic Survey. Major Findings.* Statistical Publishing House, Hanoi: GSO.

Guarnaccia, Peter J., Melissa Rivera, Felipe Franco, Charlie Neighbors, 1996. 'The Experiences of *Ataques de Nervios*: Towards an Anthropology of Emotions in Puerto Rico.' *Culture, Medicine and Psychiatry,* vol. 20, no. 3, pp. 343–78.

Hagenfeldt, Kerstin, 1994. 'Contraceptive Research and Development Today: An Overview.' In: P. F. A Van Look and G. Pérez-Palacios (eds), *Contraceptive Research and Development 1984 to 1994. The Road from Mexico City to Cairo and Beyond.* Oxford: Oxford University Press.

Haraway, Donna J., 1985. 'Manifesto for Cyborgs: Science, Technology, and Socialist Feminism in the 1980s.' *Socialist Review,* no. 80, pp. 65–108.

——, 1991. *Simians, Cyborgs, and Women. The Reinvention of Nature.* London: Free Association Books.

——, 1997. *Modest Witness@Second_Millennium. FemaleMan™_Meets _OncoMouse©.* New York/London: Routledge.

Hardon, Anita Petra, 1992. 'The Needs of Women Versus the Interests of Family Planning Personnel, Policy-Makers and Researchers: Conflicting Views on Safety and Acceptability of Contraceptives.' *Social Science and Medicine,* vol. 35, no. 6, pp. 753–66.

——, 1996. 'User-Studies on Hormonal Contraceptives: towards Experience-near Approaches.' Manuscript submitted to *Reproductive Health Matters,* May 1996.

Hastrup, Kirsten, 1992. 'Writing Ethnography: State of the Art.' In: Judith Okely and Helen Callaway (eds), *Anthropology and Autobiography.* London/New York: Routledge.

——, 1993. 'Hunger and the Hardness of Facts'. *Man,* vol. 28, no. 4, pp. 727–39.

——, 1994. 'Anthropological Knowledge Incorporated: Discussion.' In: Kirsten Hastrup and Peter Hervik (eds), *Social Experience and Anthropological Knowledge.* London/New York: Routledge.

——, 1995. *A Passage to Anthropology.* London/New York: Routledge.

Heise, Lori L., 1997. 'Beyond Acceptability: Reorienting Research on Contraceptive Choice'. In: *Beyond Acceptability: Users' Perspectives on Contraception.* London: World Health Organization/ Reproductive Health Matter.

Hickey, Gerald Cannon, 1964. *Village in Vietnam.* New Haven/London: Yale University Press.

Hoàng Bảo Châu, Pho Duc Thuc and Huu Ngoc, 1993. 'Overview of Vietnamese Traditional Medicine.' In: *Vietnamese Traditional Medicine.* Hanoi: The Gioi Publishers.

Hội Liên Hiệp Phụ Nữ, 1977. *Công Tác Vận Động Phụ Nữ*. Hanoi: Nhà Xuât Bản Phụ Nữ.

Holland, Dorothy and Andrew Kipnis, 1994. 'Metaphors for Embarrassment and Stories of Exposure: The Not-So-Egocentric Self in American Culture.' *Ethos*, vol. 22, no. 3, pp. 316–42.

Hsu, Francis L. K., 1971. 'Psychosocial Homeostasis and *Jen*: Conceptual Tools for Advancing Psychological Anthropology.' *American Anthropologist*, vol. 73, pp. 23–44.

Huard, Pierre and Maurice Durand, 1954. *Vietnam, Civilization and Culture*. Paris: Imprimerie Nationale/Hanoi: École Française d'Extrême-Orient.

Hue-Tam Ho Tai, 1992. *Radicalism and the Origins of the Vietnamese Revolution*. Cambridge, Mass./London: Harvard University Press.

Hwang, Kwang-kuo, 1987. 'Face and Favor: The Chinese Power Game.' *American Journal of Sociology*, vol. 92, no. 4, pp. 944–74.

Hy Văn Lương, 1989. 'Vietnamese Kinship: Structural Principles and the Socialist Transformation in Northern Vietnam.' *The Journal of Asian Studies*, vol. 48, no. 4, pp. 741–56.

——, 1990. *Discursive Practices and Linguistic Meanings. The Vietnamese System of Person Reference*. Amsterdam/Philadelphia: John Benjamins Publishing Company.

IPAS, Women's Health Initiatives, 1995. *Provider and User Perspectives of Reproductive Health Services at Four Sites in Vietnam*. Final Report of a Baseline Assessment for the Reproductive Health Program.

Jackson, Michael, 1983. 'Knowledge of the Body.' *Man*, vol. 18, pp. 327–45.

Jain, Sagar, Ruth Kornfield, Jean Lecomte and Patricia Guzman, 1993. *Thematic Evaluation. Quality of Family Planning Services Vietnam*. UNFPA.

Jamieson, Neil, 1993. *Understanding Vietnam*. Berkeley: University of California Press.

Johansson, Annika, H.T. Hoa, L.T. Nham Tuyet, M.H. Bich and B. Höjer, 1996a. 'Family Planning in Vietnam – Women's Experiences and Dilemma: a Community Study from the Red River Delta.' *Journal of Psychosomatic Obstetrics and Gynecology*, no. 17, pp. 59–67.

——, Le Thi Nham Tuyet, Nguyen The Lap and Kajsa Sundström, 1996b. 'Abortion in Context: Women's Experiences in Two Villages in Thai Binh Province, Vietnam.' *Family Planning Perspectives*, vol. 22, no. 3, pp. 103–7.

JPRS (Joint Publications Research Service on East and Southeast Asia), 1989. JPRS-SEA-89-007, 8 February. Reprinted as 'Vietnam's New Fertility Policy.' *Population and Development Review*, no. 15, pp. 169–72.

Kaptchuk, Ted J., 1983. *The Web That Has No Weaver*. New York: Congdon & Weed.

Kaufman, Joan A., Zhang Zhirong, Qiao Xinjian and Zhang Yang, 1989. 'Family Planning Policy and Practice in China: A Study of Four Rural Counties.' *Population and Development Review*, vol. 15, no. 4, pp. 707–29.

Khuất Thu Hồng, 1990. *Rural Women in Northern Vietnam: Attitudes towards Family Planning*. International Population Dynamics Program, Department of Demography, Research School for Social Sciences, The Australian National University, Canberra.

——, 1991. 'Overview of Sociological Research on the Family in Vietnam.' In: Rita Liljeström and Tuong Lai (eds), *Sociological Studies on the Vietnamese Family*. Hanoi: Social Sciences Publishing House.

Kleinman, Arthur, 1980. *Patients and Healers in the Context of Culture*. University of California Press, Berkeley, Los Angeles, London.

——, 1982. 'Neurasthenia and Depression: A Study of Somatization and Culture in China.' *Culture, Medicine, and Psychiatry* , no. 6, pp. 117–90.

——, 1986. *Social Origins of Distress and Disease. Depression, Neurastenia, and Pain in Modern China*. New Haven/London: Yale University Press.

——, 1988. *The Illness Narratives*. New York: Basic Books.

——, 1992. 'Pain and Resistance: The Delegitimation and Relegitimation of Local Worlds.' In: Mary-Jo DelVecchio Good, Byron J. Good and Arthur Kleinman (eds), *Pain as Human Experience: An Anthropological Perspective*. Berkeley/Los Angeles/Oxford: University of California Press.

——, 1995. *Writing at the Margin*. Berkeley/Los Angeles/London: University of California Press.

——, and Byron Good (eds), 1985. *Culture and Depression*. Berkeley: University of California Press.

——, and Joan Kleinman, 1991. 'Suffering and Its Professional Transformation: Toward an Ethnography of Interpersonal Experience.' *Culture, Medicine, and Psychiatry*, no. 15, pp. 275–301.

Knodel, John, Phan Thuc Anh and Dao Xuan Vinh, 1995. *Vietnam's Population and Family Planning Program as Viewed by Its Implementers*. Bangkok: The Population Council, Regional Working Papers No. 2.

Kroeger, Axel, 1983. 'Health Interview Surveys in Developing Countries: A Review of the Methods and Results.' *International Journal of Epidemiology* vol. 12, no. 4, pp. 465–81.

Ladinsky, Judith L., Nancy D. Volk and Margaret Robinson, 1987. 'The Influence of Traditional Medicine in Shaping Medical Care Practices in Vietnam today.' *Social Science and Medicine*, vol. 25, no. 10, pp. 1105–10.

Latour, Bruno, 1993. *We Have Never Been Modern*. Cambridge, Massachusetts: Harvard University Press.

——, and Stephen Woolgar, 1979. *Laboratory Life: The Social Construction of Scientific Facts*. Beverly Hills, California: University of California Press.

Lê Thị Nhâm Tuyết, 1991. 'Women and Their Families in the Movement for Agricultural Collectivisation in Vietnam.' In: Haleh Afshar (ed.), *Women, Development and Survival in the Third World*. London/New York: Longman.

——, Annika Johansson, Mai Huy Bich, Hoang Thi Hoa, 1994. 'Women's Experience of Family Planning in Two Rural Communes (Thái Bình province).' *Vietnam Social Sciences*, vol. 1, no. 39, pp. 55–72.

Liljeström, Rita and Tuong Lai (eds), 1991. *Sociological Studies on the Vietnamese Family*. Hanoi: Social Sciences Publishing House.

Lock, Margaret, 1990. 'On Being Ethnic: The Politics of Identity Breaking and Making in Canada, Or Nevra on Sunday.' *Culture, Medicine, and Psychiatry*, no. 14, pp. 237–52.

——, 1993a. *Encounters with Aging. Mythologies of Menopause in Japan and North America*. Berkeley/Los Angeles/London: University of California Press.

——, 1993b. 'Cultivating the Body: Anthropology and Epistemologies of Bodily Practice and Knowledge.' *Annual Review of Anthropology*, vol. 22, pp. 133–55.

Lockhardt, Greg, 1992. 'Nguyễn Huy Thiệp's Highly Diverting Writing.' Paper submitted to the NIAS Conference 'Problems of Literature, Culture, Society, and History in Vietnam', held at the University of New South Wales, Australia.

Low, Setha M., 1981. 'The Meaning of *Nervios*: A Sociocultural Analysis of Symptom Presentation in San Jose, Costa Rica.' *Culture, Medicine, and Psychiatry*, no. 5, pp. 25–47.

Lutz, Catherine A., 1988. *Unnatural Emotions*. Chicago/London: The University of Chicago Press.

—— and Lila Abu-Lughod (eds), 1990. *Language and the Politics of Emotion*. Cambridge: Cambridge University Press/Paris: Editions de la Maison des Sciences de l'Homme.

—— and Geoffrey M. White, 1986. 'The Anthropology of Emotions.' *Annual Review of Anthropology*, vol. 15, pp. 405–36.

Lyon M.L. and Barbalet J.M., 1994. 'Society's Body: Emotion and the "Somatization" of Social Theory.' In: Thomas J. Csordas (ed.), *Embodiment and experience*. Cambridge: Cambridge University Press.

Madsen, Richard, 1984. *Morality and Power in a Chinese Village*. Berkeley/London: University of California Press.

Mai Huy Bích, 1991. 'A Distinctive Feature of the Meaning of Reproduction in Confucian Family Tradition in the Red River Delta.' In: Rita Liljeström and Tuong Lai (eds), *Sociological Studies on the Vietnamese Family*. Hanoi: Social Sciences Publishing House.

Mai Thị Tu and Lê Thị Nhâm Tuyết, 1978. *Women in Vietnam*. Hanoi: Foreign Languages Publishing House.

Marr, David G., 1981. *Vietnamese Tradition on Trial*. Berkeley: University of California Press.

——, 1987. 'Vietnamese Attitudes Regarding Illness and Healing.' In: Norman G. Owen (ed.), *Death and Disease in Southeast Asia*. Singapore, Oxford, New York: Oxford University Press.

McDonald, Margaret, 1995. *Women in Development: Vietnam*. Asian Development Bank, Programs Department (West).

Merleau-Ponty, Maurice, 1995 [1962]. *The Phenomenology of Perception*. London/New York: Routledge.

Migliore, Sam, 1994. 'Gender, Emotion, and Physical Distress: The Sicilian–Canadian "Nerves" Complex.' *Culture, Medicine, and Psychiatry*, no. 18, pp. 271–97.

Milwertz, Cecilia Nathansen, 1997. *Accepting Population Control*. Richmond: Curzon Press.

Morsy, Soheir, 1997. 'Biotechnology and the Taming of Women's Bodies.' In: Jennifer Terry and Melodie Calvert (eds). *Processed Lives. Gender and Technology in Everyday Life*. London/New York: Routledge.

Mosher, Steven, 1983. *Broken Earth*. New York: The Free Press.

Munro, Donald J., 1969. *The Concept of Man in Early China*. Stanford, California: Stanford University Press.

NCPFP, 1992. *Strategy for Information-Education-Communication of Population and Family Planning*. Hanoi: Hanoi Publishing House.

——, 1993a. *Resolution on Population and Family Planning* (Adopted at 4th meeting of the Party Central Committee, 7th session). Hanoi.

——, 1993b. *Population and Family Planning Strategy to the Year 2000*. Hanoi.

——, 1994a. *Dân Số và Gia Đình*. 'Đặc San Năm Quốc Tế Gia Đình 1994.' [Special edition, The International Year of the Family 1994]. Hanoi.

——, 1996. *Population and Family Planning Programme in Vietnam*. Hanoi.

Needham, Joseph, 1969. *Science and Civilization in China*, vol. 2. Cambridge: Cambridge University Press.

Nguyễn Khắc Viện, 1975. 'Confucianism and Marxism in Vietnam.' In: David Marr and Jayne Werner (eds), *Tradition and Revolution in Vietnam*. Berkeley/Washington: Indochina Resource Center.

Nha-Trang Công-Huyền-Tôn-Nữ-Thị, 1973. 'The Traditional Roles of Women as Reflected in Oral and Written Vietnamese Literature.' Unpublished doctoral dissertation. Berkeley: University of California.

Nichter, Mark, 1981. 'Idioms of Distress: Alternatives in the Expression of Psychosocial Distress: A Case Study from South India.' *Culture, Medicine, and Psychiatry*, 5, pp. 379–408.

—— and Mimi Nichter, 1989. 'Modern Methods of Fertility Regulation: When and for Whom Are They Appropriate?' In: Mark Nichter,

Anthropology and International Health. South Asian Case Studies. Dordrecht/Boston/London: Kluwer Academic Publishers.

O'Harrow, Stephen, 1995. 'Vietnamese Women and Confucianism: Creating Spaces from Patriarchy.' In: Wazir Jahan Karim (ed.): *'Male' and 'Female' in Developing Southeast Asia.* Oxford/Washington DC: Berg Publishers.

Oi, Jean C., 1989. *State and Peasant in Contemporary China: The Political Economy of Village Government.* Berkeley: University of California Press.

Ong, Aihwa, 1988. 'The Production of Possession: Spirits and the Multinational Corporation in Malaysia.' *American Ethnologist*, vol. 15, pp. 28–42.

Ots, Thomas, 1990. 'The Angry Liver, the Anxious Heart and the Melancholy Spleen.' *Culture, Medicine and Psychiatry* vol./no. 14, pp. 21–58.

Oudshoorn, Nelly, 1996. 'The Decline of the One-Size-Fits-All Paradigm, or, How Reproductive Scientists Try to Cope with Postmodernity.' In: Nina Lykke and Rosi Braidotti (eds.), *Between Monsters, Goddesses and Cyborgs. Feminist Confrontations with Science, Medicine and Cyberspace.* London & New Jersey: Zed Books.

Pelzer, Kristin, 1993. 'Socio-Cultural Dimensions of Renovation in Vietnam: Doi Moi as Dialogue and Transformation in Gender Relations.' In: William S. Turley and Mark Selden (eds), *Reinventing Vietnamese Socialism.* Boulder, Colorado: Westview Press.

Petta, Carlos Alberto, Melissa McPheeters and I-Cheng Chi, 1996. 'Intrauterine Devices: Learning from the Past and Looking to the Future.' *Journal of Biosocial Science*, no. 28, pp. 241–52.

Pfaffenberger, Bryan, 1992. 'Social Anthropology of Technology.' *Annual Review of Anthropology*, no. 21, pp. 491–516.

Phạm Bích San, 1993. *Sociological Survey on Vietnamese Women Using IUD TCu 380A.* Hanoi: Institute of Sociology.

Phạm Văn Bích, 1997. *The Changes to the Vietnamese Family in the Red River delta.* Monograph from the Department of Sociology, no. 65, Gothenburg: Göteborg University.

Porkert, Manfred, 1974. *The Theoretical Foundations of Chinese Medicine.* Cambridge, Mass./London: The MIT Press.

Potter, Sulamith Heins, 1988. 'The Cultural Construction of Emotion in Rural Chinese Social Life.' *Ethos*, vol. 16, no. 2, pp. 181–208.

Rapp, Rayna, 1991. 'Moral Pioneers. Women, Men, and Foetuses on a Frontier of Reproductive Technology.' In: Michaela di Leonardo (ed.), *Gender at the Crossroads of Knowledge.* Berkeley: University of California Press.

Rebhun, L. A., 1993. 'Nerves and Emotional Play in Northeast Brazil.' *Medical Anthropology Quarterly*, vol. 7, no. 2, pp. 131–51.

Rorty, Richard, 1991. *Objectivity, Relativism, and Truth. Philosophical Papers*, vol. 1. Cambridge: Cambridge University Press.

Rosaldo, Renato, 1989. *Culture and Truth. The Remaking of Social Analysis*. Berkeley: University of California Press.

Ross, David A. and J. Patrick Vaughan, 1986. 'Health Interview Surveys in Developing Countries: A Methodological Review.' *Studies in Family Planning*, vol. 17, no. 2, pp. 78–94.

Salemink, Oscar, 1991. '*Mois* and *Maquis*: The Invention and Appropriation of Vietnam's Montagnards from Sabatier to the CIA.' In: George W. Stocking, Jr. (ed.), *Colonial Situations. Essays on the Contextualization of Ethnographic Knowledge*. Madison, Wisconsin: University of Wisconsin Press.

Samuelson, Julia, Do Thi Ngoc Nga and Khong Ngoc Am, 1995. *Health Status of Women in Vietnam*. Hanoi: UNFPA PRSD Series.

Sanjek, Roger, 1990. 'On Ethnographic Validity.' In: Roger Sanjek (ed.), *Fieldnotes. The Makings of Anthropology*. Ithaca/London: Cornell University Press.

Scheper-Hughes, Nancy, 1992a. *Death without Weeping. The Violence of Everyday Life in Brazil*. Berkeley: University of California Press.

——, 1992b. 'Hungry Bodies, Medicine, and the State: toward a Critical Psychological Anthropology.' In: T. Schwartz, G.M. White and C. Lutz (eds), *New Directions in Psychological Anthropology*. Cambridge: Cambridge University Press.

——, 1994. 'Embodied Knowledge: Thinking with the Body in Critical Medical Anthropology.' In: Robert Borofsky (ed.), *Assessing Cultural Anthropology*. New York: McGraw-Hill Inc.

—— and Margaret Lock, 1987. 'The Mindful Body: A Prolegomenon to Future Work in Medical Anthropology.' *Medical Anthropology Quarterly*, vol. 1, no. 1 pp. 6–41.

Schieffelin, Edward L., 1985. 'The Cultural Analysis of Depressive Affect: An Example from New Guinea.' In: Arthur Kleinman and Byron Good (eds). *Culture and Depression*. Berkeley: University of California Press.

Schutz, Alfred, 1973. *The Problem of Social Reality. Collected Papers*, vol. I. The Hague: Martinus Nijhoff.

Schwartz, Benjamin I., 1985. *The World of Thought in Ancient China*. Cambridge, Mass./London: The Belknap Press of Harvard University Press.

Schweder, Richard and Edmund Bourne, 1984. 'Does the Concept of the Person Vary Cross-Culturally?' In: Schweder, R.A. and R.A. Levine (eds.), *Culture Theory: Essays on Mind, Self and Emotion*. London: Cambridge University Press.

Scott, James C., 1976. *The Moral Economy of the Peasant*. Yale University Press: New Haven/London.

——, 1977. 'Protest and Profanation: Agrarian Revolt and the Little Tradition.' *Theory and Society*, vol. 4, no. 1, pp. 1–38 and vol. 4, no 2, pp. 211–46.

——, 1985. *Weapons of the Weak: Everyday Forms of Peasant Resistance.* New Haven: Yale University Press.

——, 1990. *Domination and the Arts of Resistance.* New Yale University Press: Haven/London.

Seaman, Gary, 1981. 'The Sexual Politics of Karmic Retribution.' In: Emily Martin Ahern and Hill Gates (eds),*The Anthropology of Taiwanese Society.* Stanford: Stanford University Press.

Sen, Gita and Rachel C. Snow (eds), 1994. *Power and Decision. The Social Control of Reproduction.* Cambridge, Mass.: Harvard University Press.

Shue, Vivienne, 1988. *The Reach of the State: Sketches of the Chinese Body Politic.* Stanford: Stanford University Press.

Sivin, Irving, 1994. 'IUDs: A Look to the Future.' In: P.F.A. Van Look and G. Pérez Palacios (eds.), *Contraceptive Research and Development 1984 to 1994. The road from Mexico City to Cairo and Beyond.* Oxford University Press, Delhi, Bombay, Calcutta, Madras.

——, Forrest Greenslade, Frederick Schmidt and Sandra N. Waldman, 1992. *The Copper T380 Intrauterine Device. A Summary of Scientific Data.* New York: The Population Council.

Snow, Rachel, 1994. 'Each to Her Own: Investigating Women's Responses to Contraception.' In: Gita Sen and Rachel C. Snow (eds), *Power and Decision. The Social Control of Reproduction.* Princeton: Harvard Center for Population and Development Studies.

Spicehandler, Joanne and Ruth Simmons, 1994. *Contraceptive Introduction Reconsidered: A Review and Conceptual Framework.* Special Programme of Research, Development and Research Training in Human Reproduction, Geneva: World Health Organization.

Spiro, Melford E., 1993. 'Is the Western Conception of the Self "Peculiar" within the Context of the World Cultures?' *Ethos*, vol. 21, no. 2, pp. 107–53.

Strathern, Marilyn, 1992. *Reproducing the Future.* New York: Routledge.

——, 1995. 'Displacing Knowledge: Technology and the Consequences for Kinship.' In: Faye D. Ginsburg and Rayna Rapp (eds), *Conceiving the New World Order.* Los Angeles/ London: University of California Press, Berkeley.

Sun, Lung-kee, 1991. 'Contemporary Chinese Culture: Structure and Emotionality.' *Australian Journal of Chinese Affairs*, no. 26, pp. 1–42.

Sundström, Kajsa, 1994. 'Methods for Fertility Regulation.' Consultancy report submitted to SIDA. Stockholm: Karolinska Institutet, IHCAR.

Tai Van Ta, 1997. *'Continuity and Change in Vietnamese Women's Roles through the Ages.'* Paper presented to the Euroviet III, Bi-Annual Conference, Amsterdam.

Taussig, M., 1980. 'Reification and the Consciousness of the Patient.' *Social Science and Medicine*, vol. 14B, pp. 3–13.

Taylor, Charles, 1985. *Human Agency and Language. Philosophical Papers I*. Cambridge: Cambridge University Press.

——, 1987. *Sources of the Self*. Cambridge: Cambridge University Press.

Taylor, Keith, 1983. *The Birth of Vietnam*. Berkeley: University of California Press.

Tønnesson, Stein, 1991. *The Vietnamese Revolution of 1945. Roosevelt, Ho Chi Minh and de Gaulle in a World at War*. Oslo: Prio/London: Sage.

Tran Hung Minh, Hoang Tu Anh and Vu Song Ha, 1997. *Lower Reproductive Tract Infections. Current Situation of the Diseases – the Gaps in Knowledge and Practice of Women of Childbearing Age in a Rural Area of Vietnam*. Hanoi: Hanoi Medical School, Community Health Research Unit/Danish Red Cross Field Office, Vietnam.

Trần Thị Quế and Susan Allen, 1992. *Country Gender Analysis: Vietnam*. Prepared for the Swedish International Development Agency (SIDA).

Trần Thị Vân Anh, 1995. 'Household Economy and Gender Relations.' *Vietnam Social Sciences*, vol. 1, no. 45, pp. 53–9.

Traweek, Sharon, 1993. 'An Introduction to Cultural and Social Studies of Sciences and Technologies.' *Culture, Medicine, and Psychiatry*, no. 17, pp. 3–25.

Treiman, Katherine and Laurie Liskin, 1988. 'IUDs – A New Look.' *Population Reports*, Series B, No. 5. Baltimore: Johns Hopkins School of Public Health, Population Information Programme.

——, Laurie Liskin, Adrienne Kols and Ward Rinehart, 1995. 'IUDs – an Update.' *Population Reports*, Series B, No. 6. Baltimore: Johns Hopkins School of Public Health, Population Information Programme.

Trịnh Minh-hà, 1992. 'Surname Viet Given Name Nam.' In: Trịnh Minh-hà, *Framer Framed*. New York/London: Routledge.

Tseng, Wen-Shing, 1973. 'The Development of Psychiatric Concepts in Traditional Chinese Medicine.' *Arch Gen Psychiatry*, vol. 29, pp. 569–75.

Tu Wei-ming, 1985. *Confucian Thought: Selfhood as Creative Transformation*. New York: State University of New York Press.

Tung, May P. M., 1994. 'Symbolic Meanings of the Body in Chinese Culture and "Somatization".' *Culture, Medicine, and Psychiatry*, vol. 18, no. 4, pp. 483–92.

Turley, William S., 1993. 'Party, State, and People: Political Structure and Economic Prospects.' In: W. S. Turley and M. Selden (eds), *Reinventing Vietnamese Socialism: Đổi Mới in Comparative Perspective*. Boulder, Colorado: Westview Press.

Turner, Victor, 1967. *The Forest of Symbols*. Ithaca, NY/London: Cornell University Press.

Uhrig, Jamie, 1995. 'Summary of Major Findings. Survey on Reproductive Tract Infections in Vietnamese Rural Women.' (unpublished): Hanoi.

UNFPA, 1993. *A Study of the Factors Underlying the Low Prevalence of Oral Contraceptive Pill Use in Vietnam.* UNFPA project VIE/92/PO5. Hanoi: Ministry of Health.

——, 1994. *Contraceptive Requirements and Logistics Management Needs in Viet Nam.* New York: UNFPA.

——, 1997. *Vietnam Country Brief.* Hanoi: UNFPA.

UNICEF, 1994. *Women and Children. A Situation Analysis.* Hanoi: UNICEF.

United Nations, 1989. *Viet Nam. Knowledge and Attitudes of Grassroots Family Planning Workers about Contraceptive Methods.* Asian Population Studies Series, No. 86-D. New York: UN.

——, 1995. *Poverty Elimination in Vietnam.*Hanoi: UNDP, UNFPA, UNICEF.

Unschuld, Paul U., 1985. *Medicine in China. A History of Ideas.* Berkeley: University of California Press.

——, 1987. 'Traditional Chinese Medicine: Some Historical and Epistemological Reflections.' *Social Science and Medicine* vol. 24, no. 12, pp. 1023–29.

VNA 1997, VNA news agency, in English 0726 gmt 11 July 1997, Hanoi.

Vũ Mạnh Lợi, 1991. 'The Gender Division of Labour in Rural Families in the Red River Delta.' In: Rita Liljeström and Tuong Lai (eds), *Sociological Studies on the Vietnamese Family.* Hanoi: Social Sciences Publishing House.

Vu Quý Nhăn, 1994. 'Family Planning Programme in Vietnam.' *Vietnam Social Sciences*, vol. 1, no. 39, pp. 3–20.

——, 1995. 'Vân đềgiới trong dân số kế hoạch hóa gia đình ở Việt Nam' [Gender issues in population and family planning in Vietnam]. *Thông Tin Dân Số* no. 5, pp. 21–26.

Vương Xuân Tính, 1994. 'The Need for Sons: Problems and Solutions.' *Vietnam Social Sciences*, vol. 1, no. 39, pp. 25–29.

Werner, Jayne, 1997. 'Gender and Economic Reform in Viet Nam.' Paper presented to the Euroviet III, Bi-Annual Conference, Amsterdam.

White, Christine, 1987. 'State, Culture and Gender: Continuity and Change in Women's Position in Rural Vietnam.' In: Haleh Afshar (ed.), *Women, State and Ideology.* London: Macmillan Press.

Whitmore, John K., 1984. 'Social Organization and Confucian Thought in Vietnam.' *Journal of Asian Studies*, vol. 15, no. 2, pp. 296–306.

——, 1987. 'Foreign Influences and the Vietnamese Cultural Core: A Discussion of the Premodern Period.' In: Trương Bửu Lâm (ed.), 1987. *Borrowings and Adaptations in Vietnamese Culture.*WHO, 1995. *An Assessment of the Need for Contraceptive Introduction in Vietnam.* Geneva: WHO.

Whyte, Michael, 1984. 'Clans, Culture and the Rationality of Large Families. *Antropologiska Studier* no. 35/36, pp. 56–64.

Wolf, Margery, 1972. *Women and the Family in Rural Taiwan*. Stanford: Stanford University Press.

——, 1985. *Revolution Postponed: Women in Contemporary China*. Stanford: Stanford University Press.

Woodside, Alexander B., 1971. *Vietnam and the Chinese Model*. Cambridge, Mass./London: Harvard University Press.

——, 1976. *Community and Revolution in Modern Vietnam*. Boston: Houghton Mifflin.

World Bank, 1992. *Vietnam: Population, Health and Nutrition Sector Review*. The World Bank, Asia Regional Office.

Yang, Mayfair, 1988. 'The Modernity of Power in the Chinese Socialist Order.' *Cultural Anthropology* vol. 3, no. 4, pp. 408–27.

Index

The Nordic Institute of Asian Studies (NIAS) is funded by the governments of Denmark, Finland, Iceland, Norway and Sweden via the Nordic Council of Ministers, and works to encourage and support Asian studies in the Nordic countries. In so doing, NIAS has published over one hundred books in the last thirty years.

Nordic Council of Ministers